CW01022446

Airspeed Aircraft

since 1931

Horsa gliders, with their aft fuselages detached for rapid troop disembarkation, lie in fields north of Ranville after the Normandy landings in June 1944. (*Imperial War Museum B5593.*)

Airspeed Aircraft

since 1931

H A Taylor

Revisions by D H Middleton

First published 1970

This revised edition published in Great Britain 1991 by
Putnam Aeronautical Books, an imprint of
Conway Maritime Press Ltd.,
24 Bride Lane, Fleet Street,
London EC4Y 8DR

British Library Cataloguing in Publication Data
Taylor, H. A. (Harold Anthony) *1904 –*
Airspeed aircraft since 1931.–2nd. ed.
1. Great Britain. Aircraft, history
I. Title
629.133343

ISBN 0 85177 848 8

Revisions typeset by The Word Shop, Bury, Lancs.
Printed and bound in Great Britain by
BPCC Wheatons Ltd, Exeter, Devon.

Contents

Introduction

However interesting the necessary detective work may be, the reconstruction of the history of an aircraft company which no longer exists, and of which very few official records remain available, is no mean task. The threads of much of this story have had to be woven together from discrete pieces of information culled from scores of different sources, human and otherwise, and (hopefully) intelligent guesses have had to be made in a few cases where no reliable connecting threads could be found.

Having said this—to placate in advance any former members of the staff of Airspeed and others who may not agree with every interpretation of long-past events and policies—I will add that the story of the company and the descriptions of the sixty aircraft, variants and projects are as complete (and myth-free) as it has been possible to make them from the sources of available information. Many of these sources, where human, are given in the acknowledgements which follow this introduction, or are mentioned in the various narratives, but the stories of the earlier days and aircraft of the company would have been very much less complete if I had not had the benefit of the information in *Slide Rule**, the autobiography of the late Nevil Shute Norway, and that in the diaries for 1931–36 kept by A. Hessell Tiltman—the founders and original joint managing directors of the company. Nor would I have even attempted the task if I had not myself spent nearly five years with Airspeed in the post-war period when the Ambassador airliner was being developed and produced.

This book is perhaps unusual by comparison with others in the Putnam series in that such a large number of projects are described and, in many cases, illustrated with general-arrangement drawings. These projects have been included not only because the story of Airspeed would be incomplete without this illustration of the effort continuously being put in, so to speak, behind the scenes, nor because the projects greatly outnumbered the actualities, but because they are, in many cases, extremely interesting and original, and show the advanced way in which the company was thinking during periods when orders were rare events for the British aircraft industry—and especially so for newcomers.

Two or three apparent inconsistencies should be explained. In the data summaries following each aircraft description the units and bases of

* Published by Wm. Heinemann Ltd.

performance are those which were current at the time when the particular aircraft were designed and/or flown. They are not always, therefore, similar in content.

The detail form of the designations used by Airspeed and others for type numbers varied considerably. In the narrative and tabulations the designations AS.5, AS.6, etc, are used throughout because this seems to have been that commonly used in the most recent company brochures and newsletters. As several had already been completed with the designations A.S.5, A.S.6, etc, this form was used for all the general-arrangement drawings.

Finally, in Appendix III giving the RAF serial numbers of the Oxford by manufacturer and mark number, the de Havilland-built listing will be seen to have been laid out in a slightly different form and is not broken down under mark headings. This is because the constructor's numbers were available for all these 1,500 or so Oxfords and are therefore included in parentheses following each consecutive group of serial numbers.

Very few Oxfords have survived, none in flying condition. The photograph below shows one rebuilt for the RAF Museum by those consummate craftsmen at Cardington. Another is displayed in the Imperial War Museum at Duxford whilst, in Belgium, one is to be seen in the Royal Army Museum in Brussels. One has been converted by Singapore Airlines to represent the Consul used on its early services as Malayan Airways, and the South African Air Force has a fourth machine for renovation.

With the Dan-Air Ambassador at Duxford it is believed that these five are the only complete Airspeed aircraft in existence.

Oxford MP425 before final assembly at Cardington in July 1987. (*Ian Frimston*)

Acknowledgements

One of the most pleasantly surprising discoveries for any newcomer-author of a book in this series is the way in which other researchers into aviation history have been ready to help by providing all the information which they have collected in such laborious detail. Inevitably, for a company whose effective history ended much more than fifteen years ago, there are information gaps—but the gaps would have been very much wider if the information from these enthusiasts had not been available. Alternatively, the time needed for *ab initio* research into such matters as individual aircraft histories, certification dates and RAF serial numbers would have reduced that available for the collection of other equally necessary information.

But before naming some of these helpers, I must mention someone who, in different circumstances, might even have been a co-author. Soon after being asked to write this book, I discovered that a pre-war pupil of the Airspeed Aeronautical College, Donald H. Middleton, was collecting material for a book. His primary interest was (and is) in the 'human' story of Airspeed, in an attempt to recapture the spirit of the pre-war industry, and he tape-recorded many interviews with Airspeed staff-members and others. He generously let me listen to these, or have transcriptions made; allowed me to see all the material he had collected; and provided copies of several original prints of general-arrangement drawings.

This book is about aircraft rather than people—but there would have been no aircraft without people. Although only a part of one of Don Middleton's recorded interviews has been used in the narrative, they filled many historical gaps and were very valuable as leads to events and to a better understanding of these events.

Among the many fact-finding helpers, only a few of whom can be named, A. J. Jackson takes first place. He provided me with all his notes on the individual aircraft histories of the Ferry, Courier, Envoy, civil Oxford and Consul. D. K. Fox, of Air-Britain, filled big gaps in the story of 'impressed' aircraft, and J. A. Bagley helped with Oxford, Queen Wasp, Fleet Shadower and Horsa test information. Dr A. E. Slater, supported by A. Coulson, provided nearly all the missing material about the only two Tern sailplanes completed and their later history. Bruce Robertson, in addition to providing, indirectly, most of the RAF serial-number information for the Oxford and Horsa, has also lent me one or two rare photographs, and Derek Wood allowed me to ransack his long-preserved historical treasures.

From overseas, Ken F. Smy helped to sort out the histories of the South African Envoys and later Oxfords and Consuls, providing, too, some of the pictures. From the Netherlands, B. van der Klaauw confirmed the existence of two mysterious Envoys and listed the Royal Netherlands Air Force Oxfords. From Japan, Eiichiro Sekigawa, of *Aireview,* helped to sort out the Mitsubishi-built and other Envoys. Kenneth Meehan of New Zealand provided pictures of, and additional information about, the New Zealand Oxfords. In addition to those whose names appear in the narrative, or in photographic credits, other essential help has been given by the Air Historical Branch of the Ministry of Defence.

London 1970 H. A. TAYLOR

NOTE TO SECOND EDITION

Airspeed was fortunate in the calibre of its designers. Hessell Tiltman and his successor, Arthur Hagg, were outstanding in their day and produced some beautiful designs – doubtless influenced by their earlier mentor, Geoffrey de Havilland. The Envoy and the Queen Wasp revealed Tiltman at his best whilst Hagg's de Havilland Albatross and Airspeed Ambassador were among the world's most beautiful aeroplanes.

I was fortunate to enjoy the friendship of Hassell from 1960 until he died in 1975 and of Miriam, his wife, until she died in 1986. This gave me the stimulus to ensure that, somehow, the story of the Company must be told so, with Tiltman's help, I began work, soon to learn that Tony Taylor was writing this book. I offered him my data. Later, in 1982, Terence Dalton published my complementary book, *Airspeed, the Company and its Aeroplanes.* This concentrated more upon the human side of Airspeed and it led, in 1987, to the Airspeed Exhibition at Portsmouth City Museum. In this context I must mention Alastair Penfold, now of Hampshire Museum Service, who planned it superbly. Many of the exhibits are now at the Southampton Hall of Aviation and it is to be hoped that, in due course, the Portsmouth Museum will find a permanent place for them with all my original archive material.

I must mention John Ainsworth who has been tireless in keeping alive the name of Airspeed and very helpful in research projects. He insists that the name of the late Bill Hodder should be recorded as one whose workmanship ensured a 'showroom' finish on the 4,961 Oxfords built by Airspeed.

Ron Clear has also offered valuable advice.

Northampton 1991 D. H. MIDDLETON

History of the Company

Paradoxically, a major air disaster led indirectly to the appearance of Airspeed. Soon after the Government-designed and -built passenger airship, the R.101, crashed in the early morning of 5 October, 1930, on Beauvais Ridge in northern France during a rashly programmed flight to India, via Egypt, the decision was made to abandon Britain's airship building and development programme. Although its Government-sponsored, but fixed-price, and industry-constructed sister ship, the R.100, had, only six weeks before the disaster, returned to England after a reasonably successful, if incident-prone, flight to and from Canada, the design and development work on this airship was also stopped. On 2 December, 1930, the Howden, Yorkshire, base of its designers and constructors—the Airship Guarantee Company, a wholly-owned subsidiary of Vickers under Sir Charles Dennistoun Burney as managing director—was closed down, and the technicians, design staff and other workers had to move on to new employment.

The original Airspeed factory—a leased section of a disused bus garage in York—with assembly work proceeding on an AS.4 Ferry; the fuselage of an AS.1 Tern is suspended from the roof. (*Courtesy Derek Wood.*)

Two members of the company's technical staff—A. Hessell Tiltman, the newly appointed chief engineer, and N. S. Norway, previously chief calculator and later deputy chief engineer under Barnes (later Sir Barnes) Wallis—had already decided to try to form an aircraft-design and manufacturing company of their own. Before joining the R.100 development team both had been with the de Havilland Aircraft Company. Hessell Tiltman had been a senior designer and Norway, very much earlier, a stress and performance calculator. While still in the airship company they had done preliminary design work on an aircraft for the private owner. Seven years later Norway was to leave the company to continue a career as a novelist, under a pseudonym made up of his first names, Nevil Shute. His books were by then becoming successful, not only in their own right, but as material for films. Much of the story of the R.100, and of the earlier days of Airspeed, is told in his autobiography, *Slide Rule*.

In the event, Tiltman and Norway succeeded, after a great deal of what would now be called 'hard selling', in obtaining some, if inadequate, financial support for their venture. On 13 March, 1931, a company was formed in York under the name of Airspeed Ltd, with a nominal capital of £50,000 in £1 shares and with promises of a barely sufficient starting capital of a little more than £5,000. In addition to Tiltman and Norway,

Three of the original directors of Airspeed: from left to right, Nevil Shute Norway, A. Hessell Tiltman and Lord Grimthorpe (chairman). Behind them is the first production AS.5 Courier which was about to be handed over to Aircraft Exchange and Mart. (*Flight 10076s*.)

Sir Alan J. Cobham, another of the original directors, photographed in a Tiger Moth at the introductory ceremony of National Aviation Day at Hanworth Air Park in April 1932. (*Flight 11495.*)

who were appointed joint managing directors, the original board consisted of Lord Grimthorpe (who was later to sponsor North Eastern Airways, one of the earlier operators of British domestic air services) as chairman; Sir Alan J. Cobham (famous as a long-distance pilot and pioneer of new air routes, and then sponsoring National Aviation Day displays); and A. E. Hewitt, a York solicitor. The name Airspeed, incidentally, was proposed by Mrs Tiltman.

The two originators were to work together in their joint capacity for more than seven years in the day-to-day running of the company. Except in the very earliest days, when he helped with stress calculations, Norway was primarily concerned with the commercial, sales and general management side of the business, while Tiltman concentrated mainly on the technical and design side. He was personally responsible for the overall design of every Airspeed aircraft, actual or projected, up to and including the AS.51 Horsa military glider and the projects of the 1941–42 era. Some of the general-arrangement drawings reproduced in this book have been based on prints from those originally drawn and signed by Tiltman—all of them meticulously and beautifully delineated.

From the period when design work on the AS.4 Ferry was getting under way in July 1931 and onwards, Tiltman was assisted, on detail design, by A. E. Ellison, who was associated with him on the R.100 before joining Airspeed and who remained with the company through the earlier AS.57 Ambassador design and development era until 1951, when he joined the English Electric Company to work later on the Lightning fighter and to become a special director.

When designing the Ferry, and more particularly the Courier, there was no data on which to work and everything had to be done from first principles—helped obviously by Tiltman's earlier experience with Airco from 1916 to 1920 and with the de Havilland Aircraft Company from 1922 until 1929, when he joined the Airship Guarantee Company.

During the first three years of the life of Airspeed many of the shareholders were employed by the company and at one period nine of them were working full time. Lord Grimthorpe continued, in the earlier days, to provide much of the financial support, as well as personal guarantees for overdrafts, but other shareholders were also helping to keep the company solvent. During one very difficult period, about two years after the formation of the company, four of them got together and offered financial support with bank guarantees and a total sum of about £10,000 in the form of debentures.

The best-known of these working shareholders was Capt. T. E. Laing, who was one of the first supporters of the company and was, for several years, works manager. He remained with Airspeed throughout all its vicissitudes until his death in a motorcar accident in 1948. Others included D. D. Little, who was appointed company secretary in November 1931; Lord Ronaldshay, who worked at Airspeed in York for some months before deciding to invest in the company; and R. D. King, who joined in April 1932 to become business manager.

At the first official board meeting, on 17 April, 1931, Sir Alan Cobham stated a requirement for two passenger-carrying aircraft with good take-off and landing characteristics for use on his touring air display project. An order for these aircraft, at a price of about £5,000 each, was not immediately possible and, with the limited funds available, the building of a projected two/three-seater private-owner's aircraft was considered to be rather too ambitious and commercially uncertain a programme for a start.

The original prospectus, sent out on 20 March to invite support for the proposed company, concentrated almost entirely on the value of the likely market for a really well-turned-out and comfortable private aircraft. The prospectus went into considerable detail about the requirements—such as 'motorcar-like' interior and furnishings, which, it said, had not yet been met by any then-existing, or proposed, light aircraft. Somewhat optimistic forecasts were made of the sales prospects for such an aircraft and of the ensuing profitability of the whole operation. The intentions were serious enough and general-arrangement drawings of the proposed private-owner type were completed. But financial support, in those very lean years for the British economy, was not forthcoming in anything like an adequate amount, and Airspeed, starting on a financial shoestring, had to look, initially, at less expensive projects.

So the first Airspeed designation, the AS.1, was an advanced soaring glider, or sailplane, named the Tern. At the first unofficial board meeting, on 20 February, 1931, Sir Alan Cobham had suggested that a boom in gliding in Britain could be expected, and design work on the AS.1 was under way before the end of that month in a room leased at 10 Piccadilly Chambers, York. Later the shared leasing of an empty bus garage in Piccadilly was arranged for the manufacture and assembly of the Tern and of the small AS.4 airliner, for which an order from Sir Alan had been confirmed towards the end of June.

The prototype AS.4 Ferry, G-ABSI, flying at Hanworth Air Park, London, during the special showing in May 1932 before it joined National Aviation Day tours. (*Flight 11531.*)

Until the early 1930s, Germany had been building the best (and almost the only) high-efficiency soaring gliders. Airspeed's directors believed that there was a market, if small, for a British-built sailplane and that this could be designed so that it would be assembled and dismantled more easily for necessary ground transport than the esoteric German sailplanes —yet be just as efficient. At that time, following demonstrations of hill and thermal soaring by German pilots, enthusiasm in Britain had been rapidly (if temporarily) increasing. The first trials of the Tern were made in August 1931. The German gliding champion, Carli Magersuppe, took part in later trials, and the Tern, for a short period, held the British altitude and distance records. One remaining Tern, much rebuilt, was still flying more than fifteen years later.

Advanced though it was, the Tern can be considered as little more than a sinew-stretching exercise for the new company. Even before the first Tern was airborne at the end of a tow-rope, work had started on the design of the less aerodynamically pleasing, but more practical and prospectively profitable AS.4 already mentioned. For his National Aviation Day touring company, Sir Alan Cobham needed an aeroplane which would carry a reasonably large number of passengers on short flights at low cost, while providing them with something in the way of an airliner environment. This had certainly not been provided by many of the aircraft which in the past had been used for so-called joy-riding. In fact, the old joy-ride idea had to be dispelled if Sir Alan's project was to succeed. He wanted a first flight to appear normal, commonplace and comfortable, and not some brief once-and-for-all adventure. The travelling air display was, of course, designed to make money—but also, quite seriously, to make the public more air-minded.

The AS.4 Ferry, ordered by Cobham towards the end of June 1931, was a somewhat extraordinary affair by today's standards—but it did its job. It was a miniature three-engined airliner of the period, but with the third engine not, as was usual, in the nose, but mounted on the top wing, so that the pilot had a better view forward. The first Ferry, G-ABSI, was designed, built and delivered in ten months—including tests early in April at Sherburn-in-Elmet and for four days at RAF Martlesham Heath, where in those days civil as well as military aircraft were tested for official approval of airworthiness. Cobham's second Ferry, G-ABSJ, was delivered in early June. Two more, the only others to be built, were completed in 1933 for John Sword of Midland and Scottish Air Ferries.

In September 1932 a decision had already been made to move to a new factory at the municipally-owned aerodrome at Portsmouth and work on its construction started on 2 December. The terms offered by the Portsmouth Corporation were extremely good, because a manufacturing tenant such as Airspeed was wanted. The factory was designed as a hangar-type building so that it could be used for other purposes if Airspeed failed to succeed. The price was £4,000, with a down payment of £1,000 and the remainder, to be paid back over ten years, loaned at 5 per cent interest. The ground rent was 1 per cent on sales turnover up to £60,000, with a reduced rate for higher figures.

Ground staff hold down the tail of the prototype AS.5 Courier during a pre-test engine run at Portsmouth. The early flights of the Courier were made without the Townend ring cowling. (*Flight 12891.*)

The first production AS.5 Courier, G-ACJL, photographed in the air after being handed over to the newly appointed distributors for Britain and Ireland, Aircraft Exchange and Mart, whose symbol can be seen on the fin. (*Flight 10078s.*)

While the AS.4 Ferry was approaching completion Tiltman had been doing initial design work on the AS.5 Courier—a very advanced aircraft for its day. His preliminary sketches were approved at a board meeting on 17 November, 1931, and design went ahead while efforts were being made to find a means of financing the construction of a prototype. Sir Alan Cobham had tentative plans to make a very-long-distance non-stop flight with the use of air-to-air refuelling and he approached Lord Wakefield—who was always ready to give support for worthwhile projects in the civil aviation field—for financial assistance.

Soon after the first flight of the Ferry, in April 1932, satisfactory talks were held, and Lord Wakefield provisionally promised to put up £10,000, of which £5,000 was for the aircraft, and Sir Alan signed a contract early in May. The price was £5,000, excluding the cost of the Armstrong Siddeley Lynx engine, which was to be provided free. Construction of this single-engined, five-passenger, low-wing monoplane with a retractable undercarriage (the first in any production type British aircraft) started in September.

It was also in September 1932 that Airspeed obtained a contract to build the SM.1, a two-seat parasol monoplane of pusher layout which had been planned and designed by W. S. Shackleton and C. Lee Murray in an effort to find a way towards a simple, easy-to-fly ‘everyman’s’ aeroplane for club and other use. The SM.1 (G-ACBP, Airspeed constructor’s number 8) flew in 1933.

The move to the Portsmouth factory, a major operation, was made in March 1933 and among the important items transported by road from York was the almost complete prototype Lynx-engined AS.5. On 11 April this made its first flight, and in June it went to Martlesham Heath for official trials. Two months later three more Couriers were under

Portsmouth Airport as it was in the autumn of 1933, with the new Airspeed factory in the middle distance near the shore of Langstone Harbour. Extensions were put in hand in 1934. (*Flight 10074s.*)

construction and a larger twin-engined aircraft on the same lines (to be the AS.6 Envoy) was already being considered. The first, G-ACJL, was handed over on 4 September to Aircraft Exchange and Mart, who had obtained the sales rights for England, Wales and Ireland. The sales rights for India and Burma were in the hands of R. K. Dundas Ltd, a company which had been formed by Lord Ronaldshay and R. D. King, then Airspeed's business manager, and was later to take over the British sales agency for Airspeed on the completion of AEM's initial contract. Another production Courier, G-ACLF, this time the 'Colonial' or 'Overseas'

In March 1933 Airspeed moved into a new, specially-built factory at Portsmouth Airport. In the right foreground is an AS.4 Ferry—second for Midland and Scottish Air Ferries. (*Flight 12871.*)

version with the more powerful Cheetah V engine, was shown at Hanworth Air Park on 9 December before leaving on a demonstration tour to India. During the tour G-ACLF was chartered by the Viceroy of India for a flight from Delhi to Patna and return—a distance of about 1,100 miles, and by then the aircraft had put in 200 hr since leaving England.

Although preliminary air-refuelling tests had been proceeding with the prototype Courier, a non-stop flight to Australia, planned by Sir Alan Cobham with Sqn. Ldr. W. Helmore, who had joined him in the venture, continued to be delayed. The attempt—then with India as the goal—was not in fact made until 22 September, 1934, and failed because of a minor mechanical fault. During a refuelling contact over the Mediterranean, a split-pin in the Courier's throttle-linkage came out, and an undercarriage-up forced landing had to be made at Halfar aerodrome in Malta. However, using a Handley Page W.10 as a tanker, the previous tests had shown the feasibility of the system, and the Air Ministry had shown a practical interest after a demonstration in April 1934, during which 120 gallons had been piped to the Courier, and two-gallon oil tins transferred by connecting line, in 2 min 20 sec. A development company, Flight Refuelling Ltd, was formed.

The third production AS.5 Courier, the Cheetah-engined 'Colonial' version, at Almaza Airport, Cairo, in December 1933 while on a flight to India for a demonstration tour by R. K. Dundas Ltd, who had the sales rights for India and Burma.

This company, still in existence more than thirty-five years later after reconstitution in 1948, has been the confirmed leader in air-to-air refuelling techniques. Earlier tests culminated in the use of the system for the first British commercial two-way experimental services over the North Atlantic when in August 1939 the Imperial Airways Short Empire flying-boat *Caribou* was topped up with fuel over Foynes, Shannon, Ireland, for the difficult westward crossing.

Air-to-air refuelling experiments were made with the prototype AS.5 Courier using one of Sir Alan Cobham's National Aviation Displays Handley Page W.10s. Sqn. Ldr. W. Helmore is handling the fuel line in this posed picture taken in October 1934 before the England–India non-stop flight attempt.

After World War II the system was for some time under trial by BOAC and also by the USAF which, in February 1949, completed a non-stop round-the-world flight when a Boeing B-50 was refuelled by pairs of B-29 Superfortress tankers using this British equipment.

Meanwhile, however, Flight Refuelling had been working on a much-refined and more operationally practical system on which tests started in April 1949. In this system the tanker aircraft trailed a refuelling hose with a conical drogue which was entered by a probe in the nose of the receiving aircraft. The 'probe-and-drogue' method of flight refuelling is now in use by all the major air forces of the world.

Because of the Courier's aerodynamic cleanliness and advanced design it was of interest to operators other than airlines and private owners. One was bought by the RAF and delivered in February 1934, and later modified by Airspeed for experiments at the Royal Aircraft Establishment (RAE) with a then unusual system of flaps and slotted flaps. Another, G-ACNZ, was bought by D. Napier & Son, the engine manufacturer, for tests and demonstrations with the company's 350 hp Rapier engine.

The first commercial flight by the Courier was made early in May 1934 when two were used for a cargo-carrying trial between London and Manchester by Bouts-Tillotson Transport, the aircraft being leased for the demonstration by Aircraft Exchange and Mart. The service, if it can so be described, was not developed, but the operation was given a big send-off at Hanworth Air Park by Sir Philip Sassoon, Under-Secretary for Air, and members of Parliament.

The really important events for Airspeed in 1934 were the take over agreement, announced early in July, with Swan Hunter and Wigham Richardson Ltd, the big shipbuilding company of Wallsend, Newcastle-upon-Tyne, and the completion and first flight of the twin-engined AS.6 Envoy on which a decision to go ahead had been made in the previous November.

In August 1933 Airspeed had once again run into serious financial difficulties, with too much money going out and too little coming in from sales. The overdraft was standing at nearly £13,000, including an unsecured sum of £4,000. This was when, as recorded earlier, four of the working shareholders had saved the day by taking up some £10,000 in 6 per cent debentures. At about the same time Leonard Tetley joined the board after taking up £5,000 in ordinary shares and £5,000 in debentures and was appointed London representative. Towards the end of the year Throgmorton Securities, representing a company interested in entering the aircraft manufacturing business, approached Airspeed with certain proposals, but after long negotiations the proposals were turned down. Negotiations were then opened with Armadores Trust, who were associated with Swan Hunter, and these were successful.

The agreement, involving the voluntary liquidation of the original

A comfortably relaxed group await the time of take-off with the Napier Rapier powered AS.5 Courier in the heats for the King's Cup race in July 1934. From left to right are Air Vice-Marshal A. E. Borton, and Messrs Winter, Smith and Savage. (*Flight 10629s.*)

The prototype AS.6 Envoy flying over the Solent with the *Queen Mary* below moving through Cowes Roads. (*Flight 12573s*.)

company and the registration of a new publicly-subscribed company, Airspeed (1934) Ltd, put the business in a very much stronger position—though it was to be several years before profits were being made. Until that moment the small, privately financed company had had a hard struggle to survive in days which were difficult—and not only for the aircraft industry. In the new company the original directors remained, at least initially, but they were joined by C. S. Swan, Sir Philip Wigham Richardson and George Wigham Richardson (later to be chairman in succession to Lord Grimthorpe). The nominal capital was £220,000, with 640,000 six per cent preference shares and 240,000 ordinary shares of 5s.

A. Townsley of Swan Hunter was appointed general manager after a period during which he was attached to Airspeed to investigate the production capacity and efficiency of the company before deciding whether to accept the transfer. He was later to join the board. Another member of the management who arrived after the Swan Hunter takeover, and who remained with Airspeed to the end, was J. Liddell. He became company secretary, was later appointed to the board and, in the final period, was joint managing director with Major Hereward de Havilland.

The AS.6 Envoy made its first flight on 26 June, 1934, in the hands of Flt. Lt. C. H. A. 'Percy' Colman, who had joined the company from Midland and Scottish Air Ferries. It was a seven-passenger aircraft powered by two 200 hp Wolseley AR.9 nine-cylinder radials. The Envoy was one of the very new aircraft shown at the display of the Society of British Aircraft Constructors at Hendon on 2 July. Of incidental interest is the fact that it was the first British civil aircraft for which a preliminary test-to-destruction wing had to be constructed to meet new and more stringent certification requirements.

1934 was also the year in which the long-remembered England-Australia race for the Mac.Robertson Trophy was held, in October, and for it a development of the Envoy, the AS.8 Viceroy, was designed and built at short notice. This was fitted with two NACA-cowled Armstrong Siddeley Cheetah radials of greater power than the AR.9s of the first Envoy and had long-range tankage. Because time was short the Viceroy was tested for its certificate of airworthiness at Portsmouth by an RAF pilot from Martlesham Heath. It was not successful in the race, in which it started in the scratch position in the handicap section; it was withdrawn after reaching Athens. A Courier, however, was also in the race and this was placed third in the handicap section when it completed the course in a flying time of 100 hr 24 min at an average speed of 123 mph, excluding the time at refuelling stops. Late that year an indirect set-back was suffered when an Envoy, built for a trans-Pacific flight by C. T. P. Ulm, was lost in the Pacific between San Francisco and Honolulu.

In the first month of 1935 the capital of the company was increased by £130,000 with a new share issue so as to be able to finance developments following an agreement with the Dutch designer and manufacturer, A. H. G. Fokker. This included not only a licence to build Fokker-designed aircraft and to sell them in the British Empire, but also to build and sell in Britain the American Douglas DC-2 for which Fokker held the licence for Europe. Fokker was appointed technical advisor to Airspeed. Apart from £20,000 on the execution of the licence, a royalty of £600 was to be paid for each DC-2 manufactured up to 20 and another £20,000 when sales reached a value of £150,000. Fokker was to receive 1 per cent of

The Airspeed factory at Portsmouth seen from the Langstone Harbour side after extensions had been made in 1934. (*Courtesy Richard Worcester.*)

C. T. P. Ulm's AS.6 Envoy, originally registered G-ACYJ, being loaded aboard at Southampton for transport to Montreal, Quebec, before being flown to Oakland, California, for its unsuccessful Pacific proving flight.

gross receipts—an apparently small proportion which was to cost Airspeed a great deal of money in the future—and had an option on preferred shares.

In the end, the agreement came to nothing, but the various aircraft that might have been built under it were covered by the Airspeed type numbers from the AS.16 (Fokker F.XXII transport) to the AS.23 (Douglas DC-2). The arrangement probably gave Airspeed new knowledge and confidence, and one of the indirect results may have been the continuing design work on a 15-passenger high-wing project, the AS.14—the originally named Ambassador. A mock-up was made, but no airline was sufficiently interested, and Airspeed was soon to find its energies diverted more towards the development and manufacture of military trainers and other types. In the period following the Fokker agreement Airspeed worked on a large number of projects, mostly still-born and including a few startlingly original ones, such as the 1936 AS.31, which was a fighter with the pilot's cockpit in the boom-mounted tailplane.

At this time Airspeed, like other aircraft companies, was finding great difficulty in obtaining qualified engineers and draughtsmen, so in 1935 the company founded the Airspeed Aeronautical School (later College) at Portsmouth Airport, offering courses for those who wanted to enter the aircraft industry.

By the end of 1935 the Envoy was really beginning to get about the world. In that year examples with Walter Castor II radial engines were already being operated by Czechoslovak State Airlines. Some were operated by Japan Air Transport; the Japanese bought six Envoys and a licence for the Mitsubishi Aircraft Co to manufacture them. One of the first production Envoys, G-ACVI, was sold to Ansett Airways of Melbourne and, registered VH-UXM, was one of the two aircraft with which R. M. Ansett started airline services in 1936. It was still flying in Australia (re-engined with Wright Whirlwinds) in the mid-1940s.

Towards the end of 1935 an order came from South Africa for seven Envoys which were to be of a new convertible civil-military version; four of them to be laid out as civil aircraft for South African Airways and three to be military versions for the Air Force. The first two left for South Africa on 4 July, 1936. One, a civil version, made a very fast time to Johannesburg; the other, a military version, remained for a while in Egypt for demonstrations.

The greatest travellers among the Envoys, however, were two which were delivered by air to Liu Chow, Kwangsi Province, China, in January and June 1937, over a distance of about 9,000 miles. The first was taken out by Flt. Lt. Colman and the second by G. B. S. Errington. George Errington had joined Airspeed in 1934 as an inspector, became a test pilot with the company in 1935 and was chief test pilot from 1939 until the company was finally absorbed completely by de Havilland in the early 1950s. The flights were made without trouble, even in those days of limited navigational aids and other facilities, though George Errington, who left rather too late in the year, ran into difficult monsoon weather during the final part of his journey.

The AS.6 Envoy, G-AENA, *Gabrielle*, being prepared for the start of the Portsmouth–Johannesburg race in 1936. The Envoy, carrying the racing number 13, crashed on take-off at Abercorn, Rhodesia, killing two of the crew of four. (*Flight 13478s*.)

One of the less fortunate in the Envoy series was the stock model Cheetah IX engined Series II, G-AENA, which was entered by Max H. Findlay and Ken Waller in the England (Portsmouth)–South Africa (Johannesburg) race for the Schlesinger Trophy in September 1936. In itself the race was something of a disaster, with very few finishers, but it was a positive disaster for the crew of the Envoy. It crashed at Abercorn, Rhodesia; Max Findlay and the radio operator, A. H. Morgan, were killed.

Meanwhile, a British domestic airline, North Eastern Airways, sponsored by Airspeed's chairman, Lord Grimthorpe, had used Envoys in an

One of the AS.6 Envoys used by North Eastern Airways, G-ADAZ, earlier named *Tynedale*, on the apron at Doncaster Aerodrome in October 1938 when mail was first carried during the second period of the airline's British east coast domestic services—this time between Croydon Airport and Perth, with stops at Doncaster, Leeds and Newcastle. (*Courtesy John Stroud.*)

abortive attempt to develop an air service by the east coast route from London to Scotland. On 8 April, 1935, this airline started operations on a London (Heston)–Edinburgh (Turnhouse) service, which was, however, closed down at the end of July because of inadequate navigation aids and poor traffic. Operations were re started in July 1936, using Croydon Airport for a London base, with a London–Leeds–Newcastle–Perth service, but this venture was also, in due course, to be abandoned.

An event in September 1936 which had a considerable effect on the plans of Airspeed was the decision by Lord Nuffield to stop the development and production of Wolseley aero-engines. Until then some of the Envoys had been powered by these engines, and Wolseley had been asked to tender for the delivery of them for the 'Envoy trainer' which was later to become the AS.10 Oxford. In his autobiography, N. S. Norway described the decision as a 'major disaster' for Airspeed, but it is likely that the decision was a blessing in disguise. At any rate the Oxford got

The prototypes of the AS.30 Queen Wasp and the AS.10 Oxford taxying in at the Royal Air Force Display, Hendon, in June 1937, when both were seen for the first time in public. (*Flight 14568*[s].)

along very well with Armstrong Siddeley Cheetah engines and at the time of the decision there was no Wolseley engine available of comparable power.

The reasons for the decision were typical of a period when the individual was still all-powerful in big business. The Government had decided that future Air Ministry contracts should be on a cost-plus-agreed-profit basis. In this, all costs were to be examined by Ministry accountants. Lord Nuffield, who had already spent about £200,000 on Wolseley aero-engine development and production, was not prepared to accept this system, which he looked upon as an unreasonable interference with the liberty of an individual industry.

Airspeed was asked to take over the production of Wolseley engines, but the company was not then able to finance the project, nor were its shipbuilding backers, Swan Hunter, in favour of extended adventures in the aviation business—or not, at least, until profits were being made. So the Wolseley aero-engine died.

At the end of 1936 the company's chairman, then George Wigham Richardson, who had taken over on 31 December from Lord Grimthorpe,

Another view of the prototype AS.10 Oxford as it taxied in at Hendon during the 1937 RAF Display. (*Flight 14570*[s].)

King George VI disembarks from the King's Flight Envoy III, G-AEXX, during his tour of RAF stations in May 1938. (*Charles E. Brown 5775–2.*)

announced a loss on the year's trading but mentioned important new contracts. The loss, he said, was due almost entirely to the small turnover but the total orders in the books were worth about £700,000. The contracts from the Government were for three different types of aircraft. These, as it later turned out, were for the AS.10 Oxford advanced twin-engined trainer, a military development of the Envoy which was destined to become the best-known and most important of Airspeed products, the AS.30 Queen Wasp target drone and the AS.27 'special defence' aircraft.

The invitation to submit designs for the trainer had been received in 1935. This was required not only to be a transitional trainer for twin-engined conversion and instrument flying, but also to provide instruction in navigation, night flying, radio operation, gunnery and vertical photography. So, in the course of project design development, there were considerable changes from the originally considered Envoy variant.

The Queen Wasp was intended to supplement and replace the radio-controlled Queen Bee modification of the de Havilland Tiger Moth which was already being used for gunnery training. The AS.30 was a Cheetah IX engined cabin biplane with folding wings (for operations from aircraft carriers), interchangeable wheel and float undercarriage, and was designed for catapult launching. It successfully completed carrier trials from HMS *Pegasus* (ex-*Ark Royal*) late in 1937. However, only five aircraft were completed, and the remainder of a large series of intended orders was not placed. The AS.27 'special defence' aircraft, intended, in its later form, to trail cables carrying explosives, was never built. The Queen Wasp and the Oxford were seen for the first time officially at the RAF Display at Hendon in June 1937. The first Oxford to go into service went to the RAF Central Flying School at Upavon in November of that year.

The real beginning of the King's (now Queen's) Flight came with an order—very much a feather in Airspeed's cap—for a special Envoy Series III for the transport of Royalty and State personages. As recorded in the section on the AS.6 Envoy, it was in the news in May 1938 when HM King George VI used it for a tour of four RAF training stations during which he saw some of the new Oxfords at work. Two Envoys were delivered to the RAF in India for use by the Viceroy and his staff, and five more Envoys were also sold to the RAF in 1939.

In June 1938, following the placing of big additional Government orders for the Oxford, it was announced that the type was to be built on a sub-contract basis by the Percival Aircraft Company and the de Havilland Aircraft Co. This can be said to be the beginning of an association with de Havilland which was to lead, in June 1940, to the completion of negotiations for the purchase by de Havilland of the ordinary shares held by Swan Hunter and Wigham Richardson, and, some ten years later, to the complete absorption of Airspeed by de Havilland.

By this time, June 1938, Norway had left the company after a disagreement and was devoting his whole time to writing. As managing director, Hessell Tiltman was now supported by A. Townsley (ex-Swan Hunter) as director and general manager, a post he had held since July 1936. Otherwise the board remained the same as before. At the end of the company's financial year, now in July, the chairman announced a profit on the year's trading and a consequent reduction in the deficit to less than £70,000. He also referred obliquely to 'an order for two prototypes'.

These turned out to be for the AS.39 Night or Fleet Shadower, another of the interesting types which were built or projected by Airspeed, but destined to come to nothing. Although the requirement lapsed after the start of the war, the AS.39 was a remarkable aircraft. It was designed to meet a specification which required long airborne endurance (about seven hours) with the ability to fly extremely slowly (down to 33 mph) while 'shadowing' a fleet. It was to be carrier-borne and therefore had to have folding wings, which, for such a four-engined aircraft, offered a considerable design problem.

In September 1939, while the first, and only completed, Fleet Shadower was being built, work had also been proceeding at Portsmouth on the design of the AS.45, a Bristol Mercury engined trainer intended as a back-up for North American Harvard trainers, if deliveries of these slowed

Only one AS.39 Fleet Shadower, N1323, was completed and flown though two prototypes were originally ordered to meet Admiralty requirements for a carrier-based observation aircraft of long endurance and low minimum speeds.

down, and for the Miles Masters. Two were eventually built and flown, but by that time, 1941, the training requirements were seen to be being met and no plans were made for production.

Meanwhile, in June 1940, as already recorded, the de Havilland Aircraft Co had bought the Swan Hunter shareholding in Airspeed and the board membership now included four DH directors: Alan S. Butler (chairman), F. T. Hearle, F. E. N. St Barbe and W. E. Nixon; while George Wigham Richardson remained on the board, Townsley continued as director and general manager and J. Liddell, secretary of the company (also ex-Swan Hunter), became a board member.

Hessell Tiltman, the last of the original directors, left the company in 1942, presumably to make way for design-leadership changes.

The war, coupled with the effects of the de Havilland take-over and the bombing attacks on Portsmouth, produced some considerable complications for Airspeed and its staff. Not only did the project design team find it necessary to move to Hatfield, but the building of a shadow factory at Christchurch (completed in 1941), to be managed by Airspeed and eventually to be taken over by the company, caused further dispersal of manpower. Although the factory at Portsmouth continued to be the main centre, with the production drawing office remaining there throughout the war, the project design team made a number of moves, the first of which was in 1940 to Hatfield, where the DH Technical School was initially used as a drawing office.

After the move to Hatfield, the design team started work on the AS.48, a Napier Sabre engined fighter. This project was dropped when it was seen that twin-engined radar-equipped aircraft, the Bristol Beaufighter and, afterwards, the de Havilland Mosquito, would be more effective. Work was also started on the AS.49, a Gipsy Six engined single-seat fighter trainer. A hit-and-run raid by a Junkers-Ju 88 on Hatfield in October 1940 put an end to this project. It not only destroyed the mock-up but burnt all the drawings and design calculations. The Ju 88 was also destroyed.

The design team then moved to Salisbury Hall, London Colney, and it was there, late in 1940, that work started on a project which was destined to be another famous and successful Airspeed aircraft, the AS.51 Horsa troop-carrying and, later, vehicle-carrying glider. Ten months after the specification had been received, the prototype was air-towed out of the Fairey company's Great West Aerodrome (now part of London's Heathrow Airport) for its first flight.

In the meantime, production drawings were being completed at Portsmouth, and contracts for the quantity production of the various airframe sections were given to different manufacturing centres. When completed, these sections were taken to RAF maintenance units for assembly, test and delivery. The work of manufacture and assembly was also done at the Christchurch shadow factory, the only plant where complete Horsas were in fact made and flown. Altogether more than 3,500 Horsas were put together in the different assembly units. Little was said, and nothing written, about tne Horsa in those days. The first picture of it was not published until February 1943.

The first prototype AS.51 Horsa glider, DG597, is rolled out in September 1941 at Fairey's Great West Aerodrome, now a small area within Heathrow Airport, London. (*Crown copyright.*)

A sea of Horsa gliders picketed down in 1945 at Netheravon, Wiltshire, which was then an RAF Transport Command training station. (*Imperial War Museum CH16367.*)

After project work on the Horsa I had been completed, the majority of the Airspeed design team returned to Portsmouth to continue work on Horsa development, including that on the Mark II, with a hinged nose to take vehicles and guns, and on a powered version with two Cheetah engines, and to start design work on the AS.55, a four-engined military transport freighter project.

Two members of the team, however, joined A. E. Hagg at Walton-on-Thames to work on the AS.56, a Napier Sabre engined fighter which used a new fan-cooled annular radiator. Arthur Hagg had previously been chief designer of de Havilland and was largely responsible for such aircraft as the Fox Moth, the Dragon Rapide and the Albatross airliner. He had later been concerned, at his own company at Shepperton, Surrey, with the design of air-sea rescue boats and tenders. He was working as consultant and designer in charge of engine installations for Napier when, in 1942, he was invited by the Ministry of Aircraft Production to work on the fighter. As an Airspeed project the AS.56 was dropped, but development continued on the annular radiator.

Among the recommendations of the Brabazon Committee, which was formed to decide on the types of commercial transport aircraft which should be built after the war, was one for medium-haul services. Airspeed was asked to start work on the design of the Type 2 (later Type 2A), a 'DC-3 replacement'. Although there was an agreement between Britain and the United States that the United Kingdom should concentrate on military production and development, work on this project was considered to be justified in relation to its prospective use as a military transport.

Arthur Hagg was asked to take charge of the project, which was given the type number AS.57 (Specification C.25/43), and the nucleus of a design team was built up at Fairmile Manor, Cobham, Surrey, where they remained until moving to their final home at the Christchurch factory in September 1944. Hagg was officially appointed technical director and director of design for Airspeed from 1 January, 1943. The original team who chose, or were chosen, to work on the AS.57 under him were: H. V. Clarke, chief engineer; A. E. Ellison, project engineer; G. P. Jewett, development engineer; J. F. Foss, chief aerodynamicist; C. Chapleo, chief stressman; J. Johnston, chief draughtsman; F. J. Jupp, experimental manager; and D. G. Riches, assistant experimental manager. Ellison was, as already recorded, a founder member of the Airspeed technical staff; he had joined the Airship Guarantee Company from de Havilland and had then moved on to the original Airspeed group at York.

On 25 January, 1944, the name of the company was changed again from Airspeed (1934) Ltd, to Airspeed Ltd.

Since 1941 the Christchurch factory had been a production centre for

The nucleus of the design and development team for the Ambassador airliner. From left to right they are D. G. Riches (assistant experimental manager); C. Chapleo (chief structures engineer); G. P. Jewett (chief development engineer); A. E. Ellison (chief project engineer); J. F. Foss (chief aerodynamicist); H. V. Clarke (chief engineer); A. E. Hagg (technical director and chief designer); F. J. Jupp (experimental manager); J. Johnston (chief draughtsman); G. B. S. Errington (chief test pilot).

Oxfords and Horsas and was later to do Supermarine Seafire conversions, and to make de Havilland Mosquito VIs and 35s. Altogether, 550 Oxfords and some 700 Horsas were made at Christchurch. With its ample assembly space, a 1,700-yard-long grass aerodrome and room for development, it was considered to be an ideal base for the development of the AS.57, which was later to be named the Ambassador. Soon after the design team had moved in, much of the planned accommodation—design and drawing offices, research laboratories and the technical block—was ready for initial habitation.

Although the Airspeed head office remained at Portsmouth until the company was finally taken over by de Havilland, the Christchurch base, seen here, originally built as a Government shadow factory, was the design and main assembly centre for the Ambassador airliner in the 1944–53 period.

Originally the AS.57 was envisaged as a more or less directly comparable replacement for the DC-3, but with an improved performance and modern design features, such as the nosewheel undercarriage. It was proposed as an airliner with a 40,000 lb gross weight and a payload of about 7,000 lb (30 passengers) powered by two Bristol Hercules engines. However, the conviction grew, maintained in particular by Arthur Hagg, that a medium-range aircraft in this class for post-war European services would need to have something like twice the passenger payload of the DC-3 if it were to meet traffic demands, and to have a much-improved economic performance while carrying the equipment likely to be demanded by the airworthiness authorities and the operators. So, with the selection of the more powerful Bristol Centaurus engines, the AS.57 project became first a 45,000 lb aircraft with an 8,000 lb (40-passenger) payload, and, later, a 52,000 lb plus aircraft with an 11,000 lb (50-passenger) payload. But it was still envisaged as a big twin, though plans were made from the start for the alternative use of four propeller-turbines, examples of which were then in the early stages of development by three manufacturers—Rolls-Royce (Dart), Napier (Naiad) and Armstrong Siddeley (Mamba).

Two prototypes of the AS.57 had been ordered by the Ministry of Aircraft Production (later the Ministry of Supply) and by mid-1946 control cabin and other mock-ups had been built, and the first of the prototypes was beginning to take shape in the experimental shop at Christchurch, where the assembly shops continued to complete Ministry contracts for Horsas and Mosquitos, the production of which was gradually tapering off. Already other variants of the Ambassador were being worked upon. A model of a projected military freighter, the AS.60, named the Ayrshire, was shown in 1946 during a four-day exhibition at the Royal Aircraft Establishment, Farnborough, and at the display of the Society of British Aircraft Constructors held that year, and in 1947, at Radlett aerodrome.

The first hand-made Ambassador, G-AGUA, made its initial flight on 10 July, 1947, and the second, G AKRD, pressurized prototype flew a little more than a year later, on 26 August, 1948. The first prototype was not designed to be pressurized, but a decision had been made in June 1947 that all production aircraft should have their fuselage structures designed for pressurization and have space provision for cabin blowers and other associated equipment.

During the summer and autumn of 1947 the production future of the Ambassador continued to remain in the balance. British European Airways could not be sure whether to order it and the Ministry was obviously helpless without support from the airline for which the aircraft was now primarily intended. However, after a great deal of heart-searching,

The Ambassador prototype, G-AGUA, is held off for landing at Christchurch after its first flight on 10 July, 1947. Note the missing tab on the central rudder which was later locked to become part of a fixed fin. (*Courtesy W. F. Shaylor.*)

Government and airline comings and goings, and threats by Airspeed and de Havilland to put the assembly space at Christchurch to other uses, a decision was made. BEA announced, early in December 1947, that the Ambassador was the aircraft 'best suited to meet its requirements'.

The airline's understandably difficult dilemma was the result of the fact that it had also been sponsoring the development of the Vickers V.630 Viscount, one of two experimental propeller-turbine powered airliners being built as a result of changes in the Brabazon Committee's original recommendations to meet short/medium-haul requirements. With its first flight still a year or so away, BEA and the Ministry had to decide whether to take the risk of ordering the Dart-engined Viscount (known

Consultation after the initial flight of the first prototype Ambassador. From left to right those in view in the foreground are John Roberts, the resident technical officer of the Ministry of Aircraft Production; F. J. Jupp, experimental manager; A. Townsley, director and general manager; J. F. Foss, chief aerodynamicist; A. E. Hagg, technical director and chief designer; and G. B. S. Errington, chief test pilot.

until August 1947 as the Viceroy), with its then unproven and commercially uncertain engines, or to take the more immediately practical course of ordering a bigger-capacity, conventionally powered aircraft with a more or less equivalent performance and with better-understood and reliable operating economics. In the end, of course, BEA was to order a larger version of the V.630, the V.700, thus becoming the airline pioneer of operations with propeller-turbine aircraft.

The history of the Ambassador and, consequently, of Airspeed was to be influenced to some considerable extent by the progress of the Viscount, by the question of whether or not BEA ordered it, and by its eventual success in service. The decision by BEA to buy the Ambassador was a heavy blow for Vickers at the time; although there was no question of stopping the programme of development of the Viscount, its future became somewhat nebulous. BEA had earlier given an undertaking that the Viscount would eventually be ordered and this plan was left in abeyance. The prototype Viscount 630 made its first flight on 16 July, 1948, and was soon found to have outstanding prospects as an airliner if only because of its smoothness and quietness. BEA, already thinking again about the turboprop, was requiring an aircraft of larger capacity than the V.630. The development of this larger version, the V.700, was announced in March 1949, and a firm contract for 28 aircraft was eventually signed in August 1950. The prototype was then being used experimentally by BEA on scheduled services between London and Paris, and London and Edinburgh. Passengers were delighted with the experience, though they were to learn later that the Ambassador was very little inferior in terms of comfort and quietness.

On the basis of a verbal understanding of December 1947, Airspeed started production of the Ambassador (later to be named the Elizabethan by BEA), and a firm contract for 20 was signed on 23 September, 1948. As a consequence of the promised order, the second prototype, which had been planned as a four-turboprop variant and had a wing structure designed to take these engines (Napier Naiads were envisaged at that time), was fitted instead with two Bristol Centaurus engines so as to be able to take part in the flight-test programme of the aircraft as ordered by BEA. As development progressed and changes were made, the need for a third prototype, designed to production aircraft standards, became obvious. This, G-ALFR, later named *Golden Hind*, flew in May 1950.

Meanwhile, at the Portsmouth factory, a comparatively little publicised but more immediately profitable exercise had been in progress—the conversion of surplus Oxford trainers into civil transports. This conversion, aptly named the Consul, was largely the brain-child of W. F. 'Bill' Shaylor, who had been the commercial manager of the company since September

The first definitive version of the Ambassador, the production prototype G-ALFR, later named *Golden Hind*, made its first flight in May 1950 and was later used as a flying test-bed for the Napier Eland propeller-turbine.

1937. He had realized that there would be a considerable demand for smaller charter/executive-type aircraft and that post-war designs would not be available in time to meet this demand. Oxfords were bought from the Government at very low prices and either collected virtually unused, from RAF maintenance units, or taken from the production line. Engines, where required, were bought at similarly low prices in their crates, before being stripped and rebuilt by the makers to meet the necessary standards for civil use.

The first Consul was given its certificate of airworthiness in March 1946, and nearly 130 of these modified twin-engined trainers were sold to British business owners and airline operators. Altogether, more than 200 Consuls, Consul variants and sundry Oxford conversions of various types were produced cheaply and sold profitably while development was proceeding on the Ambassador at Christchurch. During this earlier period Airspeed's Portsmouth factory had also been kept busy with sub-contract work for de Havilland on Vampire fighter fuselages and was later to make structural sections for the production Ambassadors.

The ownership of Airspeed by de Havilland became complete in 1948 when the holders of 6 per cent preference shares were, in May that year, offered one DH ordinary £1 share for every four preference shares, an offer which was accepted by the directors. But Airspeed continued to retain its independence in all but major policy matters. Even after the retirement of Arthur Hagg as technical director in the early summer of 1949, when he handed over to George H. Miles as chief designer, the revised board still included two earlier Airspeed members, though none of the originals. W. E. Nixon was now chairman in place of Alan S. Butler; joint managing directors were Major Hereward de Havilland and J. Liddell, and the other directors were F. T. Hearle, F. E. N. St Barbe, Philip E. Gordon-Marshall (who had been appointed to the board late in 1946 as sales director with primary responsibility for the Ambassador) and A. Townsley. Bill Shaylor was also appointed a director in 1950 to look after commercial affairs at board level. Among the originals, as already recorded, Norway (joint managing director since the formation) had left in 1938, and Hessell Tiltman (joint managing director 1931–38 and afterwards managing director) and Sir Alan Cobham had left the company in 1942.

But the end for Airspeed, even as a quasi-independent organization, was soon to come. The complete merger with de Havilland was announced in June 1951, thus confirming a situation which had been effectively a fact since the owners of the Airspeed 6 per cent preference shares (the only ones outstanding) had exchanged them in 1948 for DH shares. After 20 years of real or partial independence, the company became the Airspeed Division of de Havilland. Even this title, with its reminder that a company of such a name once existed, was to disappear within a comparatively short time.

Apart from the genuine doubts which the parent company harboured about the sales prospects of the Ambassador/Elizabethan airliner, the development and production of which was now running about a year behind earlier schedules, there were other factors behind the decision to take over the Airspeed facilities, to call off the continuing negotiations for the sale of Ambassadors to other customers and to limit the production to the 20 aircraft ordered by BEA. The most important of these factors was the Korean war and the positive, if relatively minor, rearmament programme to which Britain was consequently committed. The design office, the experimental shop and the assembly capacities at Christchurch were needed for the essential production of aircraft which were also more profitable than the Ambassador seemed likely to be. Another factor was the knowledge that the Ambassador was still by no means through its development problems, coupled with the probability that any prospective sales would cost an unprofitable amount of money in necessary technical support. Finally there was the unspoken conviction that, if any civil transport was, at that time, to be given priority over the existing military requirements, the de Havilland Comet jet transport should have that priority.

Strengthened by technical staff from Hatfield, the Christchurch plant was, with the original factory at Portsmouth, to do valuable work in aircraft design and production as the Airspeed Division of DH and, later, simply as The de Havilland Aircraft Company, Christchurch. Earlier the factory had designed and built the prototype DH.115 Vampire Trainer (the first flight of which was made from Christchurch on 15 November, 1950) and production versions. Later, the team redesigned the DH.112 Venom for the Royal Navy and built 50 of them. The most notable effort was the 80 per cent redesign, under W. A. Tamblin, of the D.H.110 as a shipborne fighter, the Sea Vixen, with hydraulic nosewheel steering, power-folding wings and long-stroke undercarriage.

In 1960 the Hawker Siddeley Group took over the de Havilland assets and, in 1961, it was announced in the local newspaper that 1,500 workers would be redundant within a year. In October 1962 the last completed DH assembly left the factory, leaving only the Machine Shop employing 500 workers in two Bellman hangars. In the second a small group was engaged upon a few Sea Vixen and Trident components.

In 1963 the aircraft interests of Hawker Siddeley became Hawker Siddeley Aviation and Sea Vixen production tailed off leaving only a few Trident parts to be completed.

When the civil Comet was developed into the Nimrod maritime reconnaissance aircraft in 1966 part of the main factory was re-opened to build wings and sub-assemblies with Trident front fuselage sections and engine cowling components. The signs were encouraging as the work-force slowly increased but, suddenly, the factories at Portsmouth and Christchurch were closed, the sites being sold to developers.

It was left to George Statham, the works manager, to express a fitting epitaph to this fine company: 'I came here as a de Havilland man but I soon recognised the strength of the Airspeed tradition. Frankly I now look upon myself as an Airspeed man.'

Today not even the airport at Portsmouth remains as a focus for the nostalgia felt by so many people; attempts to persuade the developers to name some of the roads after Airspeed people met with no sympathy so the name dreamed up by Miriam Tiltman in her York home in 1931 has disappeared. It is fitting that other new industries are growing on the site. FTP Industries is the only tenuous link with the past; that is now in the Westland Group.

Technically, most Airspeed aircraft were in advance of their time but the difficulty in prospering in the civil market was, and still is, immense. The Ambassador was the last chance but, being in a quasi-competitive position with its own parent and, therefore, the Comet, Airspeed had no chance of success.

One of the only two AS.1 Tern sailplanes built was still flying in 1948. It is seen here being towed off at Dunstable in July 1938 during the National Gliding Contests in which, flown by G. A. Little and A. H. Reffell, it took fourth place in the Seager Trophy Race.

AS.1 Tern

The first aircraft to be designed and built by Airspeed, the AS.1 Tern sailplane, was in fact something of a stop-gap venture—though no less carefully thought-out, designed and made for that reason. Before the company had been formed and manufacturing and design premises leased in York, the two primary sponsors, N. S. Norway and A. H. Tiltman, had, as recorded in the historical summary, planned to start by making a two/three-seat, high-wing, de Havilland Gipsy engined private-owner-type cabin aircraft. They believed that there was a market for a 'different' and better light aeroplane, and quite a lot of work had already been done on its preliminary design.

However, at the company's first post-formation board meeting, Sir Alan Cobham had announced his need for a small multi-passenger, multi-engined aircraft, with what would now be described as a 'good field performance', for use by his National Aviation Day venture. A firm order could not then be placed and something had to be built in the meantime. The light aircraft was too ambitious a project within the limited available funds and with the prospect of an order for Sir Alan's projected airliner-in-miniature.

So work on the sailplane was started. With the growing interest in gliding in Britain, Airspeed believed that there was quite a good market prospect for a British sailplane which matched the existing German sailplanes in efficiency, but which, at the same time, could be dismantled and assembled more easily at the gliding site than some of the more esoteric aircraft already in use.

At an earlier informal board meeting Sir Alan had predicted a boom in gliding, and a provisional decision had been made to proceed with design work on a sailplane in parallel with that on the private-owner type. Initial work was therefore fairly well advanced when the go-ahead was finally agreed. Airspeed then estimated that there might be a market for about 40 gliders per annum at a price of £110–£125 each.

In the event, only two (constructor's numbers 1 and 2) were completed, with components for a third (c/n 3), and these were offered at the somewhat high price, ex-works at York, of £248. The venture was, in cash terms, unsuccessful, but the Tern helped to make known the name of Airspeed, and its minor successes encouraged the new shareholders. Initial, motorcar-towed, tests were made at Sherburn-in-Elmet aerodrome early in August 1931 by N. S. Norway, who had learned to fly in 1923–24 at the de Havilland School of Flying at Stag Lane, had maintained his pilot's licence, and had, in expectation of the need, obtained his 'A' in a Lowe-Wylde glider at Sherburn in February. Later, soaring tests were made by Carli Magersuppe, the German sailplane pilot, then chief instructor of the Scarborough Gliding Club, from Sutton Bank, near Thirsk, and later from sites near Ravenscar and at Ingleby Greenhow, in the Cleveland Hills.

The first British sailplane distance record was made on 24 August, 1931, by Magersuppe with the Tern, flying from Stoupe Brow, Ravenscar, to North Beach, Scarborough—a straight-line distance of 8·3 miles, but covering about 16 miles in the process of 33 minutes of cliff soaring. This record distance, miniscule by present-day soaring standards, was beaten a year later with one of 13 miles in another type of sailplane. The Tern also held, for a time, the British altitude record of about 800 ft. Maj. H. Petre also flew the Tern on record attempts, but newspaper reports from the period name Magersuppe as the pilot on the record flights.

The story of the two completed Terns is interesting in that one, much rebuilt, was still flying in 1948. After being used by the London Gliding Club and lying at the club's Dunstable site during the war, it was bought 'in very small parts' by an Ashington, Northumberland, dental surgeon, A. Coulson, in 1947. He rebuilt it in high-wing form by 'flat-topping' the fuselage, and gave it dihedral. The second Tern, earlier used by the Southdown Club, went to a group at Lulsgate Bottom, Bristol (now Bristol Airport). After being damaged there, it was bought by Coulson for spares. His original Tern was eventually sold to an RAF gliding group.

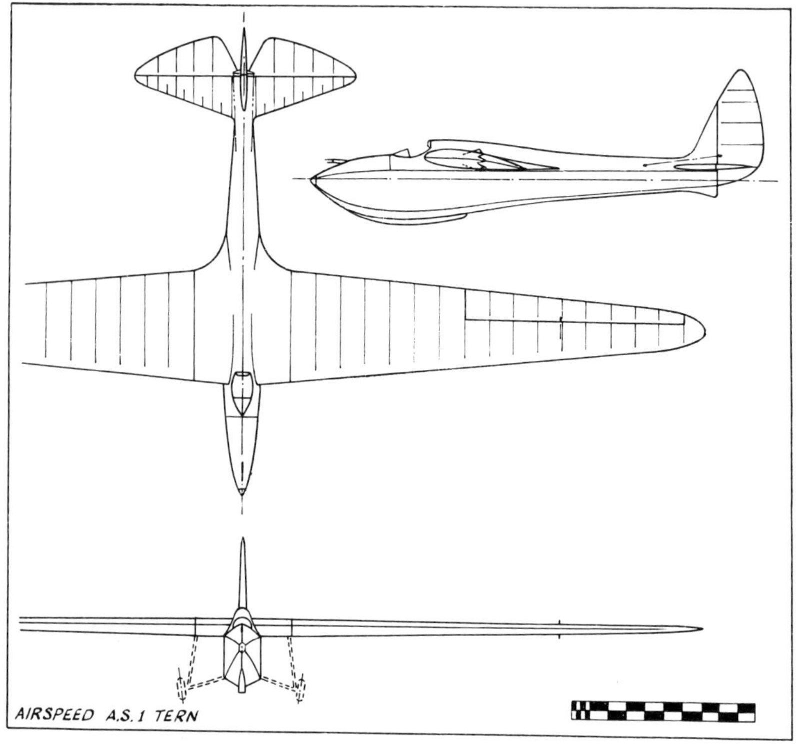

The Tern was described by *The Sailplane* (later *Sailplane and Gliding*) in 1931 as bearing 'no resemblance, except in cleanliness, to other high-efficiency craft . . . The great feature of the machine is the easy way in which it may be assembled or taken to pieces. The minimum of bolts are used and these may be easily extracted.' Airspeed records say that assembly took 'about five minutes'. The cantilever wing was in three parts—a 5 ft-span centre-section attached permanently to the fuselage, with each extension plane attached by two bolts vertically placed at the front and rear Warren-girder-braced spars. The aileron controls connected themselves automatically at the centre-section. Each tailplane, with elevator, was attached similarly with the bolts on each side. The pilot's seat was immediately forward of the front spar with a head fairing continuing to the tail to form the top part of the fuselage. Construction was of spruce, three-ply and fabric.

Span 50 ft (15·2 m); length 24 ft 7 in (7·45 m); wing area 201 sq ft (18·7 sq m). Loaded weight, approximately 400 lb (181 kg); wing loading 2 lb/sq ft (9·8 kg/sq m). Stalling speed 25 mph (40 km/h); cruising speed 35–40 mph (55–65 km/h); gliding angle at cruise 1:20. Stressed for air-towing up to 70 mph (112 km/h).

The Ferry in pleasure-flying action during its first appearance in a National Aviation Day display at Stag Lane Aerodrome, London, in May 1932. (*Flight 11530.*)

AS.4 Ferry

The ideas for that quaint but ingeniously efficient AS.4, which was later to be named the Ferry, were initially proposed at Airspeed's first post-formation board meeting on 17 April, 1931. Sir Alan Cobham, one of the company's original directors, wanted a miniature multi-engined airliner for use on his National Aviation Day (later National Aviation Displays) tours. Because the displays would usually be operated from comparatively small fields, the proposed aircraft had to have an exceptional take-off and landing performance while carrying a maximum passenger payload on local 'air-experience' flights. Towards the end of June an order for two of these ten-passenger aircraft was placed at a price of £5,195 each for delivery in April 1932. As developed, the design was for an equal-span biplane with two upright 120 hp de Havilland Gipsy II four-cylinder engines on the lower wing and one inverted 120 hp Gipsy III in the upper wing centre-section. This arrangement, apart from other aerodynamic advantages, gave the pilot a clear view forward.

Design and construction at York were completed in fewer than ten months and at the end of March 1932, the prototype, G-ABSI, was towed to Sherburn-in-Elmet, the nearest suitable aerodrome. The exercise was not without its problems and difficulties, but the alternative was to dismantle and reassemble at great cost in time. Without its extension wings the Ferry still had a span of about 16 ft, and the operation was

The prototype AS.4 Ferry at Hanworth Air Park, London, where it was shown for the first time in public in May 1932 before joining National Aviation Day tours later that month. (*Flight 11536.*)

planned to take place at night with the support of the local police. All went well until, at 2 a.m. near Tadcaster, the motorcade met (or nearly met) the vehicle carrying the rudder of the SS *Berengaria*, which was being transported in the opposite direction. The matter was, however, resolved and the Ferry reached Sherburn at dawn. On 5 April, after assembly and inspection, the first flight, of 19 minutes, was made by Capt. H. V. Worrall, chief pilot of National Flying Services at Yeadon, now Leeds/Bradford Airport. The only two serious faults, easily adjusted on the spot, were a mildly overbalanced rudder and a slight nose-heaviness. The Ferry had by now been weighed and found to be within hoped-for limits. The tare weight had been estimated at 3,460 lb and came out at 3,436 lb. The centre of gravity with ten passengers was also about right. The original estimated gross weight was 5,400 lb, and an increase to 5,600 lb was later cleared. On 8 April it was loaded to 5,400 lb on its third flight. The take-off run was not considered satisfactory at 570 ft, and the time to 10,000 ft, at 45 minutes, was longer than estimated. However, the rpm were low on take-off and the fitting of finer-pitch propellers improved both take-off and climb when the Ferry was tested again on 9 April.

National Aviation Day tours were now ready to start and time was of the essence. With the help of the Air Ministry and the RAF test pilots concerned, the Ferry got through its Martlesham Heath certification trials in four days and was officially delivered on 24 April after a total of 13 hours' test flying to join NAD later as *Youth of Britain II*. (*Youth of Britain I* was a Handley Page Clive.) It was nearly a fortnight too late to take part in the initial launching ceremony for National Aviation Day at Hanworth Air Park on 12 April. However, a special showing was arranged for it there on 4 May, after which it joined Sir Alan's fleet and was very much a part of the touring assembly at the special display at Whitchurch Airport, Bristol, on 5 June. The Ferry made its initial appearance with NAD at Stag Lane aerodrome in May, following the opening display at Ilford, Essex, on 16 April, 1932.

Prototype test and certification programmes are rarely trouble-free and those for the Ferry provided no exception. Apart from delays caused by RAF routines at Martlesham—such as parades and half-days—there was trouble with an exhaust manifold and with a sheared bolt in the undercarriage after the tests had been completed, so that the delivery flight was delayed by three days.

A second Ferry for NAD was already, by then, under construction at York, and plans were made to build essential parts of two more 'for stock'. This second AS.4, G-ABSJ, was delivered to NAD early in June as *Youth of Britain III* (later *Youth of Africa*), but, because of an accident in July (in which nobody was hurt), did not contribute proportionately to the season's work.

By the standards of the period, the Ferry did a remarkable job. G-ABSI, during its first three months with NAD, completed 288 hr on the short-period flights, made 3,600 landings and carried about 36,000 passengers. Turnrounds were sometimes accomplished in fewer than 30 seconds and refuelling in 1½ minutes. The two aircraft together, notwithstanding the crash-damage repair delay, logged 640 hr in the first season's operations, making 9,100 landings and carrying 92,000 passengers. Out of the revenues

This view of the AS.4 Ferry prototype taken when on initial show at Hanworth Air Park emphasizes both the cranked lower wing and the arrangement of the one inverted and two upright engines. (*Flight 11537.*)

The prototype AS.4 Ferry being refuelled in June 1932 at Whitchurch Airport during the Bristol Aero Club meeting at which the National Aviation Day touring display took part. The blister on the nose is the fairing which covered exterior control gear. (*Flight*.)

from the displays Sir Alan was paying for the Ferries at a rate of £400 a week to Airspeed—but this sum was more than swallowed up by the increasing costs of the company's design and manufacturing work.

The only two other AS.4s to be built, G-ACBT and G-ACFB, were sold to Midland and Scottish Air Ferries, the first being delivered in February 1933 and the second, from the company's new Portsmouth factory, in June of that year. This pioneer domestic airline was owned by John C. Sword and his wife, Christina. Although Sword was a director and western manager of Scottish Motor Traction (which was also, at that time, flirting expensively with air transport) there was no financial connection between the two organizations. The first down-payment for the second Ferry was Sword's 6½-litre Bentley motorcar. This was valued, for the purpose of initial payment, at £900 but when it was sold Airspeed obtained £700 for it. This second Scottish aircraft was fitted with radio and had a lavatory; a gross weight of 5,950 lb was by then permitted, so the payload remained reasonable.

At that time the Ferry was being offered for £3,975. Earlier, Edward Hillman, the motor coach operator who started Hillman's Airways, had been a possible buyer, but he broke off negotiations in August 1932 and later ordered the twin-engined DH.84 Dragon, which was built more or less to his specification and was sold for £2,700. The appearance of the Dragon and the inevitably lower cruising speed of the special-requirement Ferry were the main reasons for the failure of the latter to win orders in a hard world of unprofitable airline operations.

The Ferries, in their distinctive red and white styling, were used by MSAF for a variety of operations, mostly charters, and notably on the Hooton Park (Liverpool/Birkenhead) – Castle Bromwich (Birmingham) and Heston (London) – Castle Bromwich services in connection with the British Industries Fair of 1933 and 1934, which was held at Birmingham in February/March of the two years.

The MSAF venture was, however, to be short-lived; services were suspended on 30 September, 1934, after little more than 18 months of operations. One of the Ferries, G-ACBT, remained unsold at Renfrew Airport, Glasgow, and was still there in 1939. The other, G-ACFB, was sold in April 1936 to C. W. A. Scott Air Displays, which was already using G-ABSI, one of the two NAD aircraft. The other NAD Ferry, G-ABSJ, was sold in September 1934 to the Himalaya Air Transport and Survey Co with whom it was re-registered VT-AFO and named *Dragoman*. It was

The fourth and last AS.4 Ferry to be built was one of two operated by Midland and Scottish Air Ferries. After this pioneer airline went out of business G-ACFB was used by C.W.A. Scott Air Displays and later by Air Publicity of Heston, who re-engined it.

used for six months in 1934 to carry pilgrims part of the way to Badrinath, now in Uttar Pradesh, but was withdrawn from service soon afterwards. Interestingly, G-ABSI and G-ACFB were, after sale to Air Publicity of Heston, modified in the winter of 1936–37 to take inverted Gipsy Major engines in place of the two upright Gipsy II engines and were used for pleasure-flying trips until the end of the summer of 1938, after which G-ABSI was sold to Portsmouth Southsea and Isle of Wight Aviation, though it was little used on their Solent Ferry.

The prototype AS.4 Ferry after it had been re-engined in the winter of 1936–37 by Air Publicity of Heston with inverted Gipsy Major engines in place of the two outer upright Gipsy IIs. G-ACFB was similarly modified. (*Courtesy Richard Riding.*)

The AS.4 was described by its designer, Hessell Tiltman, at the time when it made its first appearance, as an aircraft with 'a large cabin and a small petrol tank'. In fact it had fuel capacity available for about five hours at cruising speed, but with full tanks it could not carry its capacity payload of ten passengers. More to the point was its high ratio of dis-

The 10-passenger cabin of the AS.4 Ferry was spartan but practical in its pleasure-flight furnishings. The occupants had a reasonably good view of the world at large and could also see what was going on in what would now be called the flight deck. (*Flight 11532.*)

posable load (passengers and/or fuel) to power, which worked out at about 6 lb per hp or, with ten seats filled, at 36 hp per passenger.

The Ferry ran into 'regulations' difficulties in its early development days. The ruling at the time was that any aircraft with ten seats or more was required to have radio equipment, but, had the tenth seat been taken up with radio, no such equipment would have been needed. In the end,

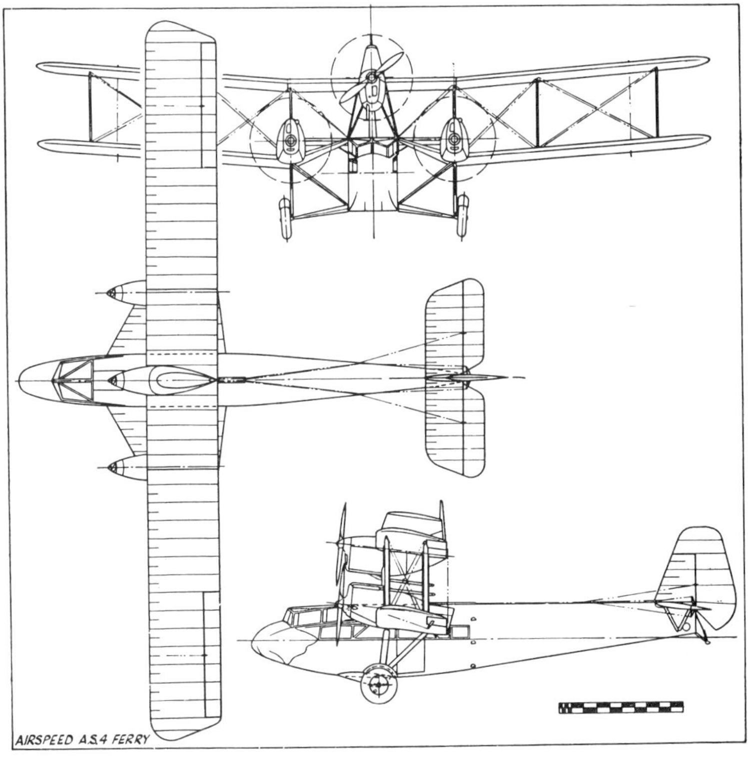

because the Ferry was to be used only for local flying by NAD, no radio was required, and the Ferry was used with Cobham's 'circus' as a ten-passenger aircraft without radio.

Although it was first intended specifically for pleasure-flying or short-haul work, the designers took some trouble to calculate its performance in other rôles. A six-passenger (plus luggage) payload could, for instance, be carried for four hours at cruising speed on the assumption of the failure of one engine and maintenance of height at 5,000 ft. If an 8,000 ft engine-out cruise case was to be assumed, the payload would need to be reduced to the equivalent of five passengers and luggage.

In design the Ferry was unusual for its era mainly because of the arrangement of the engines, with two on the cranked lower wing and the third not in the nose, as was then normal, but in the upper-wing centre-section, giving the pilot, as already mentioned, an unobstructed view forward. The fuel was carried in a gravity-feed, 65-gallon tank above and behind the central engine, which was fed also by pump. To provide rapid refuelling there was a pipeline to the tank from a union on the side of the fuselage. Other mildly unusual features included the aerofoil-section fairing enclosing the radius-rods of the split-axle type undercarriage, which may or may not have provided extra lift but would have had a useful ground-cushioning effect.

Structurally the Ferry was straightforward and mainly of wood. The fuselage was a flat-topped monocoque of spruce and plywood covering and had two passenger doors. The wings had box spars with spruce flanges and ply walls. Steel tubes were used for the compression drag struts.

Span 55 ft (16·76 m); chord 5 ft 9 in (1·75 m); overall length 39 ft 8 in (12·09 m); overall height 14 ft 3 in (4·34 m); wing area 641 sq ft (59·5 sq m); cabin dimensions 12 ft 7 in (3·86 m) by 3 ft 9½ in (1·16 m) by 5 ft 9 in (1·75 m). Weight empty, including furnishing, 3,440 lb (1,560 kg); pilot, fuel and oil (3·75 hr cruise), 660 lb (298 kg); payload 1,500 lb (681 kg); loaded weight 5,600 lb (2,540 kg); wing loading 8·7 lb/sq ft (42·75 kg/sq m); power loading 15·5 lb/hp (7·1 kg/hp). Maximum speed at sea-level 108 mph (173 km/h), at 5,000 ft (1,524 m) 103 mph (165 km/h); cruising speed at 1,000 ft (305 m) 85–90 mph (136–144 km/h); stalling speed 49 mph (79 km/h); take-off in still air 200 yd (183 m); distance to 80 ft (24·4 m) 500 yd (457 m); initial rate of climb 520 ft/min (2·65 m/sec); time to 5,000 ft (1,524 m) 14 min; time to 10,000 ft (3,048 m) 38 min; absolute ceiling 13,000 ft (3,960 m); range 320–340 miles (510–545 km).

(Performance figures are from the Martlesham test report.)

The prototype Courier, in its initial development form, flying on test from Portsmouth in 1933. (*Flight 12890.*)

AS.5 Courier

With design work on the Ferry virtually complete it was possible for A. H. Tiltman to start thinking in more detail about a follow-up project. Earlier ideas for a private-owner type had changed and developed, and this follow-up aircraft, the AS.5, was to become a five/six-seater with a much wider range of usefulness and was, for its day, of extremely advanced design. Tiltman's initial sketches of the proposed AS.5 had been approved by the other members of the board of Airspeed at a meeting in November 1931, and good progress was being made on the design by early March 1932.

The story has been told that the decision to design and build a low-wing cantilever monoplane with a retractable undercarriage stemmed from seeing a photograph of a Lockheed Orion in an aviation magazine. By 1931 three or four American manufacturers were beginning to move towards the present-day concept of the 'clean' transport aeroplane, and the single-engined six-passenger Orion was an advanced and still unique civil example. Nothing of the kind was yet being considered by British manufacturers, and Airspeed was later to find that there was a certain amount of disagreement about the economic advantages of speed and of prejudice against such new-fangled and 'unnecessary' complications as retractable undercarriages.

Whether this story of the origin of the AS.5 is apocryphal or not, Airspeed needed something more than the simple ambition to design such an advanced aircraft if a go-ahead decision was to be made. This 'something more' appeared in the form of the interest which Lord Wakefield was being encouraged to take in the possibility of a very-long-distance non-stop flight by Sir Alan Cobham (later to be joined by Sqn. Ldr. W. Helmore) to demonstrate the practicability of air-to-air refuelling. An expected order for the first AS.5, named the Courier, provisionally signed on 6 May, 1932, was confirmed in August and construction started in September.

In April, as recorded in the company history, there had been satisfactory talks between Sir Alan and Lord Wakefield, who was ready to put up £10,000, of which £5,000 was for the airframe. Promise had also been received of a 240 hp Armstrong Siddeley Lynx IVC seven-cylinder radial engine. The agreement of 6 May involved difficult penalty clauses, including one that the AS.5 must be ready for delivery by 6 April, 1933. Although the first aircraft was to have special tankage (up to 275 gallons) and other equipment related to the air-refuelling rôle, Tiltman was already determined, however difficult this might be, not to compromise its basic design as a fast medium-sized transport/private-owner aircraft.

The decision had not, apparently, been reached without heart-searchings by some members of the Airspeed board. One of the leading British designers of the day had told the chairman of Airspeed, Lord Grimthorpe, that a retractable undercarriage would be more trouble than it was worth. However, the two managing directors were convinced that the only hope for Airspeed was to be in the van of design progress, and Lord Grimthorpe finally agreed to the go-ahead.

Like self-sealing tanks (indirectly an Airspeed innovation), the retractable undercarriage was ignored by the authorities of the day, but both were to be taken up seriously in due course. Airspeed was eventually paid £10,000 by the Government for use of the patented retractable undercarriage in Oxford production, but, because of tax, only a relatively small proportion

The prototype Courier G-ABXN completed its initial period of test flying without the Townend ring cowling fitted later to this and to all other Couriers, whether Lynx- or Cheetah-engined. (*Flight 12895.*)

The AS.5 Courier photographed head-on with undercarriage up and down. This aircraft was ordered by Commercial Airways of Abridge Aerodrome, Essex, but does not appear to have been operated by them. (*Flight 10292*[s] and *10293*[s].)

of this sum reached the company's bank account. Other manufacturers had meanwhile infringed the patent without possible redress.

By October 1932 the design of the Courier had been finalized to the extent that general-arrangement drawings and details were made available to visiting journalists from the technical aviation press. Of primary interest was the undercarriage, for which it was then claimed that no more than about 30 lb of additional weight had been incurred in return for an advantage of about 20 mph in cruising speed. Apart from the hydraulic jacks, no proprietary components or indicator mechanisms were available, so Airspeed had to design these from first principles. For its time the undercarriage geometry was ingenious. Each main oleo-pneumatic leg was, with its half axle, hinged to the forward wing spar. The radius-rod, which ran to the lower edge of the rear spar, was hinged, the shorter section being attached to the undercarriage leg. A hydraulic jack was attached at one end to the top of the rear spar and at the other to the radius-rod just behind the hinge point. When the leg was in the fully extended position the stop in the radius-rod hinge was designed so that it was slightly past 'dead centre', and landing loads thus tended to lock the undercarriage in its down position. The hydraulic pressure was provided manually from a hand pump operated by the pilot. When retracted the wheels projected sufficiently below the level of the underside of the wing to be usable as solidly mounted 'half-wheels' in case the lowering system failed.

Two normal fuel tankages were offered: either one or two tanks each

This picture of the prototype AS.5 Courier, by then with vivid new styling and fitted with its Townend ring cowling, shows how the wheels protruded slightly when retracted, so that a not-too-damaging landing could be made even if the undercarriage failed to extend. (*Courtesy Richard Worcester.*)

of 28 gallons capacity, in the outer centre-section, feeding by engine pump into a scuttle-mounted header tank of 10 gallons—making a total of 38 gallons for a full-payload endurance of about 3½ hours or 66 gallons for an endurance of some 6 hours and an appropriately reduced payload. The prototype was, however, as already explained, being built specially for flight-refuelling experiments, and at that time Sir Alan proposed attempting a non-stop flight to Australia. Consequently extra tankage was installed, with fuel in five tanks—three in the centre-section and one in each outer wing. The idea was to take-off at a weight just below the normal maximum and to top-up the tanks when airborne. Later, this prototype, G-ABXN, was to be seen, unusually enough, with two permitted weights inscribed on the rear fuselage: 'Max weight on ground, 3,500 lb', and 'Max weight in air, 5,050 lb'. When the tanks were topped up to this weight (including that of Sir Alan and Sqn. Ldr. Helmore), the original plan was that the Courier should carry fuel up to 275 gallons, sufficient for about 25 hours' flying, or a range of nearly 3,000 miles.

Airspeed's move to Portsmouth from York was made in March/April 1933, and the not-yet-completed prototype had to be transported there and re-erected for its first flight from Portsmouth Airport on 11 April. For this initial flight, Flt. Lt. G. H. Stainforth, the Royal Aircraft Establishment test pilot and former member of the Schneider Trophy team and holder of the world's speed record, was engaged for a small fee. He was keen to fly the Courier and, with the approval of the RAF authorities, took leave in order to be able to do so. Experienced though he was, Flt. Lt. Stainforth had had no opportunity of flying an aeroplane with a retractable undercarriage, and he took very great care to become accustomed to its operation. The story goes that he spent something like five hours in the prototype, which was jacked up in the hangar, checking and practising retraction and lowering before making the first flight. In all, he flew the Courier for about five hours initially, during the course of which he made a successful forced landing after power failure, caused probably by a fuel restriction, soon after take-off. When the engine stopped, the undercarriage was already up and the aircraft was heading towards Langstone Harbour; he put the nose down, lowered the undercarriage and turned downwind back to the airport.

During these first few hours the Courier had been flown without the Townend ring cowling for the Lynx engine. Even so, the initial tests showed that the performance was well up to the estimates, with a top speed

The first production AS.5 Courier is taxied out at Portsmouth after it had been handed over to Aircraft Exchange and Mart, who then had the sales rights for Britain and Ireland. (*Flight 10079s.*)

of 160 mph at 1,000 ft and medium weight, a cruising speed of about 140 mph and an initial rate of climb of nearly 1,200 ft/min. The corrected stalling speed was about 52 mph. When, in June, the Courier went to Martlesham Heath for its official tests, the long-chord Townend ring had been fitted. The growing official interest in this advanced aeroplane was shown by the fact that the principal British aircraft designers were invited to Martlesham to inspect the Courier and to see it perform.

The prototype had by then logged nearly 60 hours, and four different pilots, including Sir Alan Cobham, had flown it solo. There had been the usual misadventures. A heavy landing on rough ground, after the engine failure, had buckled both radius-rods and a hydraulic ram, but the undercarriage had not collapsed. Later a hydraulic coupling came adrift; luckily the failure was in the cockpit area and the two parts of the line could be held together by N. S. Norway who was flying in the second pilot's (or front passenger's) seat. There was another radius-rod failure while it was being flown on test at Martlesham, and the undercarriage, this time, collapsed, but there was comparatively little damage and the Courier was flying again in less than a week. The original 6 April, 1933, deadline for delivery to Sir Alan had, of course, long passed, but he was not ready, either, for the proposed flight to Australia.

In the meantime, construction had been started on three more Couriers, and the first of these, G-ACJL, was delivered on 4 September to Aircraft Exchange and Mart, who had been appointed distributors for Britain and Ireland. A fortnight later, on 18 September, this aircraft was used for a fast trip to Scotland for (among other reasons) a demonstration to John Sword of Midland and Scottish Air Ferries and to officials of Scottish Motor Traction. The outward flight from Portsmouth to Renfrew Airport was made at an average speed of 131 mph and the return trip at 138 mph. In December there was a joint demonstration by AEM and R. K. Dundas Ltd, who now held the agency for India and Burma.

Two basic variants of the Courier were then being offered—one, the 'English' (AS.5A) version, fitted with the Armstrong Siddeley Lynx IVC and the other the 'Colonial' (AS.5B) model, fitted with a 305 hp Armstrong Siddeley Cheetah V seven-cylinder radial. The first Colonial version, G-ACLF, was certificated early in December 1933 and left for a demonstration tour of India on 16 December flown by C. E. Kelly and carrying Lord Ronaldshay, chairman of R. K. Dundas, as passenger.

The Air Ministry had also shown practical interest in the Courier by ordering a Lynx-engined AS.5A, which was delivered to the RAF as K4047 in February 1934. This was an important event not only in itself, but because the aircraft was returned to Airspeed in the following year for the fitting of drag and high-lift devices which were tested by the RAE at

The Air Ministry's AS.5 Courier, K4047, which was later modified for flap/slot experiments made at RAE Farnborough in 1935–36 before being used by the RAF for communications work. (*Flight 10297s.*)

Entry to the front and rear seats of the AS.5 Courier was made through this triangular door on the port side. (*Flight 10296s*.)

Farnborough between November 1935 and October 1936. As pilots found, the Courier was, even with the undercarriage down, 'clean' enough to make the approach and landing a somewhat difficult operation. The speed had to be held down very accurately if it were not to 'float' for an uncomfortably long period when held off for the landing. Handley Page slotted flaps were fitted to the trailing edges of the extension wing inboard of the ailerons and split flaps (then known as Schrenk flaps) across the centre-section. In addition, the controls were modified so that the ailerons could be lowered symmetrically to act as flaps while still retaining their movement for lateral control. The split flaps provided drag and some small additional lift, while the HP flaps and drooping ailerons provided additional lift, thus steepening the approach, lowering the minimum control speed and reducing the tendency to float.

Several premature attempts were made in 1934 to develop domestic air services, and the Courier, as a fast, small-capacity transport, was of interest to the operators concerned. About half-a-dozen were on order during that year, on what Nevil Shute (Norway) described in his autobiography as 'tenuous hire-purchase deals', and some went into temporary service. Four were ordered, for instance, by London Scottish and Provincial Airways, but only two of these, G-ACSY and G-ACSZ, appear to have been operated on experimental services between London, Nottingham, Manchester and Glasgow, and later on a Southampton–Hull service. Using Couriers, LSPA started services on the Leeds–London–Paris route

The scene at Hanworth Air Park in May 1934 when an experimental cargo service to Manchester was operated by Bouts-Tillotson Transport with two AS.5 Couriers leased from Aircraft Exchange and Mart. For the occasion the Couriers carried the words 'Bouts Airlines London—Manchester Express Freight'. The service was not repeated.

on 6 August, 1934. But like so many other airline attempts of the period, the effort was unsuccessful. A Courier was also seen for a short period in the colours of Commercial Airways of Abridge, Essex.

Another abortive exercise involving Couriers was a one-off experimental cargo service between London and Manchester, organized by Bouts-Tillotson Transport on 9 May, 1934. Two aircraft were leased from AEM and pilots hired for the occasion, and each flew north with 1,000 lb of cargo, returning in due course with assorted loads, including cotton goods, newspapers and a racing greyhound complete with boy handler. The aim was to start a London–Manchester–Belfast service, but nothing came of it.

An outstanding success for the Courier in 1934 was its performance in the England–Australia race from Mildenhall to Melbourne for the

The first production Courier, G-ACJL, at Mildenhall before the start of the 1934 England–Australia race in which, flown by Sqn. Ldr. D. E. Stodart, it finished third in the handicap section. (*Flight 10920*[s].)

Mac.Robertson Trophy in October 1934. Four Couriers, G-ABXN, G-ACJL, G-ACVF and another, unspecified, had originally been entered for the race, but only one eventually competed. This was the first production Courier, G-ACJL, flown by Sqn. Ldr. D. E. Stodart (who had originally entered G-ACVF) accompanied by his cousin, K. G. Stodart. There were two sections in the competition: the speed race, which was on a first-over-the-line basis (i.e. the shortest elapsed time), and the handicap race, which was won by the competitor whose flying time (excluding ground stops) beat by the biggest margin the handicap-adjusted time calculated according to a much-criticized formula which took into account the loaded weight, payload, horsepower and wing area. The Stodarts' Courier averaged 123 mph, with a flying time of 100 hr 24 min and a net time (actual flying time minus the allowance) of 79 hr 32 min, to take fourth place in the handicap race. The winners (C. W. A. Scott and T. Campbell Black, in one of the original de Havilland Comets) won the speed race, so were ineligible for the handicap prize, thus leaving Sqn. Ldr. Stodart and his companion effectively in third place. The Courier remained in Australia, where it was re-registered VH-UUF.

Following the successful flight-refuelling demonstration for the Air Ministry in April 1934 (described in the company history), the prototype Courier, G-ABXN, had by then finally made the planned attempt on a long-distance non-stop flight—though to India, not Australia. Experiments with the new techniques had not been entirely without difficult

The accuracy of flying needed during early air-to-air refuelling tests is emphasized in this picture of the Courier seen from the Handley Page W.10 tanker with Sqn. Ldr. W. Helmore at the receiving end. See also the picture on page 10. (*Flight 10837s*.)

incidents. One of these had very nearly ended in disaster on one of the early trials when the ballasted trailer-cord (for pulling in the tanker's fuel line) had jammed in the Courier's aileron-hinge gap before fuel was being passed. Control was regained at low altitude by using full opposite aileron to release the cord. This near-accident led to a minor revision of the system. The bag of sand, used until then to weight the fuel-line cord, was replaced by a toy balloon filled with water. In the repetition of any similar event the balloon could be expected to burst and reduce damage and danger.

For the flight to India it was planned to air-refuel the Courier initially over Portsmouth, soon after dawn, and over Malta the same evening from Sir Alan's two Handley Page W.10s used for passenger flying with National Aviation Displays. The later air-refuellings were to be made at dawn over Aboukir aerodrome, and over Shaibah aerodrome, Basra, in the evening, for the final leg to Karachi (then in India), arriving at dawn. These two refuelling operations were to be handled by RAF air-tankers based at these two points. The original proposal had, as already explained, been to fly non-stop to Australia late in 1933, but this was found rather too ambitious and expensive at this relatively early stage in the development of the air-refuelling techniques so the destination of the flight had, in April 1934, been changed to India. At the beginning of September, the decision was reached to make the flight to Karachi that month, starting at dawn on 21 September from Portsmouth.

After a 24-hour delay because of a forecast of bad weather, the Courier took off from Portsmouth Airport at 05·30 on 22 September with 100 gallons of fuel on board. In the first air-refuelling, near Selsey Bill, from one of the two W.10s, G-EBMR *Youth of New Zealand*, the Courier's tanks were topped up with another 80 gallons before it was headed across the Channel below low cloud. The other NAD W.10, G-EBMM, was already based in readiness at Halfar aerodrome, Malta, for the second refuelling operation. The Courier arrived over Malta at 16·15 GMT, and contact was made with the W.10.

During a second contact to top up the tanks after Sqn. Ldr. Helmore had checked their contents, Sir Alan found that there was no shut-down response when the throttle lever was pulled back. The control had become disconnected. He immediately broke contact with the W.10 and headed for Halfar. Unfortunately the disconnected control at the engine end did not hold the throttle open; power was gradually being lost, and an arrival at Halfar was touch and go. By leaving the undercarriage up, and with the good fortune of the fact that the throttle was closing only slowly, the Courier just scraped into Halfar over the boundary wall to make a safe belly landing on the protruding wheels. In spite of the very excessive landing weight, of about 4,500 lb with nearly full tanks, no serious damage was involved except to the propeller. A junction pin in the throttle linkage had lost its split-pin and had fallen out into the tray of the engine cowling. The attempt, even if a failure, at least showed that air-refuelling in real-life conditions was practical, so long as the weather and visibility were good enough for successful contacts to be made.

Although entirely unconnected with the long-distance air-refuelling attempt as such, a related accident should be recorded here. After the initial refuelling by G-EBMR, this W.10 returned to the Flight Refuelling base at Ford, Sussex, to have its special tanks removed and seats re-installed. It crashed on a positioning flight to rejoin National Aviation Displays, then operating at Coventry, following fatigue failure of a tailplane bracing-wire bolt, and the crew of four were killed.

The Courier was probably the only civil aircraft of its time capable of providing a satisfactory flying platform for the Napier Rapier which was installed for test and demonstration work. G-ACNZ was later re-engined with an Armstrong Siddeley Lynx and used on the Solent ferry. (*Flight 10470s.*)

One not-to-be-forgotten variant of the Courier was the AS.5C, G-ACNZ, ordered by D. Napier & Son, the aero-engine manufacturers, and fitted by Airspeed with a 350 hp Rapier IV sixteen-cylinder H-type engine for test and demonstrations. Delivered in June 1934, this clean, fast version of the Courier was normally flown by AVM A. E. Borton, a director of Napier. It was not, unfortunately, fast enough to beat the over-optimistic handicappers in the heats for the King's Cup Race of July 1934—one of its earliest appearances.

As can be seen in Appendix II (B), 16 Couriers were built and at least nine survived into the World War II period—and one of them, for a time, even into the post-war period. The prototype, G-ABXN, was still airworthy and flying in 1940. After service alongside G-ABXN with North Eastern Airways during and after 1937, G-ACLF, G-ACLT and

At one period, Portsmouth Southsea & Isle of Wight Aviation had seven Couriers operating on their Solent ferry service. This, G-ADAX, was one of several bought initially by the airline and remained in operation for five years until requisitioned for taxi service with the Air Transport Auxiliary in 1940. (*Courtesy Richard Riding.*)

G-ACVF had gone to Portsmouth Southsea and Isle of Wight Aviation, which also operated G-ACNZ (after re-engining with a Lynx), G-ACZL, G-ADAX and G-ADAY—all with the retractable undercarriages later locked permanently down.

Apart from the retractable undercarriage and the fact that it was, by British standards, unusual in that it was a cantilever low-wing monoplane, the Courier was structurally conventional. The 10 ft 3 in span centre-section was integral with the fuselage and the outer-wing structure consisted of two box spars of spruce and three-ply, girder-type former ribs

Four Couriers in a line-up at Portsmouth Airport of the fleet of Portsmouth Southsea & Isle of Wight Aviation who operated the Solent ferry on which seven Couriers were eventually deployed. On the right are two Monospars and a Fox Moth.

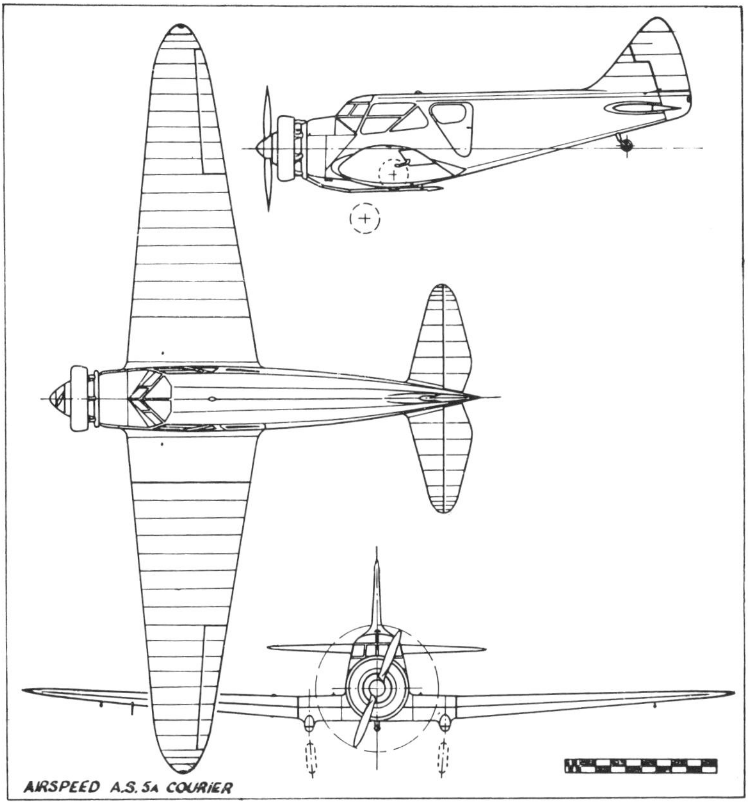
AIRSPEED A.S. 5A COURIER

G-ACVF
G-A

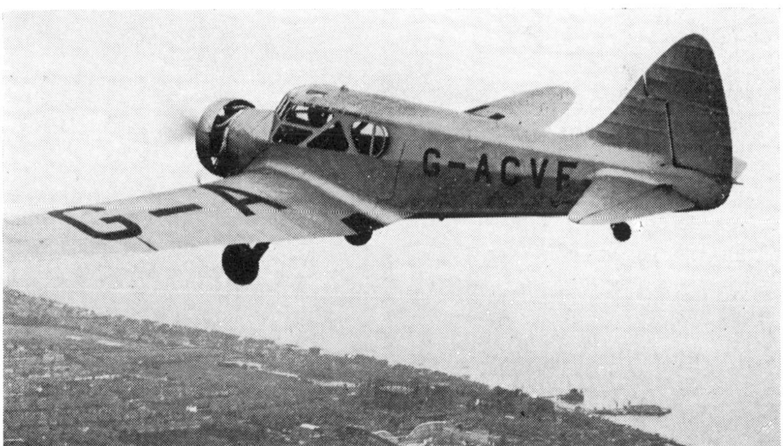

The only surviving post-war AS.5 Courier was that bought early in 1946 by East Anglian Flying Services, later Channel Airways, of Southend, and used for pleasure flying and taxi work for three years until scrapped for lack of spares. (*Courtesy Richard Riding*.)

and inter-spar bracing of built-up diagonal struts. The wing was fabric covered apart from the leading edge. The fuselage was in three sections. The forward one (back to the instrument panel) was of welded tube; the centre and aft sections were built up of spruce longerons and bulkheads, with plywood covering. The tailplane, adjustable by screw-jack, and the fin were cantilever.

Span 47 ft (14·3 m); length 28 ft 6 in (8·68 m); wing area 250 sq ft (23·2 sq m); cabin 8 ft long by 3 ft 8 in wide and 5 ft 3 in high (2·4 m by 1·1 m and 1·6 m).

AS.5A (Lynx IVC). Empty weight 2,344 lb (1,064 kg); pilot, passengers and baggage 1,200 lb (545 kg); fuel and oil for 5-hour cruise 490 lb (222 kg); loaded weight 3,900 lb (1,771 kg). Maximum speed at sea-level 154 mph (246 km/h); maximum speed at 5,000 ft (1,525 m) 148 mph (238 km/h); maximum speed at 10,000 ft (3,048 m) 143 mph (230km/h); cruising speed at 1,000 ft (305 m) 132 mph (212 km/h); landing speed 56 mph (90 km/h). Initial rate of climb 730 ft/min (3·7 m/sec); service ceiling 13,500 ft (4,120 m). Maximum range 600 miles (965 km).

AS.5B (Cheetah V). Empty weight 2,328 lb (1,056 kg); pilot, passengers and baggage 1,056 lb (524 kg); fuel and oil 516 lb (234 kg); loaded weight 4,000 lb (1,814 kg). Maximum speed at sea-level 165 mph (264 km/h); maximum speed at 5,000 ft (1,525 m) 160 mph (257 km/h); maximum speed at 10,000 ft (3,048 m) 155 mph (249 km/h); cruising speed at 1,000 ft (305 m) 145 mph (233 km/h); landing speed 58 mph (93 km/h). Initial rate of climb 940 ft/min (4·7 m/sec); service ceiling 17,000 ft (5,180 m). Maximum range 640 miles (1,030 km).

AS.6 Envoy

The logical successor to the Courier was a larger, twin-engined version and Airspeed's thinking on these lines began soon after the first flight of that advanced aircraft. The decision to go ahead with the AS.6, or Envoy, was made at a board meeting in November 1933; six (including the AS.8 Viceroy variant specially built for the England–Australia Race and described separately) were in various stages of construction by January 1934. The prototype, G-ACMT, flew on 26 June, 1934, in the hands of Flt. Lt. C. H. A. Colman. It was shown at the one-day SBAC Display, Hendon, on 2 July, and was at Martlesham Heath, for certification tests, by September.

Although three of the first batch, including the Viceroy, were powered by 240 hp Armstrong Siddeley Lynx IVC or 350 hp Cheetah engines, both seven-cylinder radials, the design of the Envoy was initially based on the use of Wolseley engines, and the connection between Airspeed and Wolseley Motors remained very close until, in September 1936, Lord Nuffield suddenly decided, after a disagreement with the authorities, to stop the development and production of these engines. The events leading

The prototype AS.6 Envoy flying near Portsmouth in 1934. It was later modified as the prototype Mark II with split flaps and re-engined with Wolseley Scorpio Is in place of the original AR.9s.

to this decision are outlined in the company history summary and in the story of the AS.10 Oxford, but are mentioned here to explain the otherwise curious diversity of powerplants used in the first dozen or so Envoys which were constructed. In fact, two of the first three Envoys, as such, to be built, G-ACVH and G-ACVI, were ordered respectively by Wolseley Motors and Lord Nuffield himself for test and demonstration purposes. Like the prototype, G-ACVH was fitted with 200 hp AR.9 Mk IIs, and G-ACVI with 225 hp Wolseley Aries IIIs, both nine-cylinder radials; the prototype was later fitted with 250 hp Wolseley Scorpio I nine-cylinder radials and brought up to Series II standard, with flaps, early in 1936.

The prototype AS.6 Envoy, less port rear engine cowlings, gives a very dated appearance to the RAF Hawker Furies and Vickers Virginias during a Service visit to Portsmouth Airport in 1935. (*Courtesy Richard Worcester.*)

The first of the Lynx-powered AS.6 Envoys was G-ACVJ. This was taken over by R. K. Dundas, the sales agents, for demonstrations in India, leaving in mid-January 1935.

The story of the early days of the Envoy is closely concerned with long-distance racing and demonstration flights. Apart from the special Viceroy, the original entries for the England–Australia race for the Mac.Robertson Trophy in October 1934 included two Envoys—one entered by Lord Nuffield and one by Lady Cobham. Neither, in fact, was flown in the race. The entry from Lady Cobham, listed as an AS.7 (a projected military version) was cancelled, and Lord Nuffield's aircraft, G-ACVI, by then named *Miss Wolseley*, and flown by George Lowdell, was force-landed near St Neots, Huntingdonshire, while on the way to the starting and assembly aerodrome, RAF Mildenhall. Later demonstration and test flights by this Aries III engined aircraft included one to Cape Town and back by Sqn. Ldr. D. Hilton in 1935; the out-and-home journey was completed in 119 hr. This Envoy undoubtedly put in more hours than any other. It was sold to Ansett Airways, in Australia, where it was registered VH-UXM in 1936, was re-engined with 350 hp Wright Whirlwind seven-cylinder radials early in 1944, and by the autumn of 1945 had completed something like 10,000 hours.

The fourth Envoy to be completed, G-ACYJ, was a 350 hp Cheetah IX engined long-range variant built to the order of C. T. P. Ulm, the Australian pilot, for a proving/demonstration flight across the Pacific via Honolulu in preparation for possible regular services. After being test-flown at Portsmouth, it was dismantled and shipped, on 8 November, 1934, from Southampton to Montreal. Already re-registered VH-UXY, it was flown to Oakland, California, for the Pacific crossing. With G. M. Littlejohn as navigator and radio operator, the Envoy left Oakland on 3 December, but failed to reach Honolulu, which may have been overflown. Radio signals were being received after the estimated time of arrival and a seven-day search by the US Navy was unsuccessful, though debris was reported to have been found.

Meanwhile, following the Courier tradition, a 'Colonial' or 'Overseas' variant, G-ACVJ, had been built and flown. This, fitted with 240 hp Armstrong Siddeley Lynx IVCs, had been built to the order of R. K. Dundas, the Airspeed sales agents, and left in mid-January 1935, via Spain, for demonstrations in India, being flown out by Flt. Lt. H. C. Johnson, accompanied by Sir Alan Cobham. It was taken over by Commercial Air Hire in 1936 before being sold, among many other Envoys, to Spain, where the civil war had broken out. As the then joint managing director of Airspeed, Nevil Shute (Norway), put it in his autobiography many years later, 'wars came eventually to clean up the position for us'. Several of the Envoys built before 1937 ended their lives in Spain. Among them was the prototype, G-ACMT, which was sold for £6,000 and later hit high ground, killing, among others, Franco's General Mola; G-ADBB, after service with North Eastern Airways; G-ADCA, used by Portsmouth Southsea and Isle of Wight Aviation; G-AEBV, delivered to Brian Allen Aviation, in May 1936; and the AS.8 Viceroy variant, G-ACMU.

The first commercial airline operator to use Envoys was North Eastern Airways, whose chairman, Lord Grimthorpe, was also Airspeed's first chairman. Using Cheetah-engined variants, G-ADAZ *Tynedale*, G-ADBB *Wharfedale* and, later, G-ADBZ *Swaledale*, North Eastern Airways started a brief series of operations on 8 April, 1935, over what would now

The single-seat pilot's cabin of the AS.6 Envoy I. The white handle to the right of the seat operated the hydraulic pump for raising and lowering the undercarriage—and, in later marks, for raising and lowering the flaps. (*Flight 11138s*.)

be known as the east coast route to Scotland, from London (Heston) to Leeds, Newcastle and Edinburgh, the London–Edinburgh fare being £10 including ground transport. Although temporary permission was given for the use of RAF Turnhouse, Edinburgh, on the inaugural flights, the service could not be flown through to Edinburgh until 27 May, and much of the point of the operation was lost during the vital initial six weeks of the operation. The inaugural southbound service very nearly ended in minor disaster when the Envoy, with its little load of dignitaries, overshot on landing at Heston and slid into the boundary fence, luckily with only superficial damage. A more serious mishap occurred in May, when, through carburettor icing, power was lost and *Swaledale* had to be belly-landed near Ripon, Yorkshire. Lack of passengers and the much more serious lack of navigational aids caused the service to be closed down in July.

Envoy I, G-ADBA, under maintenance in one of the hangars at Croydon Airport while being operated by Olley Air Service who had leased it from the original owners, Cobham Air Routes. It was later used by Air Commerce, also of Croydon. (*Courtesy Richard Riding.*)

The service was re-opened over a different route in the summer of 1936, using two Envoys, G-ADAZ and, later, G-ADBA, previously operated by Olley Air Service on lease from Cobham Air Routes, and four Couriers, the prototype G-ABXN, G-ACLF, G-ACLT and G-ACSZ. This time Croydon was the base for London and the route was via Doncaster (a 'flag' stop only), Leeds and Newcastle to Perth, but the service was not a success and was discontinued in 1938.

More successful, though probably not much less uneconomic, were the services operated with Envoys by Japan Air Transport (Nihon Koku Yuso KK) from 1935—and later by Manchuria Air Transport (Manshu Koku Yuso KK)—and by Československé Státní Aerolinie (ČSA) starting later the same year. Four Envoys including G-ADCB, G-ADCC, and G-ADCE, later registered J-BDBO, J-BDCO, J-BDDO and J-BDEO, were bought directly by Japan Air Transport from Airspeed and two more, J-BAOH and possibly J-BAOI, were delivered via Mitsubishi

One of the first four Wolseley AR.9 engined Envoy Is delivered direct to Japan Air Transport by Airspeed in 1935. Two others were later delivered via Mitsubishi Heavy Industries whose aircraft plant obtained a licence to build the Envoy in its Mark II version. (*Courtesy Eiichiro Sekigawa.*)

The identities of the various AS.6 Envoys supplied by Airspeed to Japan Air Transport and later built under licence by Mitsubishi are not now easily disentangled. The Airspeed-built series appear to have been registered J-BDBO, J-BDCO and so on. This, therefore, is probably an Airspeed-built Envoy I. (*Courtesy John Stroud.*)

The Envoys bought by Mitsubishi and later built under licence were mostly registered under the initial group J-BAO, followed by letters starting at D. The registration of this Envoy, however, does not fit into the assumed pattern. (*Courtesy John Stroud.*)

Heavy Industries, who had obtained a licence to build the Envoy at their Nagoya aircraft plant. These and three more Mitsubishi-built Envoys, given the type name Hina-Zuru (Young Crane), bought between 1935 and 1939, were used by the airline on domestic scheduled services between Tokyo, Osaka and Fukuoka. At least four of the remaining seven Envoys built by Mitsubishi were operated in Korea and Manchuria. As originally delivered, the first Airspeed-built Envoys for Japan Air Transport were fitted with Wolseley AR.9s, but photographic evidence is available to show that J-BDEO, at least, was later fitted with Armstrong Siddeley Lynx IVCs. Since Mitsubishi also held the licence to build these powerplants, it is probable that some of the Envoys were re-engined, and that the Mitsubishi-built aircraft were Lynx-engined.

According to a correspondent in Japan, the first prototype Mitsubishi Hina-Zuru, built in 1936, was fitted with Japanese-built powerplants and with the split flaps of the Series II version. The first flight was made early in 1937. On 27 October of that year it crashed, killing one pilot and seriously injuring another, following a premature stall which developed in the engine-nacelle area caused, apparently, by the greater diameter of the nacelle used. Thereafter the use of this engine and nacelle was discontinued and later production aircraft were fitted either with British-built Wolseley or Armstrong Siddeley Lynx powerplants. Including the prototype, he writes, eleven Envoys were built by Mitsubishi between 1936 and 1938 and used by Japan Air Transport on domestic trunk services from Tokyo to Fukuoka and Sapporo and later in Korea. Most photographs of the Mitsubishi-built Envoys show them to be similar to those built by Airspeed. One magazine picture (of J-BAOS), however, shows additional supporting frames in the main passenger-cabin windows and a covering for the transparent cockpit canopy.

No such uncertainties are involved in the case of the two Envoys Is, OK-BAL and OK-BAM, delivered in 1935, and two Envoy IIs, OK-BAN and OK-BAO, delivered in 1936 to the Czechoslovak State airline—or of the Envoy III OK-VIT delivered to the Steel and Iron Corporation of Czechoslovakia in December 1936. All were fitted with indigenous 340 hp Walter Castor II seven-cylinder radial engines. The first two Envoys for ČSA were ferried out to Prague (OK-BAL on 6 August and OK-BAM on 9 September, 1935) in two stages via Paris, each carrying the same extremely high-level 'reception committee', consisting of the airline's general manager, a representative of the Ministry of Public Works and the airline's chief engineer, with the chief pilot and the chief radio operator doing an extremely competent high-speed ferrying job. Within little more than a month of delivery, OK-BAL made the first-ever ČSA flight, in four stages, from Prague to Moscow, averaging a flying speed of 148 mph for the

The first of four AS.6 Envoys, two Mark Is and two Mark IIs, delivered to Czechoslovak State Airlines in 1935 and 1936. All were fitted with indigenous Walter Castor radials. (*Courtesy John Stroud.*)

1,430 miles, and landing in the dark using only the Envoy's landing lights. The first two ČSA Envoys officially entered service with the airline on 1 October, 1935.

A possibly apocryphal story is told about this or the later deal. The Envoys for ČSA were late—only a few days behind schedule, but still late. While the first was being prepared for delivery, the top-level ČSA team had arrived in London. They, or some of them, were suffering from colds or similar high-temperature ailments. By arrangement, they were confined to bed at their hotel and put under medical supervision. Five days or so later they were reported fit and collected their Envoy, which was now ready for delivery.

Two years after the England–Australia race an Envoy featured, albeit tragically, in another long-distance race, that from England (Portsmouth) to South Africa (Johannesburg) for the Schlesinger Trophy in September–October 1936. For this race, after negotiations for the purchase of the AS.8

The stock Mark III Envoy which was modified with special long-range tanks for the Portsmouth–Johannesburg race in September/October 1936. It crashed on take-off at Abercorn, Rhodesia. (*Flight 13458s.*)

Viceroy, Max H. Findlay bought a stock Cheetah-engined Envoy II, G-AENA, and had it fitted with special long-range tanks giving a total capacity, in addition to the standard 78-gallon tankage, of about 116 gallons of fuel. Named *Gabrielle*, and with (the superstitious were quick to notice) the racing number 13, the Envoy also carried Ken Waller as second pilot, A. H. Morgan as radio operator and C. D. Peachey as engineer. On 1 October, after landing at Abercorn, near Salisbury, Rhodesia, there was a change of wind and the decision was made to take-off into wind, though the direction was uphill, rather than to delay departure for more favourable conditions. The Envoy, heavily loaded and operating from an aerodrome at about 6,000 ft above sea level, failed to clear trees at the end of the take-off run. In the crash, Max Findlay (who was flying the aircraft on this final sector) and Morgan were killed.

Those were brave days for the civil aircraft industry, commercially as well as otherwise. While test, delivery and airline pilots were battling

Manpower is used to tow the AS.6 Envoy *Gabrielle* at Portsmouth Airport before the Portsmouth–Johannesburg race in September/October 1936. (*Flight 13441s*.)

along with inadequate aids and information, commercial directors were sometimes selling at a cut price on little more than a pious hope that full payment would eventually be made and that the aeroplanes would not eventually find their way back on the shelf awaiting other prospective buyers. Although, recorded in retrospect, the sale by Airspeed of two Envoy IIIs to China in 1937 sounds an extraordinarily risky bit of commerce, it was probably as safe a deal as any, except for the pilots who flew them out, whether the price was paid in tons of rice or in ingots of silver.

In January 1937 Airspeed received an order for an Envoy III for the personal use of the Governor of Kwangsi Province, China. The aircraft, G-AERT, was wanted quickly, so it was flown out to Liu Chow by Flt. Lt. Colman accompanied by an apprentice, W. F. Locke, later managing director of FPT Industries of Portsmouth, as engineer.

The Envoy left Portsmouth on 27 January, 1937, with Mrs N. S. Norway as a passenger travelling as far as Calcutta. The flight was made in 13

The 6/8-passenger cabin of the AS.6 Envoy, looking forward to the pilot's cabin. Although it was pleasantly roomy even by present-day standards, the camera has somewhat distorted the perspective. (*Courtesy Richard Worcester.*)

flying days, with only three short intervening day-long delays—because of bad weather, a minor technical hitch, and for demonstrations—reaching Liu Chow on 12 February. Night stops were made at Marseilles, Pisa, Brindisi, Athens, Cairo, Basra, Karachi, Delhi, Calcutta, Rangoon, Lakhon, where there was a landing because of poor weather, and Hanoi. A month later, on 12 March, Flt. Lt. Colman cabled to say that he had obtained an order for a second Envoy. It turned out that the order for the first Envoy was from the Military Governor and that the aircraft was likely later to be armed. Trouble with the British Foreign Office was duly smoothed out and there was no difficulty over the order for the second Envoy, G-AEXE. This was flown out in more difficult monsoon weather conditions in June by G. B. S. Errington, later to be Airspeed's chief test pilot, accompanied by another apprentice, R. O. M. Graham, in 53 flying hours after leaving Portsmouth on 15 June. While in Kwangsi Province, Errington took a busman's holiday to test a locally built fighter.

Earlier, a hard, and no doubt reasonably economic order had been received for seven convertible civil/military Envoy IIIs from South Africa. Four were intended primarily for use by South African Airways, though capable of quick conversion, and three were military variants for the South African Air Force. The military variants were designed to carry bombs, had a single fixed forward-firing gun in a trough immediately beside the pilot's cockpit and a revolving gun turret on the fuselage aft of the wing. Conversion from civil to military layout, and vice versa, could be completed in 32 man-hours at a maximum.

The first of the military Convertible Envoy IIIs for the South African Air Force on test from Portsmouth before delivery by air to Cape Town in July 1936. (*Flight 12882s.*)

Two, one military and one civil, were flown out to South Africa, leaving on 4 July, 1936. The remaining five were shipped out and assembled at Wynberg Air Station, Cape Town, where they were inspected and test-flown by Errington before delivery. The four civil versions ZS-AGA–ZS-AGD were taken over by the South African Air Force in 1938 and given the serials 254–257. The three military versions, 251–253, also appeared on the South African civil register as ZS-ALD–ZS-ALF, from 3 July, 1936, to 31 December, 1937, when the registrations were cancelled. Numbers 251 and 252, and probably also 253, were fitted with camera equipment late in 1936 and formed part of the SAAF Air Survey Flight at Zwartkop Air

One of South African Airways four AS.6 Envoys, either ZS-AGA or ZS-AGC, on the apron at Rand Airport, Johannesburg, in 1937. (*Courtesy John Stroud.*)

Station, near Pretoria. Two, 252 and 253, suffered accidents—the first at Cradock on 24 March, 1938, and the second at Bloemfontein later in the same year—but two Envoys at least were flying during World War II. When, in June 1940, No. 1 Survey Flight of No. 67 Air School, Zwartkop, left for Kenya, the fleet, used initially for surveying roads in Abyssinia (Ethiopia) and Italian Somaliland, included two Envoys.

Among features of the three military Envoy IIIs sold to the South African Air Force in 1936 were metal propellers and dorsal gun turrets. The four civil Envoys sold at the same time to South African Airways were capable of quick conversion, and all seven were, at one time or another, used by the SAAF. (*Flight 12895s*.)

Much earlier, as already recorded, an Envoy had been seen in South Africa when, in 1935, the Wolseley-owned G-ACVI had been flown out to Cape Town by Sqn. Ldr. D. Hilton as part of the test programme for the Aries III engine.

But there were less 'hard' sells. One of these was of two AS.6J IIIs to E. Hoffman. He came to Airspeed in 1936 with the explanation that he was starting an aircraft factory in Jugoslavia and wanted to buy a licence to build Envoys there. The licence was sold for £4,000, together with two aircraft at about £6,500 each. These were to be used as 'working models'. Detailed drawings and data were sent to Jugoslavia when, in due course, the aircraft left the factory, but these came back to Airspeed through the dead-letter office. In the meantime Hoffman had explained his plans to the Board of Trade, which, after some hesitation, gave him an export licence, but insisted on sending an observer with the boat on which the Envoys were being shipped for Trieste, to make sure that they reached their destination. The story goes that when the ship arrived at Rotterdam to pick up further cargo the two Envoys were taken off. Learning of this and fearing the destination of the aircraft might be Spain, for use in the civil war, the Board of Trade got in touch with the Dutch Government, which impounded them. After the war Hoffman sued Airspeed for the return of the £4,000 on the grounds that the contract had not been fulfilled. The verdict went in favour of Airspeed.

These two Envoys were presumably those recorded at the time as having been ordered by Hirtenberger, an Austrian company which had obtained a licence to build. Two Envoys were certainly in the Netherlands in 1937, registered unofficially (or temporarily) as PH-ARK and PH-ARL and based at Ypenburg aerodrome, near The Hague. Their owner was D. H. Reinders, a Dutch businessman of The Hague, but their use and later history remain a mystery. One report says that they remained in Holland and were later destroyed by enemy action at Ypenburg; another says that they were in Holland only for a short time and were then returned to Britain. All that can be said positively is that two Envoys with these registrations were at Ypenburg in 1937. They may or may not have been the two which were impounded.

Another of the Envoys which cannot be completely identified is the Mark III delivered on 20 March, 1937, to Société Air Pyrénées as F-APPQ. After obtaining a French C of A at Villacoublay, near Paris, it was flown on 27 March to Toulouse, the base of the airline, which planned a regular service to Biarritz and Bilbao. Altogether 55 flights over this route (or sections of it) were made in 39 days of operation before the aircraft was attacked by Spanish fighters, forced down with damage to the port engine and propeller, and was crash-landed—luckily without serious injury to the pilot and passengers.

Of great prestige value to Airspeed was the order for an Envoy III 'for the transport of Royalty and State personages' which marked the real beginnings of the King's (now Queen's) Flight. Registered as G-AEXX, in the name of Wg. Cdr. E. H. Fielden (later Air Vice-Marshal Sir Edward Fielden), Captain of the Flight until 1962, this Envoy had accommodation for a pilot, a radio operator, four passengers, and a steward. It was fitted with Cheetah IX engines in helmeted cowlings and was styled in the colours of the Household Brigade. Delivered in June 1937, G-AEXX carried HM King George VI on a tour of four RAF stations—Northolt, Harwell, Upavon (the Central Flying School) and Thorney Island—in May 1938. After service as L7270 with No. 24 Communications Squadron during the war, it was again registered G-AEXX in 1946 and was then sold to an owner/operator in Sweden as SE-ASN, one of the only two Envoys to continue flying after the war.

The Royal Envoy III, G-AEXX, photographed before joining the King's Flight in June 1937. It was one of the only two Envoys to be re-registered, after war service as L7270, and was finally sold to an operator in Sweden. (*Charles E. Brown 5683–2.*)

The development and earlier history of this Royal Envoy were not without problems. After one flight the undercarriage was found to be damaged at Renfrew Airport, Glasgow. An important trip had to be made from London, so the landing gear was jury rigged with part of a bedstead for a ferry flight to Heston Airport, to which the essential replacement parts had been flown from Portsmouth.

Profitable in a more direct way were the sales in 1938 of two Envoy IIIs, G-AFJD and G-AFJE, later N9107–9108, for communications work with the RAF in India and, in 1939, of five more, P5625–5629, to the RAF for similar duties in Britain. The story of these five aircraft has not previously been recorded in detail and the fact of their existence has been overlooked in some earlier reports of Airspeed's activities. One, P5626, was the only other Envoy to survive the war; it was registered as G-AHAC early in 1946 after apparently resting in good order at an RAF maintenance unit

One of a batch of five sold to the RAF in 1939, this AS.6 Envoy (originally P5626) was civil-registered after the war as G-AHAC and used by various owners until it was dismantled in 1950. The only other Envoy to continue flying after the war was the King's Flight G-AEXX, pictured above. (*Courtesy Richard Riding.*)

Split flaps were fitted to the Mark II version of the Envoy. This is the prototype Mark I, G-ACMT, as modified to Mark II standard in 1936. (*Flight 12470s*.)

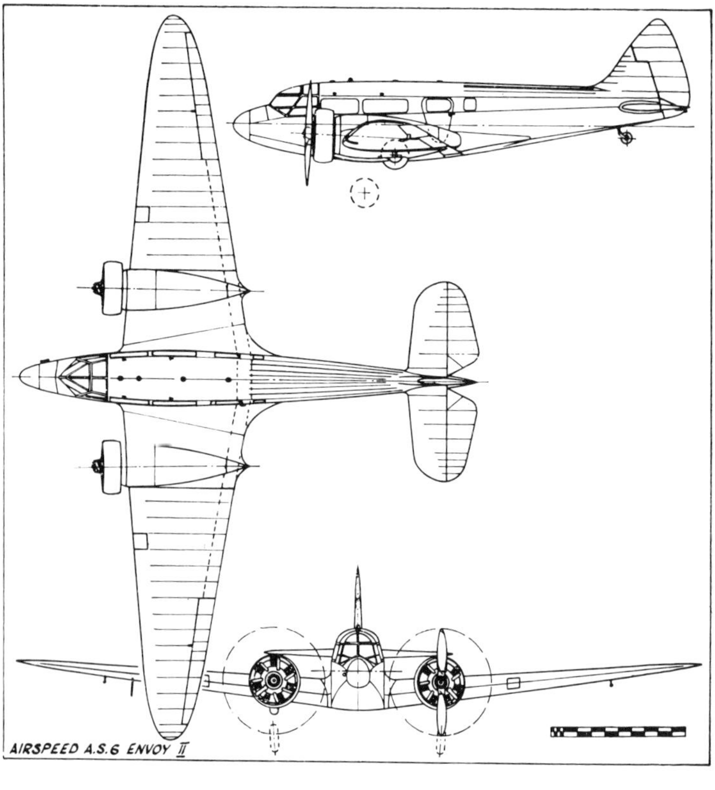

AIRSPEED A.S.6 ENVOY II

through most of the war period, and served several owners before finally being broken up at Tollerton, Nottingham, in 1950. The then commercial manager (later director) of Airspeed, W. F. 'Bill' Shaylor, remembers that, while negotiating the contract, the Air Ministry Director of Contracts, when told that the price would be that listed for the standard aircraft plus the cost of any military requirements, commented that no Envoy had previously been sold at the list price. To this Bill Shaylor retorted that there was no reason why a start should not be made in this case.

There had been earlier, more specifically military, variants of the Envoy which had got no further than the project-design stage. Two of these were given the designation AS.7, with letter suffixes denoting the use of Cheetah VI (J) or Scorpio II (K) radials, and Airspeed had also worked, at very short notice, to meet an Air Ministry requirement for a Coastal Command variant of the AS.6.

The Envoy was developed in three principal successive variants: the Series I without flaps, the Series II with flaps, and the Series III with flaps, stressed-skin wing and other modifications. The structure, of wood and stressed plywood skin, was conventional for the period and followed closely that of the Courier, with, in the Series I, similar extension wings outboard of the centre-section. The aspect ratio was 8·16, the mean dihedral was 5 degrees, and the incidence was 2 degrees at the fuselage with a 2 degree wash-out on the extension wings. The centre-section was integral with the semi-monocoque fuselage. The undercarriage was similar in geometry to that of the Courier. Normal fuel capacity was 78 gallons in two centre-section aluminium tanks, with provision for two 30-gallon tanks in the extension wings. Accommodation was for one pilot and eight passengers, but only six passengers if a lavatory was installed. Baggage was carried in a separate aft compartment reached through a door on the starboard side. The passenger door was on the port side.

Apart from the military variants and proposed variants already mentioned, the Envoy was projected also as a floatplane (the AS.6B and C) and as a photographic survey version (the AS.6F).

Span 52 ft 4 in (15·94 m); length 34 ft 6 in (10·53 m); height 9 ft 6 in (2·9 m); wing area 339 sq ft (31·5 sq m).

AS.6 (Wolseley AR.9). Empty weight, inclusive of all equipment, 3,077 lb (1,395 kg); pilot 170 lb (77 kg); fuel (78 gal, 355 litres) 600 lb (273 kg); oil (8 gal, 36·4 litres) 76 lb (34·5 kg); disposable load 2,223 lb (1,010 kg); balance available for payload, etc, 1,377 lb (625 kg); loaded weight 5,300 lb (2,405 kg); wing loading 15·6 lb/sq ft (76·2 kg/sq m); power loading 13·5 lb/hp (6·13 kg/hp). Maximum speed at sea-level 170 mph (273 km/h); cruising speed at 1,000 ft (305 m) 150 mph (241 km/h); best climbing speed 97 mph (156 km/h); stalling speed (full load) 63 mph (101 km/h); landing speed 55 mph (88·5 km/h); take-off run (no wind) 265 yd (242 m); initial rate of climb 914 ft/min (4·65 m/sec); service ceiling 17,000 ft (5,180 m); range at cruising speed 403 miles (650 km).

AS.6A/G (Armstrong Siddeley Lynx IVC or Wolseley Scorpio I). Empty weight 3,642 lb (1,643 kg); disposable load 2,070 lb (934 kg); loaded weight 5,850 lb (2,650 kg). Maximum speed at sea-level 174 mph (280 km/h); maximum speed at 5,000 ft (1,525 m) 170 mph (273 km/h); maximum speed at 10,000 ft (3,048 m) 166 mph (267 km/h); cruising speed at 1,000 ft (305 m) 153 mph (246 km/h); landing speed 64 mph (103 km/h); initial rate of climb 1,070 ft/min (5·4 m/sec); service ceiling 16,500 ft (5,020 m); range with 1,340 lb (608 kg) payload, normal tanks, 400 miles (644 km).

AS.6D (Wright Whirlwind R.760 E.2). Empty weight 3,834 lb (1,742 kg); disposable load 2,296 lb (1,041 kg); loaded weight 6,300 lb (2,860 kg); wing loading 18·6 lb/sq ft (9·1 kg/sq m); power loading 9·85 lb/hp (4·4 kg/hp). Maximum speed at sea-level 192 mph (307 km/h); speed at 5,000 ft (1,525 m) 186 mph (298 km/h); speed at 10,000 ft (3,048 m) 179 mph (286 km/h); cruising speed at 75% power at sea-level 172 mph (275 km/h); cruising speed at 62·5% power at 5,000 ft (1,525 m) 168 mph (269 km/h); climb to 5,000 ft (1,525 m) 5 min; climb to 10,000 ft (3,048 m) 12 min; service ceiling 18,000 ft (5,490 m); absolute ceiling 20,000 ft (6,100 m); normal maximum cruising range at 62·5% power at 5,000 ft (1,525 m) 625 miles (1,006 km).

AS.6E (Walter Castor II). Empty weight 3,970 lb (1,802 kg); disposable load 2,160 lb (979 kg); loaded weight 6,300 lb (2,860 kg); wing loading 18·6 lb/sq ft (9·1 kg/sq m); power loading 10·65 lb/hp (4·76 kg/hp). Maximum speed at 3,450 ft (1,050 m) 185 mph (298 km/h); speed at 10,000 ft (3,048 m) 175 mph (282 km/h); cruising speed at 75% power at 3,450 ft (1,050 m) 165 mph (264 km/h); cruising speed at 62·5% power at 13,000 ft (3,965 m) 167 mph (267 km/h); climb to 5,000 ft (1,525 m) 5·5 min; climb to 10,000 ft (3,048 m) 12 min; service ceiling 16,500 ft (5,030 m); absolute ceiling 8,000 ft (5,490 m); normal cruising range at 62·5% power at 13,000 ft (3,965 m) 635 miles (1,022 km).

AS.6H (Wolseley Aries III). Empty weight, inclusive of all equipment, 3,551 lb (1,612 kg); disposable load 1,949 lb (884 kg); loaded weight 5,500 lb (2,496 kg). Maximum speed at sea-level 166 mph (267 km/h); maximum speed at 5,000 ft (1,525 m) 161 mph (259 km/h); maximum speed at 10,000 ft (3,048 m) 155 mph (249 km/h); cruising speed at 1,000 ft (305 m) 143 mph (230 km/h); landing speed 62 mph (100 km/h); initial rate of climb 850 ft/min (4·32 m/sec); service ceiling 14,700 ft (4,490 m).

AS.6J (Armstrong Siddeley Cheetah IX). Empty weight 4,057 lb (1,842 kg); cabin equipment (for 6 passengers) 170 lb (77 kg); disposable load 2,073 lb (941 kg); loaded weight 6,300 lb (2,860 kg); wing loading 18·6 lb/sq ft (9·1 kg/sq m); power loading 9 lb/hp (4·02 kg/hp). Maximum speed at 7,300 ft (2,226 m) 210 mph (338 km/h); speed at 10,000 ft (3,048 m) 208 mph (333 km/h); cruising speed at 75% power at 7,300 ft (2,226 m) 192 mph (309 km/h); cruising speed at 62·5% power at 10,000 ft (3,048 m) 180 mph (290 km/h); climb to 5,000 ft (1,525 m) 3·5 min; climb to 10,000 ft (3,048 m) 8 min; service ceiling 22,500 ft (6,860 m); absolute ceiling 24,000 ft (7,315 m); normal cruising range at 62·5% power at 10,000 ft (3,048 m) 650 miles (1,045 km).

AS.8 Viceroy

The designation AS.8 and the type name Viceroy was given to the AS.6 modified for the England–Australia Mac.Robertson Trophy Race in October 1934 although it was not much more of a variant in the Envoy series than that for the race to South Africa in 1936. The AS.8 Viceroy G-ACMU was built to the order of Capt. T. Neville Stack, who flew it in the race with S. L. Turner as co-pilot. In the event it withdrew early in the race after initially being forced down with electrical trouble at Abbeville, in Northern France, but it had in any case been out-handicapped. As explained earlier, when discussing the AS.5 Courier, there were two sections in the race, one for absolute speed (first-over-the-line at Melbourne) and the other under a handicap system based on flying times excluding stops—though, to be eligible, the course had to be completed inside a fixed maximum elapsed time.

The handicap formula put the Viceroy in the scratch position at Mildenhall, the starting aerodrome, giving more than 35 min even to the three faster de Havilland Comets. To have stood a chance of winning the handicap race, the AS.8 would have had to average well over 180 mph between stops, an impossible target for an aircraft capable of a top speed of no more than about 210 mph and a cruising speed of 190 mph. The AS.8 had been ready only just in time to take part in the race after certification trials had been completed at Portsmouth Airport by an RAF test pilot who had, to save time, flown down specially from Martlesham Heath to the Airspeed factory.

There was an unhappy sequel to this failure of the Viceroy in the England–Australia race. Because the retirement had stemmed initially from an electrical fault, alleged to have been the responsibility of the

Specially built for the England–Australia race in 1934, the Viceroy was a modified version of the Envoy and was given the special designation AS.8. It was fitted with Cheetah VI supercharged engines in long-chord NACA cowlings. (*Flight 10842s*.)

The Viceroy is seen here taxying in at Mildenhall Aerodrome before the start of the England–Australia race from which it was withdrawn after reaching Athens. (*Flight*.)

manufacturers, Capt. Stack and Turner sued Airspeed. The case was eventually settled out of court, with the costs as they fell, £1,850 for Airspeed and the Viceroy for Capt. Stack.

Apart from its long-range tankage, the Viceroy differed from the prototype Envoy, which had made its first flight only two months earlier, in having two 280 hp Armstrong Siddeley Cheetah VI seven-cylinder supercharged radial engines, in long-chord NACA cowlings with annular oil coolers, and metal propellers. The engines were, in fact, the only two of the Series VI then in existence and were designed to give a maximum of 315 hp at a height of 7,000 ft. In addition to the two centre-section and two outer-wing tanks the Viceroy had, for the race, a 270-gallon tank along the port side in the fuselage. The undercarriage was specially strengthened to permit a maximum gross weight of 6,300 lb at take-off. Later Envoys were also certificated at this take-off weight. For its time, the radio and instrument-flying equipment was unusually complete.

But for the Spanish Civil War in 1936, the Viceroy might also have been an entry for the England–South Africa (Portsmouth–Johannesburg) race for the Schlesinger Trophy in September of that year. Following the lawsuit after the Australia race failure, the AS.8 was back at Portsmouth in the early summer of 1935, and Airspeed was negotiating a secret sale to the Emperor of Ethiopia (then normally known as Abyssinia) when the Italo-Ethiopian war came to an end. It was afterwards about to be sold to Max Findlay and Ken Waller for the South Africa race when an unusually good offer came from Spain and was accepted. A special long-range Envoy was, as already recorded, fitted up to take its place as an entry for the race.

The dimensions and weights of the AS.8 were as for the Envoy except that the permitted maximum loaded weight was 6,300 lb (or 1,000 lb higher than that of the early Envoy Is) and that it had a slightly narrower fuselage. Maximum speed at 7,000 ft (2,135 m) 210 mph (338 km/h); cruising speed 190 mph (306 km/h); stalling speed 72 mph (116 km/h); rate of climb at sea-level 1,000 ft/min (5·1 m/sec); range 1,400 miles (2,253 km).

AS.10, AS.40–43 and AS.46 Oxford

Little official Government interest, at least of a financially rewarding kind, appears to have been taken in Airspeed before 1936. As a comparative newcomer to the aircraft industry, the company had suffered under the handicap of the ruling made in the early 1920s that military contracts of value should first be offered to the 'grandfathers' among the British manufacturers. Only odds and ends in the way of design and initial development contracts had come their way. However, the Air Ministry was impressed enough with their design strength—and, no doubt, with their prospective production capacity, now that Airspeed had the financial backing of Swan Hunter—to invite the company to submit proposals for a twin-engined trainer to meet the specification T.23/36. Based on the Envoy, it was given the designation AS.10 and afterwards, in January 1937, the name Oxford.

The situation for Airspeed, at the time of design and development progress on the AS.10, was nothing if not difficult. Part of the factory at Portsmouth Airport had to be replanned to deal with a component subcontract programme, described later by the company's chairman as 'unremunerative' business which Airspeed had been 'compelled' to accept, and there was no certainty that worthwhile orders would be placed. However, in the reasonable expectation of such orders, factory extensions were put in hand. After some considerable negotiation and resistance to an

Among the first air-to-air photographs of the Oxford was this one of L4576, a turretless Mark I, taken in May 1938. (*Flight 16039s*.)

Another air-to-air view of L4576. The author was in the second pilot's seat admiring the then-so-modern control cabin layout. (*Flight 16036*[s].)

initially offered ITP (instruction to proceed) for a relatively small number of AS.10s, an ITP was received in October 1936 for more than 160, including those for expected overseas orders. RAF serials for 136 were allotted. Because of the delay in ordering and the effects of the earlier changes in the factory layout, there was an inevitable delay of something like a year before production could be got under way on the necessary scale.

The prototype Oxford, L4534, was flown for the first time on 19 June, 1937, by Flt. Lt. C. H. A. Colman, and it made a first public appearance in the 'new and experimental' park at Hendon during the Royal Air Force Display at the end of that month. The final acceptance test was completed by G. B. S. Errington on 29 September. The first small batch of production Oxfords, L4535–4537, was handed over to the RAF in mid-November and these were followed by L4540 in December and by L4541–2 in January 1938, four of the six going to the Central Flying School, Upavon, and two to No. 11 Flying Training School.

The first Oxfords to go overseas were five for the Royal New Zealand Air Force. These were shipped out in 1938, and the first two assembled at Auckland in August and September under the supervision of W. F. Locke (who, as an Airspeed apprentice, had flown as engineer on the first of two Envoy delivery flights to China). They were based at the RNZAF HQ at Wigram in South Island.

The Oxford was, for its era, a very remarkable aeroplane both in itself and as an advanced trainer. It was the first British military type to have a scientifically planned and logically laid-out cockpit in which all essential controls and instruments were either duplicated or grouped around the central throttle pedestal so that they could be reached by both pupil and instructor. Visiting pilots, such as the writer, were most impressed when taken for demonstration or air-to-air photographic flights in one of the early production aircraft during 1938. I, for one, was just as impressed two years or so afterwards when, without any dual instruction or even a demonstration circuit, I ferried one for the first time from Portsmouth to a maintenance unit in the north of England. On later RAF maintenance unit test-flying duties, when an Oxford was often the communications 'hack', we learned to appreciate its qualities as an advanced twin-engined trainer and to take special pleasure in executing accurate three-pointers followed by dead-straight landing runs without using more than a touch of correcting differential brake.

For the Oxford was not—and was not intended to be—an easy aeroplane to fly. It would, if not handled carefully, swing on take-off, and any residual drift had to be kicked off accurately just before touchdown if it were not to try very hard to career off the runway in a so-called ground-loop. If you could handle the Oxford with reasonable competence, you could tackle almost anything in the way of recalcitrant twins and multis. A wag once described the Lockheed Hudson, which had somewhat terrifying ground and near-ground handling characteristics, as an excellent interim conversion type for those about to fly an Oxford.

On production testing and, to a lesser extent, on routine post-modification testing at maintenance units, the Oxford could occasionally demonstrate some heavy pre-stall buffeting. This was almost always

The well-fenestrated control cabin of the early Oxfords could be extremely hot when flying above cloud or under cloudless skies; the upper canopies were tinted later to reduce the pressure of light and heat. (*Flight 16035s*.)

attributable to faults such as badly fitting cowlings and other similar defects which caused a premature stall at the wing root on one side or the other. Though strange to us at maintenance units, the characteristics were, as I was to discover much later, well known to the RAE at Farnborough. In 1939, or thereabouts, the RAE did tests on a 'rogue' Oxford, N6410, from Cranfield, Bedford. They found that the trouble was much

Three among the first AS.10 Oxford trainers to be delivered to the RAF. The polished cowlings were a feature of the early Oxfords.

reduced by fitting leather seals in the gap between the engine nacelles and the leading edge and could be more or less completely cured by fitting 'deflectors' above the wing between the nacelles and the fuselage. These interfered with engine starting by the handle so were not used. Ron Clear, having seen an Oxford land safely with most of one wing missing after a collision, thought that a very strong venturi effect between the nacelle and the fuselage side created a very critical airflow pattern.

Another of the early Oxfords, actually the sixth in initial serial order, L4539, was fitted experimentally in 1938 with the McLaren 'drift-correcting' undercarriage. In this the directional 'set' of the main wheels could be adjusted to match any reasonable cross-wind component, so that, when taking off or landing out of wind, the undercarriage wheels would be square to the direction of the runway even though the aircraft itself might be heading as much as 30 degrees off the runway to match the amount of cross-wind drift at touchdown speed. The idea was that of making a single runway direction practicable for nearly all wind-direction conditions. There were, however, obvious difficulties in ground control, both on take-off and after landing, and in undercarriage retraction arrangements; the development lapsed. L4539 was modified back to normal after the tests and sent to work at No. 2 FTS.

Experimental and special variants of the earlier Oxfords included the fourth production aircraft, L4538, which was initially retained as a civil transport by Airspeed and later used, as G-AFFM, by the Department of Civil Aviation and by British Airways, from October 1938, for blind approach and other associated radio-navigation development and training work. Another was a Mk II, AS504, which was fitted experimentally with two 250 hp de Havilland Gipsy Queen six-cylinder air-cooled inline engines in place of the standard 375 hp Armstrong Siddeley Cheetah X seven-cylinder radials, and flown in 1940.

There has been—and still remains—some slight confusion about the different marks of Oxford and about the manufacturer's designations (in addition to the basic AS.10) given to some of these variants. Historically, there were five different marks, though their original and later descriptions have not always agreed in the various records. These were: the Mark I, a general-purpose, bombing and gunnery trainer, normally with an Armstrong Whitworth dorsal gun turret; the Mark II, a pilot, navigation

Two of the Oxfords (NZ1260 and NZ1261) among the 297 bought by the Royal New Zealand Air Force. The first arrived in New Zealand in 1938, and they continued in service until 1948. (*Courtesy Kenneth Meehan.*)

Two of the few Oxford IIs (P8832 and P8833) which were fitted out for ambulance duties and appropriately marked before delivery by Airspeed from their Portsmouth factory. (*Crown copyright.*)

NZ1902 was one of six Royal New Zealand Air Force Oxfords which were converted to AS.65 Consul standard after the war and used for a short time. (*Courtesy Kenneth Meehan.*)

Oxford AS504 which was fitted experimentally with two Gipsy Queen six-cylinder inline engines and flown in 1940.

The only Mark III Oxford to be built made its first flight in March 1940. It was fitted with Cheetah XV engines and Rotol constant-speed propellers, one of which is feathered in this picture. (*Flight 18434*[s].)

and radio-operation trainer, without a turret; the Mark III, a projected development—of which one initial experimental version, P1864, was built and flown on 12 March, 1940—fitted with Cheetah XV engines and Rotol constant-speed propellers; the Mark IV, a projected pilot-training version of the Mk III; and the Mark V (the prototype of which was AS592) which was the pilot, navigation and radio trainer version with 450 hp Pratt & Whitney R985-AN6 Wasp Junior seven-cylinder radials and Hamilton Standard constant-speed propellers.

Another view of the experimental Mark III Oxford, P1864. All other Oxfords except the Wasp Junior powered Mark Vs had fixed-pitch propellers. (*Flight 18430*[s].)

Oxford LX119 was converted in 1947 by Miles Aircraft for Alvis Leonides engine tests and was seen variously under its U-7 experimental marking or with the civil registration G-AJWJ. Its Airspeed type designation was AS.41.

Of these, the redesignated variants were the AS.40, which was the civil version, typified by L4538 (G-AFFM), and externally similar to the AS.10 Mark II; the AS.41, which was the designation given to another experimental version and applied to LX119, registered G-AJWJ, which was taken over by Miles Aircraft for conversion to Alvis Leonides power in 1947; the AS.42, which was an Oxford I redesigned to specification T.39/37 for the Royal New Zealand Air Force; the AS.43, a survey version of the AS.42; and the AS.46, which became the Oxford V.

The Mk V was, in fact, the only production version of the Oxford to have the constant-speed (or variable-pitch) propellers which were originally intended to be fitted. Other production Oxfords had, however, to the left of the central control pedestal, a lever for propeller control. This was not connected to anything and was used only for cockpit-drill training in preparation for the operation of aircraft with active controls for the propellers.

As outlined in the introductory history, and mentioned also in the story of the Envoy, the future of the Oxford might have been somewhat different had there not been an important change of policy in a section of the British aero-engine industry. In September 1936 Lord Nuffield decided to stop the production of Wolseley aero-engines. The decision was reached because Lord Nuffield did not approve of the likely effects of the Government plan for controlled profits on a cost-plus basis. Wolseley had already been asked to tender for an order for 200 engines for the Oxford. A price had been quoted, and an 'instruction to proceed' had been given, when this decision to drop aero-engines was made after the company had spent something like £200,000 on development and initial production. Airspeed was, according to *Slide Rule*, asked to take over the production of Wolseley engines, but the programme would have been too big for the company which had, at that time, no direct means of financing such a major operation. So the Oxford went ahead with the Armstrong Siddeley

Cheetah X engines which were to power all the aircraft for British and many overseas training requirements.

The wooden structure of the Oxford followed very closely that of the developed Envoy Mk III, with stressed-skin wings and tailplane and semi-monocoque fuselage. The wing was in three parts: a centre-section, not integral with the fuselage, and two extension planes, with split flaps extending in five sections from aileron to aileron. These and the retractable undercarriage were hydraulically operated by a pump driven by the starboard engine, or by handpump with separate pipelines for undercarriage lowering in final emergency. The brakes, as was customary in British aircraft, were pneumatically operated from pressure supplied from a reservoir topped up to 200 lb/sq in by a starboard engine-driven compressor. Fuel for the two 375 hp Armstrong Siddeley Cheetah X seven-cylinder radials was in two main tanks of 49 gallons each in the centre-section and two auxiliary tanks of 29 gallons each in the extension planes at the root ends and feeding by gravity into the main tanks. The Oxford I, as a bombing and gunnery trainer, had an Armstrong Whitworth turret, with Lewis-type gun, installed amidships.

Although the crew members of the Oxford would not normally exceed three, there were six crew stations for various training duties. These were for the first pilot (or pupil), the second pilot (or instructor), bomb-aimer (prone in the nose after the dual set of controls had been removed), wireless operator (with a seat on the rear spar, facing aft on the starboard side), rear gunner and vertical camera operator. A navigator, when carried, occupied the second pilot's seat, which was slid back to make room for a folding chart-table. Equipment could be installed for alternative

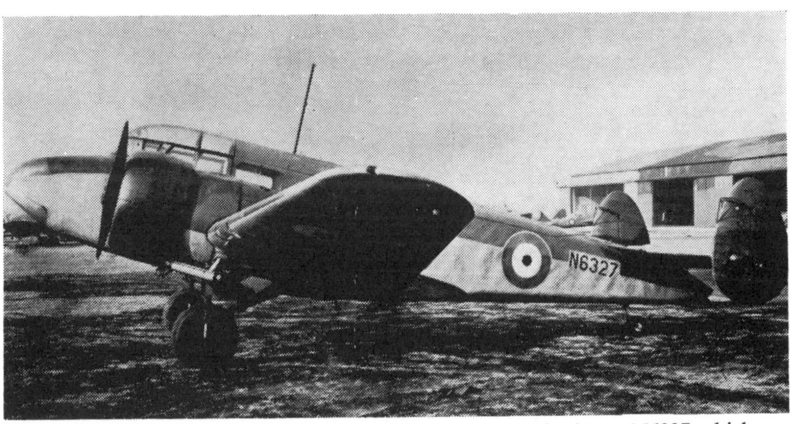

One of several experimental and other variants of the Oxford was N6327 which was fitted by Airspeed with twin fins and rudders for spin-recovery tests. (*Courtesy Bruce Robertson.*)

For its day the control cabin layout of the Oxford trainer was remarkably well-planned. All power and auxiliary controls were mounted in the central pedestal. For the first pilot, or pupil, there was a standard RAF instrument-flying panel while the instructor's panel on the right carried basic instruments including a turn-and-bank indicator. (*Flight 16242.*)

The cabin of the Oxford was spacious enough when laid out for flight-crew and navigation training. In this view the second pilot's seat has been slid back for use of the folding chart-board. The vertical object in the right foreground is the shaft for the direction-finding loop aerial.

training duties in navigation and radio operation, bombing (practice smoke bombs were carried in the centre-section well), air gunnery, aerial photography and, of course, twin-engined pilot training by day or night and instrument training under the hood. For its time, the Oxford must have been one of the most completely equipped trainers ever produced.

In the present era of all-metal construction and with civil transport utilizations running into the 3,000–4,000 hour bracket over working lives of 10–15 years, one of the most surprising things about the Oxford was its very long operating life. Aircraft built in the mid-war years, or earlier, were still flying, either as Oxfords or as converted civil Consuls, 10–15 years later. Aware of the distrust of 'wood-and-glue' methods, the producers of the original brochure for the Oxford, printed in 1938, had this to say under the heading 'Life of Wooden Aircraft': 'By the use of more advanced materials, in particular synthetic glues, and due to the improvement in manufacturing techniques, the durability of wooden aircraft compares favourably with that of all-metal machines. The old objections to wood, due to the warping of structural members and the unreliability of glued joints, have been completely overcome in recent years.'

And so it proved to be. The long lives of the Oxford variants can be attributed not only to the work of the original designers and makers, but also to that of those who were physically involved in their manufacture during years of mass production for short expected lives when an easing of standards could have been forgiven. A glance at some of the entries in the aircraft history summaries, and those of the AS.65 Consul, will uncover several Oxfords and Consuls whose serials show that they were among those assembled early in the war, or during the periods of high production rates under subcontract arrangements.

The scene at Portsmouth Airport on 14 July, 1945, when the 4,411th and last Oxford was delivered after demonstration flights by this aircraft and, on the right, the seventh Oxford (L4542) to be delivered to RAF Training Command in January 1938.

According to records compiled during the last days of Airspeed as an independently operating company, a total of 8,751 Oxfords were built.

Investigation suggests that 165 were cancelled before construction, leaving 8,586 positively accounted for. Of these, 4,411 were built at the Portsmouth factory; 550 at the Airspeed shadow factory at Christchurch; 1,515 by de Havilland at Hatfield; 750 by Standard Motors at Coventry; and 1,360 (or 1,525 if the aircraft believed to have been cancelled in the serials NJ401–607 are included) by Percival Aircraft at Luton. In addition, 2,576 Oxfords were rebuilt by various companies. The last of 4,411 Portsmouth-built Oxfords provided an occasion for a special demonstration and official party on 14 July, 1945, at Portsmouth Airport before delivery. With Portsmouth's final aircraft on show there was the seventh to be delivered to the RAF, L4542, in January 1938. The last Oxford in RAF service was, to use the long-familiar term, struck off charge when the AFTS at Pershore closed down in 1954.

BOAC had a number of civil-registered Oxfords for initial training from their Hurn base. This one was delivered in August 1946 and later went to Short Bros. Note the retractable wheel fairings which were fitted to some Oxfords. (*Richard Riding.*)

Of the grand total of 8,586 Oxfords, more than 500 went to South Africa and Southern Rhodesia; 297 were ordered for the Royal New Zealand Air Force; 188 went to Canada as airframes to be fitted there with P & W Wasp Junior engines and Hamilton Standard propellers as Mark Vs; and at least 40 went to the Middle East. Others went to Australia; to the Portuguese Air Force; to the Free French Air Force in Africa; to the United States Air Forces in Britain; to units for communications and radar calibration; to ten anti-aircraft co-operation squadrons; and to units for air-ambulance duties.

Apart from the Oxfords which were bought back from the Government by Airspeed and rebuilt as AS.65 Consul civil conversions after the end of the war, some 40 Oxfords were also civil-certificated and British-registered for various transport and training purposes. Among them were seven, G-AIAT–G-AIAZ, used by BOAC's initial training flight at Hurn, Hampshire, and civil-registered from August 1946; four which went to Air Service Training, Hamble, in 1947 and 1950; LN-LAD and LN-LAE

One of the many civil-registered Oxfords was Scottish Aviation's G-AHDZ seen on the apron at Prestwick Airport with the original hotel and control tower in the background. This Oxford was later sold to Union de Transports Aériens. (*Richard Riding*.)

Another civil-registered Oxford, G-AHXA ex-V3870, was used initially by the Brevet Flying Club and later by Payloads (Charter) before being sold to Egypt as SU-AER in 1947. (*Richard Riding*.)

These two civil-registered Oxfords, LN-LAD and LN-LAE (ex-PK262 and PK285) were operated for a while as trainers with Det Norske Luftfartselskap (now part of SAS) before being sold to the Royal Norwegian Air Force. They are seen at Fornebu, Oslo.

One of the two ex-RNZAF Oxfords, civil-registered ZK-APX and ZK-APY, which were used for a short period in 1948 for light cargo operations from Wellington by G. M. Gould. (*Courtesy Kenneth Meehan.*)

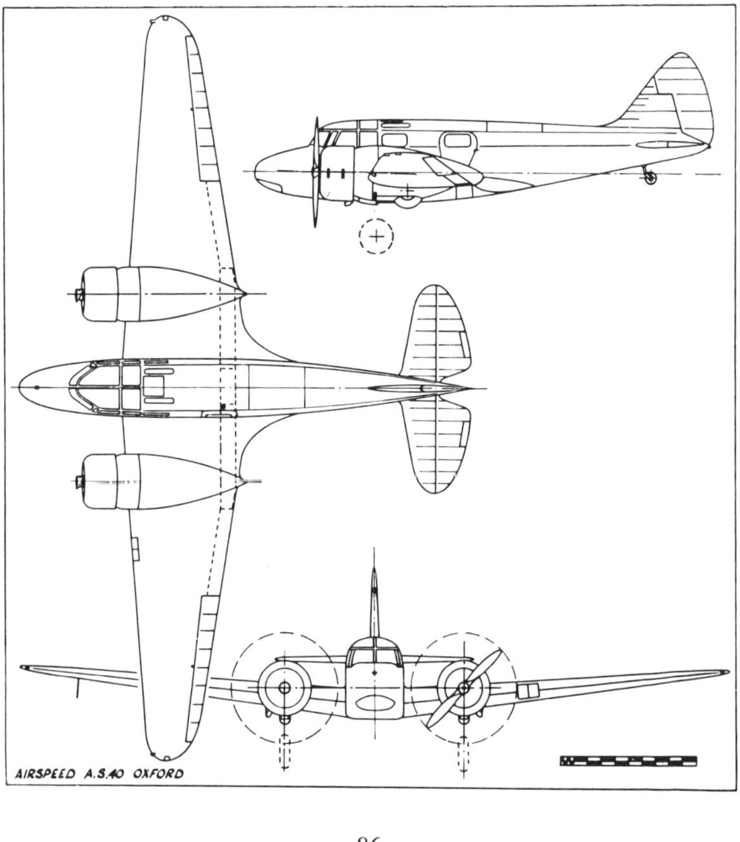

AIRSPEED A.S.40 OXFORD

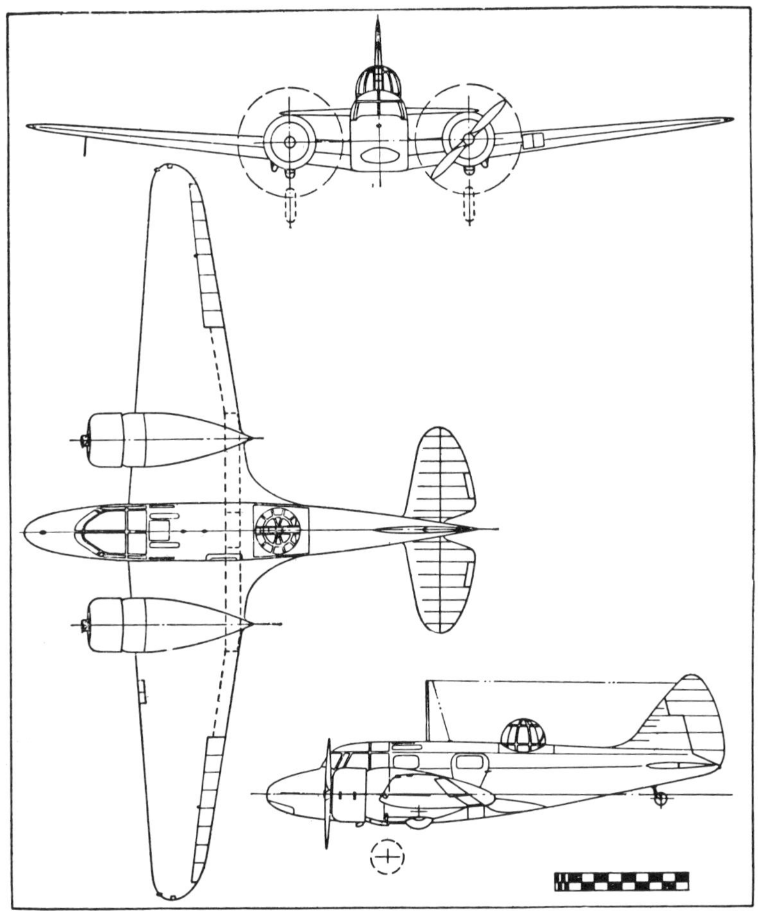

AIRSPEED A.S.10 OXFORD Mk I

which went to Norwegian Air Lines (DNL) as trainers; and two ex-RNZAF aircraft, registered ZK-APX and ZK-APY, used briefly for light cargo operations from Wellington during 1948 by G. M. Gould. In addition, BOAC had, early in 1945, at least five on loan from the RAF, which were based at Whitchurch, Bristol, on training work, as well as at Hurn and overseas; these were R6070, T1379, AP474, DF521 and NM536. Others were registered in the names of the Lancashire Aircraft Corporation, though only one of these appears to have been modified for civil use, and of Aerocontacts before these latter were sold to Britavia. Several Oxfords were used by companies in the aircraft industry, including Airspeed and de Havilland, for inter-factory communications work. At least four of these Oxfords, some still in use into the 1950s, had early single-letter RAF serials which show that they were built in, or around, 1940.

Of the 500 or so Oxfords which went to the then Union of South Africa (serials 1901–1999, 3301–3599 and 3801–3899) and operated mainly at training schools—Nos. 21 (Kimberley), 26 (Pietersberg) and 42 (Port Elizabeth)—six were on the post-war civil register. None, however, appear to have been operated and all the registrations were soon cancelled, so they are not included in the appendices giving the civil-registered Oxfords. For the record, they were ZS-AUF–ZS-AUI (1946) and ZS-BOC and ZS-BOD (1947). Their respective South African Air Force serials were 3732, 3395, 3340, 3634, 3842 and 3407. At least eight AS.65 Consuls were, however, on the South African register; these are mentioned in the Consul narrative and listed in the associated aircraft history record appendix.

Span 53 ft 4 in (16·25 m); length overall 34 ft 6 in (10·5 m); wing area 348 sq ft (32·34 sq m).

Oxford I and II (Two 375 hp Armstrong Siddeley Cheetah X moderately supercharged seven-cylinder air-cooled radials with two-blade fixed-pitch propellers).

Empty weight, with fixed equipment, 5,380 lb (2,440 kg); fuel (156 gal) 1,202 lb (545 kg); oil (15 gal) 135 lb (61·3 kg); useful load 2,220 lb (1,010 kg); loaded weight 7,600 lb (3,447 kg).

Oxford I. Maximum speed at 8,300 ft (2,530 m) 182 mph (291 km/h); rate of climb at 6,300 ft (1,920 m) 930 ft/min (4·73 m/sec); climb to 10,000 ft (3,048 m) 12·5 min; service ceiling 19,200 ft (5,850 m); endurance 5 hr.

Oxford II. Maximum speed at 8,300 ft (2,530 m) 188 mph (301 km/h); rate of climb at 6,300 ft (1,920 m) 960 ft/min (4·9 m/sec); climb to 10,000 ft (3,048 m) 12 min; service ceiling 19,500 ft (5,945 m); endurance 5½ hr.

Oxford V (Two 450 hp Pratt & Whitney R985-AN6 Wasp Junior nine-cylinder air-cooled radials with two-blade Hamilton Standard constant-speed metal propellers).

Empty weight, with fixed equipment, 5,670 lb (2,575 kg); loaded weight 8,000 lb (3,632 kg). Maximum speed at 4,100 ft (1,250 m) 202 mph (324 km/h); initial rate of climb 2,000 ft/min (10·2 m/sec); climb to 10,000 ft (3,048 m) 6 min; service ceiling 21,000 ft (6,400 m); endurance 5 hr.

The prototype AS.30 Queen Wasp, K8887, was shown for the first time publicly in the new and experimental park at the RAF Display, Hendon, at the end of June 1937. It had made its initial flight earlier in the month. (*Flight 14567s*.)

AS.30, AS.38 and AS.50 Queen Wasp

The story of the Queen Wasp is one which typifies the necessarily varying policies and requirements as the situation changed from one of imminent and expected war, through the phoney period following declaration of war and on to the real thing. This attractive little biplane was originally ordered in May 1936 and designed and built as the AS.30 to meet Air Ministry specification Q.32/35 for a faster and more effective radio-controlled, pilotless aircraft, in landplane and seaplane versions, to supplant and supplement the Queen Bee variant of the de Havilland Tiger Moth already being used for live gunnery practice. Later, a variant, the AS.38, was proposed, but not built, for use as a communications aircraft with the RAF; the designation AS.50 was applied to a production trainer version to specification T.24/40.

The Queen Wasp, much too good-looking to be shot out of the sky, was a single-bay biplane with folding wings, mainly of wood construction, and powered by a 350 hp Armstrong Siddeley Cheetah IX seven-cylinder radial. The centre-section was built integrally with the fuselage, and the outer wings were of two-spar ply-covered construction with fabric-covered slotted flaps and ailerons. The fuselage was in three sections, with the middle portion carrying the centre-section.

Access to the single-seat cockpit was by way of a door in the starboard side between the spar-mounted bulkheads. A transparent sliding panel in the roof between the bulkheads and spars provided access to the slinging gear and wing-joint pins and served also as an emergency exit. Slotted flaps were fitted to the trailing edge of the top wing, extending over the whole outer spans. Slotted ailerons were on the lower wing only and were interconnected with the flaps so that these and the ailerons were lowered together.

Two prototypes, K8887 with a land undercarriage and K8888 with floats, were built and flown in 1937, and four, or possibly five (P5441–5445) production Queen Wasps were completed and delivered to the RAF. The first of these flew on 29 March, 1940, and the second on 18 May, 1940. Five more, P5446–5450, were partially completed. The RAF serial numbers allocated shows that the expected requirement was for 325, including the two prototypes.

The Queen Wasp landplane prototype made its initial flight, in the hands of G. B. S. Errington, from Portsmouth Airport on 11 June, 1937, and was seen publicly for the first time at the RAF Display, Hendon, at the end of that month among the new and experimental aircraft. The second prototype, the seaplane, was flying soon afterwards and was successfully catapulted from HMS *Pegasus* (ex-*Ark Royal*) in November.

Those who flew the later Queen Wasps say that the slow-speed characteristics were not all that could be desired and at least one of those responsible for the detail design is critical today of the unnecessary sophistication and complication in an aircraft which was, after all, intended at first solely to provide a target which had a usefully higher speed and better automatic-flight behaviour than the Queen Bee. The tapered wings—which made it difficult to provide wash-out to promote an initial stall at the root—meant that, except for the prototype, it had a somewhat sharp wing-drop at the stall. On one stalling test the lift generated by the upper-wing centre-section sucked out the transparent panel.

The second Queen Wasp, K8888, was fitted with floats and was successfully catapulted from the carrier HMS *Pegasus* (ex-*Ark Royal*). It is seen here taking-off on test near Gosport.

The second prototype Queen Wasp, which was even more good looking with the big floats which gave it a more balanced appearance than that of the landplane version. (*Flight 15084*[8].)

One account, however, given by its designer, Hessell Tiltman – who had had the characteristic demonstrated to him while flying as a passenger with George Errington – describes the first prototype as showing extraordinary stalling behaviour. Because of some feature of the centre-section, the flow breakaway in that area appears to have been complete at low speeds, so that the Queen Wasp could be made, with full-up elevator, to sink, level laterally, but without lateral control, at a very high rate of descent and low forward speed until checked by full power, or by down elevator for an earlier diving recovery. Maybe this was the first example of a stable, but recoverable, deep stall with a conventionally configured aircraft. Neither the second prototype nor later Queen Wasps demonstrated this characteristic perhaps because changes had been made to the centre-section. These dropped a wing in the normally expected way.

The AS.30 cannot, however, have been difficult in normal conditions because both the landplane and seaplane prototypes survived the test-flying period without serious mishap. The first flight of the seaplane was made by Flt. Lt. C. H. A. Colman, who had never previously handled either a floatplane or flying-boat. Incidentally, in tank tests at Farnborough the original Short-built floats were found to be unsatisfactory because of pitching instability. After the RAF had developed a better design, Shorts produced their own alternative which, after some modifications, was equally satisfactory.

Catapult spools were fitted to the second prototypoe for trials at RAE Farnborough. The aeroplane disappeared from view as the Queen Wasp left the trolley, first one wheel and then the other bounced along the ground before the wingtip hit, rolling the machine over on its back. Miraculously there was no fire and the pilot was rescued from the rear fuselage.

Tiltman liked the Queen Wasp which must obviously have been a good flying machine to be capable, as it was, of radio-controlled pilotless flight. We are nowadays accustomed to the idea of automatic control down to the actual landing, but it is suitably humbling to realize that all this was being done much more than a quarter of a century ago with aircraft of such limited capacity and payload as the Queen Wasp – and its even more limited predecessor, the Queen Bee. It was not as if the automatic control and guidance system could be of an over-simplified, hit-or-miss kind. The system used was extremely complex, with all manner of built-in fail-safe devices to cope with such things as false gyro signals during acceleration (particularly in catapult launching) or deceleration, and radio or battery failure.

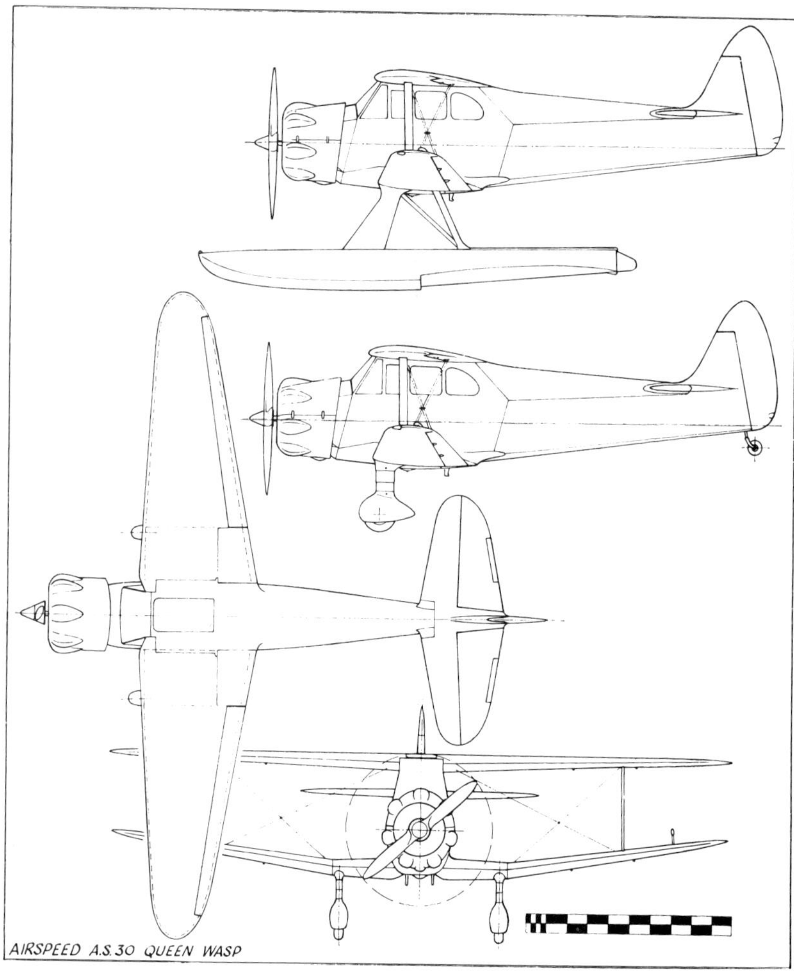
AIRSPEED A.S. 30 QUEEN WASP

Another air-to-air picture of the second Queen Wasp which emphasizes again its good looks by comparison with the landplane variant. (*Flight 15087s*.)

In automatic flight the Queen Wasp was controlled by an air-driven gyroscope unit which maintained the status quo by corrections made through pneumatic servos to the rudder and elevator (the ailerons were locked in the neutral position). Changes of heading or attitude, as signalled by radio from the ground with coded dot-dash signals, were made by suitably precessing the gyro with a system of air-driven pistons. There were three radio-controlled throttle positions—fully open, half open for cruise power, and closed. The throttle movement was interconnected with a complicated device to counteract the effects of acceleration and deceleration on the gyro. A servo motor lowered the flaps when 'landing glide' was demanded by radio signals, but only when the speed was right. Regardless of any lack of radio instructions an altimeter contact system automatically initiated a pull-out to the fast level full-throttle condition below a pre-set altitude.

A weighted trailing aerial, automatically winched out by ASI signal after take-off or catapulting, served the dual purpose of radio aerial and automatic-landing activator. When the weight struck the ground, contacts on the winch caused an electrically operated spring-loaded valve to apply up elevator and short-circuited all air supplies to the gyroscope and other valves. When the aerial touched, the Queen Wasp was thus committed finally to its own landing, for better or for worse.

This relatively straightforward autolanding system, however, provided problems of its own. In very bumpy weather the trailing aerial could snatch sufficiently vigorously to give the unthinking system the idea that a landing should be initiated. So a relay was introduced into the system to forestall automatic action before a 'landing glide' signal had been received.

When serious failures occurred the systems were arranged for the aircraft to enter a flaps-down engine-off glide in a gentle left turn, so that, at the worst, an automatic landing might be made not too far from base. Engine failure left the Queen Wasp in a flaps-down glide in a slow turn to port. Battery failure left it in a flaps-up glide—also in a slow turn to port. As a Farnborough note said: 'The aeroplane will almost certainly crash, but the flying range is limited.' To deal with radio failure, the system included a clock which, reset by all incoming signals, selected the emergency glide condition if no signals had been received after an elapsed period of two minutes. They certainly thought of nearly everything even thirty-odd years ago.

AS.30 (Cheetah IX). Span 31 ft (9·45 m); span, folded, 12 ft (3·65 m); overall length, landplane, 24 ft 4 in (7·42 m); seaplane 29 ft 1 in (8·85 m); overall height, landplane, tail-down, 10 ft 1 in (3·05 m); seaplane 13 ft (3·96 m). Loaded weight, landplane, 3,500 lb (1,588 kg); seaplane 3,800 lb (1,724 kg). Maximum speed at 8,000 ft (2,438 m) 172 mph (277 km/h); cruising speed at 10,000 ft (3,048 m) 151 mph (243 km/h); service ceiling 20,000 ft (6,096 m).

AS.38 (Cheetah X). Span 31 ft 11 in (9·73 m); span, folded, 12 ft 3 in (3·75 m); overall length 26 ft 4½ in (8·02 m); wing area 133 sq ft (12·36 sq m). Loaded weight 3,645 lb (1,653 kg). Maximum speed, sea-level, 154 mph (248 km/h); cruising speed, sea-level, 140 mph (225 km/h); rate of climb, sea-level, 1,310 ft/min (6·6 m/sec); service ceiling 22,000 ft (6,706 m).

AS.39 Fleet Shadower

Like the General Aircraft GAL.38, the AS.39 Fleet Shadower was designed to meet Air Ministry specification S.23/37. This, in turn, was drawn up to meet Admiralty requirements for a carrier-based aircraft suitable for the purpose of shadowing, or maintaining contact with, an enemy fleet at night. These requirements called for long duration (6 hr) and the capacity to operate at exceptionally low speeds. The overall dimensions were also restricted by the need for shipboard stowage, and the wings were therefore designed to fold. Not unnaturally the AS.39 and GAL.38 evolved into remarkably similar aircraft in general appearance and layout. The GAL.38, however, had a nosewheel-type undercarriage, whereas the Airspeed Shadower had a specially-long-travel British Landing Gear tailwheel assembly well ahead of the tailplane to give 'level-landing' characteristics

The basis of the design of the Fleet Shadower was the use of slipstream lift from the four propellers to give it a very low minimum cruising speed. The long-stroke undercarriage included a long mid-fuselage tailwheel strut to give it 'level-landing' characteristics. (*Imperial War Museum MH4277.*)

without, however, the natural directional stability enjoyed by the now conventional tricycle arrangement.

Both aircraft were fitted with four 130 hp Pobjoy Niagara V seven-cylinder air-cooled radials with two-blade fixed-pitch propellers. Long-period cruising at a very low speed, of less than 40 kt, was made possible by slipstream action, on the Crouch-Bolas principle, over full-span slotted flaps/ailerons. An exceptional field of view had to be provided for the pilot and the observer. The latter was accommodated in a nose compartment with clear-vision panels at the front and sides, while the pilot's

Among the many near-impossible requirements in the specification of the AS.39 Fleet Shadower was the ability to fold its wings, complete with four Niagara radial engines, for shipboard stowage. (*Courtesy W. F. Shaylor.*)

This view of the AS.39 emphasizes the incidence of the wing, designed to provide a maximum in the way of slipstream lift at low speeds and shows the long-travel rear undercarriage leg for level-attitude landings.

cockpit was on a separate raised floor, offset slightly to port to provide a passageway to the quarters of the third crew member, the radio operator. The three compartments formed the forward portion of the fuselage from the nose to the rear-spar bulkhead.

Two prototypes of the AS.39 were ordered and given the RAF serials N1323–1324, but only one was completed and flown for the first time by G. B. S. Errington on 18 October, 1940, after earlier taxying tests on 10 August. Present-day thinking about the Fleet Shadower, which was originally known as the Night Shadower, is that it was, like its unidentical twin, the GAL.38, ruined by the near-impossible requirements.

The original AS.39 design had twin fins and rudders but wind-tunnel tests at the RAE Farnborough showed inadequate directional stability, and the addition of the centre fin cured this prospective trouble. To meet the specification a C_L max (maximum coefficient of lift) of about 3·3 was needed.

The flight trials of the AS.39 certainly gave some disappointing initial results. The rate of climb was, as expected, poor; there was a large nose-down change of trim when the throttles were closed; the elevators were somewhat ineffective; and areas of the wing showed disturbed airflow even at speeds well above stall. This last characteristic was believed to have been the direct or indirect cause of the other difficulties. Such full-scale airflow breakaway could not be reliably reproduced in small-scale wind-tunnel model tests. The principal areas of premature stall were those behind the engine nacelles, where engine-cooling airflow coupled with the effects of the large exhaust pipes and other appendages were obviously not capable of being reproduced in the tunnel tests. The marked change of trim when power was cut back was probably caused by the fact that, following the loss of the propeller slipstream, there was premature stalling in the centre-section area, a result which would have been exaggerated by the greater effective angle of incidence as the rate of descent increased when the slipstream-lift was removed. The poor rate of climb was directly the result of high drag and the low power/weight ratio—and indirectly, no doubt, of the premature breakaway of the airflow in the wing-root areas.

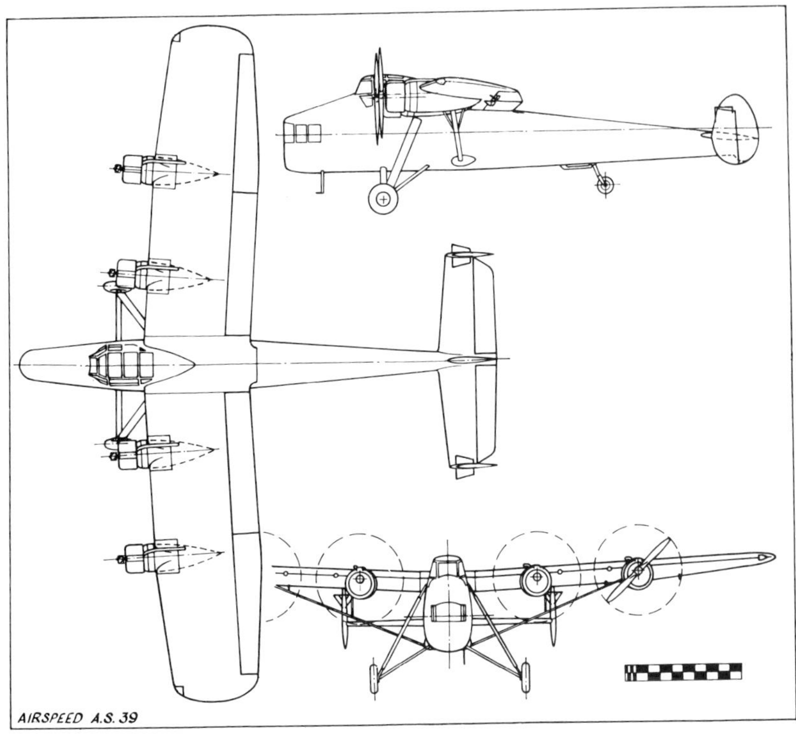

The AS.39 was of mixed construction, with the high strut-braced wing of spruce and plywood covering, and the fuselage of all-metal stressed skin built in one unit except for the observer's detachable compartment. The wing was designed for buoyancy in case of ditching, with the sections between the spars made watertight. Each outer wing, complete with two engines and an 85 gallon (386 litre) fuel tank, folded from the root, and a jury strut supported the forward spar when folded. The entire trailing edge consisted of four slotted flaps, the outer sections functioning also as ailerons. There were automatic slots on the leading edges ahead of the aileron/flap sections.

The main undercarriage was of the non-retractable divided type with each unit as a three-member pyramid consisting of a forward-inclined oleo shock-absorber leg, a radius-rod and axle. The steerable tailwheel, positioned midway between the wings and the tail, had a special long-travel shock absorber and a, necessarily, powerful self-centering device.

Span 53 ft 4 in (16·25 m); length 40 ft (12·2 m); height 10 ft 5 in (3·17 m); width folded 18 ft (5·5 m). Empty weight, with fixed military equipment, 4,592 lb (2,083 kg); removable equipment 313 lb (142 kg); crew (3 with parachutes) 600 lb (272 kg); fuel and oil 1,430 lb (649 kg); loaded weight 6,935 lb (3,146 kg). Maximum speed at 5,000 ft (1,525 m) 126 mph (202 km/h); cruising speed at 5,000 ft (1,525 m) 113 mph (181 km/h); stalling speed, full throttle, sea-level, 33 mph (53 km/h); stalling speed, full throttle, at 5,000 ft (1,525 m) 37·5 mph (60 km/h); initial rate of climb 865 ft/min (7·3 m/sec); rate of climb at 5,000 ft (1,525 m) 630 ft/min (4·5 m/sec); rate of climb at 10,000 ft (3,048 m) 365 ft/min (1·85 m/sec); time to 10,000 ft (3,048 m) 18 min; service ceiling 14,700 ft (4,480 m); absolute ceiling 16,700 ft (5,090 m); endurance approximately 6 hr.

T2449, the first of the only two AS.45 advanced trainers, provisionally named the Cambridge, to be built. (*Imperial War Museum MH5167.*)

AS.45 Cambridge

Designed to meet Air Ministry specification T.34/39, the AS.45, provisionally named the Cambridge, was an advanced trainer in the broad class of the North American Harvard and the Miles Master. At the time when design work started, it was supposed that there might be a shortage of such trainers and that a third type would be needed to fill the gap by, say, 1942. In the event two prototypes were built and flown (the first on 19 February, 1941, by G. B. S. Errington) with the RAF serials T2449 and T2453, but the type did not go into production. The prototypes are

The Bristol Mercury powered AS.45 advanced trainer. The undercarriage retracted inwards towards the fuselage. (*Imperial War Museum MH4284*).

recorded as having been taken on charge by the RAF, respectively on 7 and 15 July, 1942. Ron Clear recalls ruefully that he flew the prototype to Farnborough where it was used to fan the flames in fire-fighting trials. He wondered if the hours spent test flying it were really justified.

Although the records say that the training requirement for the AS.45 lapsed with the adequate supply of Harvards and Masters – so that it did not therefore, go into production – the fact seems to be that the AS.45 was not a particularly satisfactory aeroplane. It suffered, for instance, from somewhat ineffective aileron and elevator control at low speeds; the cause of the elevator deficiency was said to have been related to the gear ratio used. The overall drag, too, was higher than had been estimated, and there was some difficulty in reaching not only the target level-flight speed but also the required maximum diving speed. George Errington pulled out of a power dive to the accompaniment of a violent bang as a large panel of the upper wing skin disappeared. To his surprise no further disintegration took place and he was able to land at a rather higher speed than usual.

The conventional three-quarter rear view of the AS.45 shows the high tailplane and the V-shaped doors, and emhasizes the rugged crash-survival superstructure.

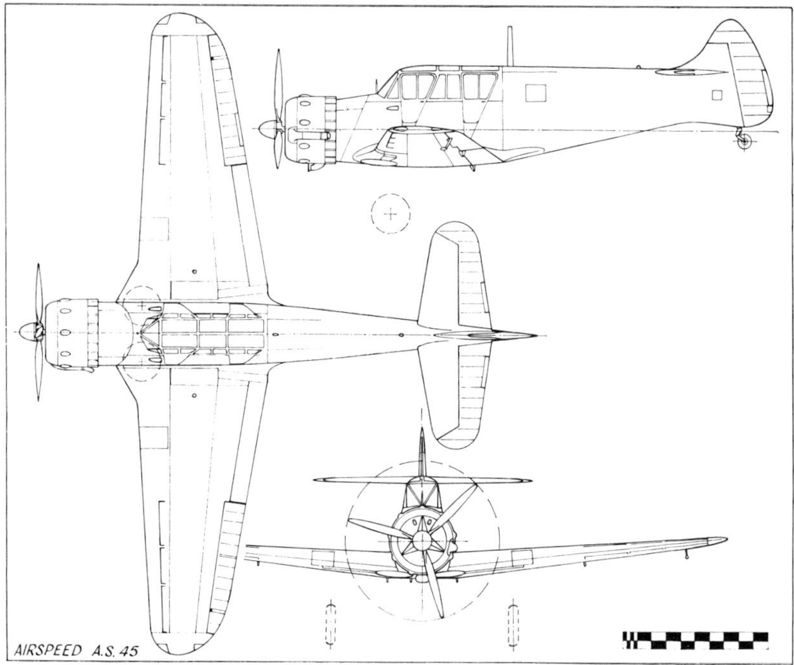

His statement that the loss made little difference to controllability sounds incredible. Experiences with the Hurricane, for instance, showed that, when gun panels tore away after being insecurely fastened, the stall-speed could rise by 20 mph or so and, for a safe landing, a fast 'wheeler' was advisable.

The control faults of the AS.45 were of a relatively minor nature and these, with the excess drag, could, no doubt, have been cured in development towards a definitive production version. The principal trouble was excessive structure weight. Wood was used for the wing and steel tube for the fuselage, which had four doors – two on each side, one normal and one emergency each for the pupil and instructor – with tubular members at root level for strength and to provide better protection in an accident.

The AS.45 was a low-wing, cantilever, tandem-seat monoplane with an inward-retracting undercarriage and powered by a 730 hp Bristol Mercury VIII nine-cylinder radial engine. Its two fuel tanks, one in each wing, had a total capacity of 130 gallons (590 litres).

Span 42 ft (12·8 m); length 36 ft 1 in (11 m); height, tail down, 11 ft 6 in (3·5 m); wing area, including ailerons and flaps, 290 sq ft (26·9 sq m). Maximum economical cruising speed at 12,500 ft (3,810 m) 228 mph (365 km/h), at 16,000 ft (4,880 m) 237 mph (381 km/h); time to 15,000 ft (4,575 m) 12·5 min; service ceiling 24,800 ft (7,560 m); range 680 miles (1,095 km).

A Horsa glider comes in to land, with large-area flaps fully down, after a training flight at the Heavy Glider Conversion Unit, RAF Netheravon, in July 1943. (*Imperial War Museum CH10345.*)

AS.51 Horsa Mk I, AS.52/53 and AS.58 Horsa Mk II

In some ways the Horsa troop- and vehicle-carrying glider was Airspeed's most remarkable achievement. Not only was it highly successful within the inevitable limitations of military use, but it was designed and flown in fewer than ten months and put into quantity production and assembled on a country-wide basis. The specification, X.26/40, was delivered in December 1940 to the Airspeed design team under Hessell Tiltman. After being bombed out of the de Havilland Technical School quarters at Hatfield in October 1940, the team was then installed at Salisbury Hall, London Colney. The construction of the sections of the first two prototypes, DG597 and DG603, was completed or directed from there, and were assembled at Fairey's Great West Aerodrome, now a small part of London's Heathrow Airport. The remaining five prototypes, DG609 and DK346, 349, 353 and 358 were assembled at Portsmouth so that trials could be done on the loading and unloading of such equipment as Bren-gun carriers.

The first prototype, flown by G. B. S. Errington, was towed off by an Armstrong Whitworth Whitley, flown by Nick Carter, from the Great West Aerodrome on 12 September, 1941. The initial designs were productionized by the drawing office at Portsmouth—no mean task, since the plan was that the Horsa should be produced in sections by woodworking factories and assembled and test flown at RAF maintenance units. Some 3,000 Horsas were produced in this way; in addition, Airspeed, at their Christchurch, Hampshire, shadow factory, constructed and assembled about 700—the only ones to be manufactured, assembled and test-flown on one site.

The first AS.51 Horsa glider, DG597, with flaps down, outside the hangars at Fairey's Great West Aerodrome where the first test flights, towed by a Whitley bomber, were made. (*Crown copyright.*)

Two versions of the Horsa were put into production: the Mk I (AS.51), which was the original troop-carrier, and the Mk II (AS.58), which differed in having a hinged nose for the direct loading of vehicles and guns, twin nosewheels, and a tow-cable attachment at the nosewheel strut and not, as in the Mk I, at the upper spar-attachments of the main undercarriage legs. At least three other variants were projected. One, the AS.52, designed to specification X.3/41, was intended to carry various combinations of bomb loads in a central 25 ft-long bay. These loads could consist of four 2,000 lb bombs, two 4,000 lb bombs, or one 8,000 lb bomb. The bay, which was circular in section when the bomb doors were closed, stretched from a point a couple of feet or so aft of the main entrance door to a point level with the wing trailing edge.

Another variant, the AS.53, was a vehicle-carrying project which was superseded by the AS.58. A third, which was apparently given no Airspeed designation, was a powered version to be fitted with two 375 hp Armstrong Siddeley Cheetah X radial engines.

There are some discrepancies (as with the Oxford) in the various records of the actual numbers of Mk Is and IIs produced by different centres. Official de Havilland figures, published in 1951, give a total of 3,655, of which 2,960 were sub-contracted and assembled at RAF maintenance units and 695 were produced complete at Christchurch. RAF serial numbers are recorded for 3,792, excluding the seven prototypes; it is possible that those with the outstanding 137 serials were never completed. However, the totals tally for the Christchurch-built Horsas (470 Mk Is and 225 Mk IIs, making 695 in all) and for those sub-contracted to the Austin Motor Company (300 Mk Is and 65 Mk IIs, totalling 365). The biggest share of sub-contracted production was handled by Harris Lebus, the furniture manufacturers, and associates, with, according to serial-number records, a total of 1,461 Mk Is and 1,271 Mk IIs, 2,732 in all, making grand totals of 2,238 Mk Is and 1,561 Mk IIs.

The Horsa went into initial full-scale action during the invasion of Sicily in 1943. As *Royal Air Force 1939–1945** puts it, 'the airborne harbingers of the Eighth Army were carried in two types of glider, the light Hadrian or Waco, of which the maximum load was 14 men and a handcart, and the larger Horsa, which could carry 30† men within its plywood belly'. But before that desperate affair, in which only the gliders towed by the RAF were even moderately successful, the British-built gliders had been towed by aircraft of No. 38 Wing all the way from England to North Africa, an operation which is rightly described as 'a most difficult and hazardous undertaking' and which must also have involved both tug and glider crews in tremendous feats of physical endurance. As the official history describes, the squadron mainly concerned, No. 295, had to fly, necessarily in daylight, within 100 miles of the German air bases in south-west France. Of the 30 Horsas which left England, 27 reached North Africa—a remarkable effort. One was ditched in the sea when its Handley Page Halifax tug was shot down by two Focke-Wulf Condors and the three pilots were rescued after 11 days in a dinghy. Another Horsa ditched after the towrope parted; its pilot was rescued after ten hours in the sea.

Only a week after their arrival in North Africa the Horsas were due to take part in the invasion of Sicily, carrying troops to strategic points near Syracuse. The multiple reasons—including bad weather, inexperience and the inadequacy of the C-47 tugs— for the near-failure of this operation have no place in this narrative, but only 12 out of 137 gliders, including ten Horsas, reached the chosen landing zone. All the successfully landed gliders were towed by the RAF, using Armstrong Whitworth Albemarles and Halifaxes. One Horsa landed within 300 yards of the primary objective, a bridge known as the Ponte Grande, south of Syracuse.

During the invasion of France in June 1944, Horsas were used by both the British and the US forces. More than 20 per cent of the material landed on the beachheads in Normandy was delivered by glider. On D-day

* *Published by HMSO.*

† *In fact maximum capacity was 25 troops and 2 pilots.*

most of the initial task was performed by dropped parachute troops, but six Horsas were successfully landed near the swing-bridge over the Caen canal, one of them within 50 yards, and this vital objective was seized. Gliders carrying 493 troops, 17 guns, 44 Jeeps and 55 motorcycles were successfully released; only 22 gliders were lost. The most valuable work done by the gliders was in the carrying, later on D-day, of reinforcements and stores for the airborne troops and 246 of them arrived at the chosen landing zone, the troops being carried in Horsas, and the Jeeps, trailers and stores in the bigger General Aircraft Hamilcars. About 95 per cent of the gliders reached their appointed destinations.

Although the outflanking attempt represented by the attack on Arnhem, in Holland, in September 1944 was—for various reasons, including a lack of transport aircraft—a magnificent failure, it was a success so far as glider operations were concerned. After paratroops had been dropped to mark the landing zones, 320 glider-tug combinations flew the first lift, with relatively few failures. But the second lift, initially of nearly 300 gliders, was delayed by bad weather and by then the situation had seriously

A solitary abandoned Horsa I sits near Syracuse after the initial attack on Sicily from North Africa in 1943. This was the first full-scale action in which Horsa gliders were used. (*Imperial War Museum BNA5543.*)

deteriorated, never to be recovered. Meanwhile, in mid-August 1944, operation 'Dragoon' had seen the successful landing of more than 400 gliders in the invasion of the south of France. The most extensive use of gliders was probably in March 1945, when more than 400 glider-tug combinations were used during the Rhine crossing. The majority of the earlier operational tows were by Short Stirlings, with Halifaxes taking over later. Whitleys and Albemarles were not much used except for delivery and test flights.

To say that it would be interesting to be able to reproduce or summarize the report on the first few test flights with the Horsa would be a considerable understatement. Press releases to the contrary, very few first flights are made without incident or trouble; that of the Horsa involved not only the unknowns of the glider itself, but also those of the towing combination. Never before had a glider of this size been aero-towed. Recollections of one who was at Heathrow on that day in September 1941 are that (as expected) the Whitley tug had disappeared almost out of sight across the aerodrome before becoming airborne; that there was a last-minute panic because the paperwork had not arrived; and that there had been an earlier near-disaster when a lifting jack pierced the fuselage.

A dazzle-striped Horsa I of the RAF Heavy Glider Conversion Unit on final approach in July 1943. (*Imperial War Museum CH10366.*)

Of later development and production test flying there are many stories. One of them concerns an accidental long-distance powerless flight, from somewhere over Windsor to RAF Netheravon, which at least demonstrated the reasonable efficiency of the Horsa as a pseudo-sailplane. During one of a series of high-altitude test flights, which were then being made without oxygen supplies in the Horsa, George Errington, who was flying the glider, said to the Halifax tug pilot, R. E. Clear, when they were climbing through 16,000 ft, that he wanted to get as high as possible. This was the last communication between the two. Evidently the communications cable contained within the towrope had broken—as it occasionally did when the line was stretched in turbulence. The Halifax/Horsa combination had reached nearly 20,000 ft just south of Windsor on the way back from a run to the Thames Estuary area when the Horsa began to oscillate more and more violently and to lose station as George Errington began to suffer the effects of oxygen shortage. A moment later the

Photographed on tow in September 1943, this early Horsa does not yet carry the invasion markings which were to become familiar a year later. The towing cables for the Mark I were at the upper spar-attachment of the main undercarriage legs; in the Mark II the attachment was at the nosewheel strut. (*Imperial War Museum CH10891.*)

glider was released. With the help of a strong north-easterly wind and, at lower levels, of a well-defined cloudstream, the Horsa got all the way back to Netheravon. Oxygen supplies were installed in Horsas the very next day.

The Aero Airborne Flight at RAE Farnborough did quite a lot of work on the Horsa, both on operational trials and in sorting out some longitudinal instability. One of the relatively early production aircraft, DP749, was used for these tests and also, in 1943, for trials of rocket assistance for towed take-offs—with rockets first applied to the glider and later to the Whitley tug. In May 1944, on a priority basis, tests were made at RAF Netheravon of snatch pick-ups, so that gliders could be retrieved for a second operation. Most of these trials were made using a Waco Hadrian (or Hadrians) but a Horsa was also involved in the trials, with a USAF C-47 (DC-3) as the snatcher.

For this operation the nylon towing cable was laid along the ground ahead of the glider and its ends arranged in a three-sided loop on wire hooks across two 12-foot-high poles placed 20 feet apart. The C-47 (or Whitley) picked up the looped tow line by means of a hook at the end of a trailing steel cable. The shock of the zero-to-80-knot or more speed differential was taken up by an automatic braking system in the drum from which the tug's cable was run out from the C-47.

For the writer, active experience with the Horsa was limited to a one-hour delivery-cum-test flight early in 1945 from the maintenance unit at RAF Cosford (a Horsa assembly centre) to RAF Netheravon, Wiltshire, with RX960. Riding for experience as second pilot, I was allowed to fly it most of the way, except for the towed take-off, initial climb and the final few minutes after casting-off from the Whitley tug, during which the vital remainder of the production test programme had to be completed.

The cable was released at about 5,000 ft and we were then on our own. First, the test pilot, Sqn. Ldr. Palmer, who had now taken over, completed a series of stalls, flaps up and down; then, having lost height down to about 1,500 ft, the Horsa was pushed into a 160 mph dive to near-ground level. It was then pulled up into the circuit and approach, using the pneumatically-operated flaps to adjust the drag to guarantee a final touchdown, with full flaps, as near as no matter within the parking area.

The final excitements were enjoyable, but I cannot say the same about the 50-minute period of towed flight. Apart from the fact that the controls were on the heavy side (those of the Horsa, which was not intended for more than a short operating life, had plain bearings) we were riding in some of the rough air left by the tug. There were two possible tow positions—high or low, either above or below the Whitley—and periodically during the flight the Horsa was moved from 'high tow' to 'low tow', or vice versa. This involved, with a twin-engined tug, trying to 'go round the slipstream'—in other words, turning one way and then the other when climbing or descending and while the Horsa was being pulled along and was not, therefore, freely controllable. With a four-engined tug, incidentally,

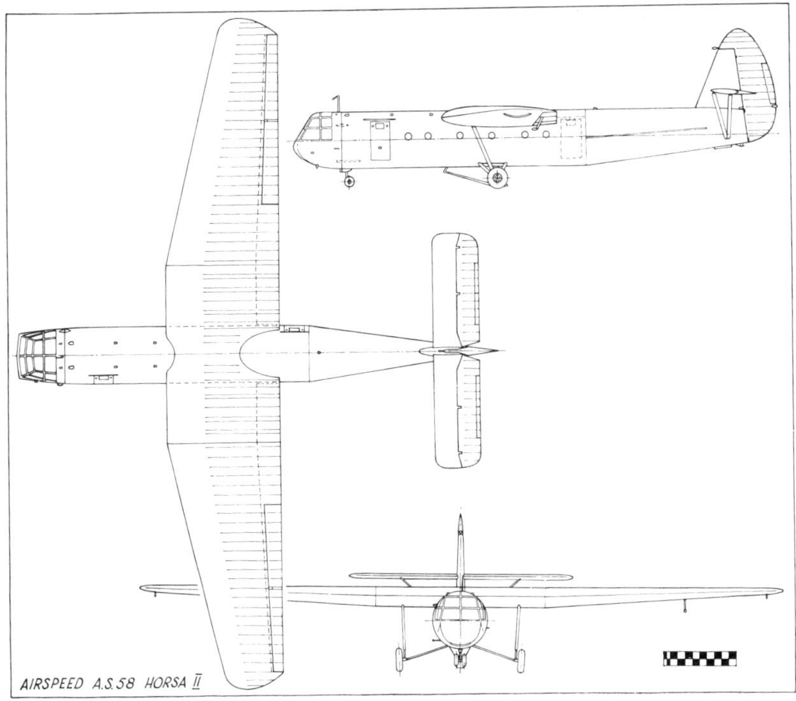

it was impossible to avoid the slipstream and the Horsa was dived or climbed through it to 'low' or 'high' tow. For an inexperienced Horsa pilot it was very hard work indeed until I discovered that aileron had to be reversed almost before bank was beginning to develop. Nor am I supposing that the pilot of the Whitley, with all these varying loads on its tail, was having a very good time, either. On take-off, as on all glider-towing operations, the Horsa was airborne long before the tug and had to be held down so that too much up load was not applied to the tail of the Whitley, thus preventing it from being lifted off.

The Horsa glider was manufactured in thirty sections which are seen here, before assembly, in an official publicity picture of airframe workers and parts taken in May 1944. (*Imperial War Museum CH13022.*)

The Horsa must have been the most wooden of aircraft ever built. Even the controls in the cockpit were masterpieces of the woodworker's skill. The impression one got was that almost everything, except the instruments, was made of wood—with no attempt to disguise it. Between the dual controls and their aileron wheels a small central pedestal carried duplicated air-brake control levers, the tow-release control, the undercarriage-jettison lever, the flap control and, of course (on the first pilot's side), a large-diameter fore-and-aft trimming wheel.

Because the Horsa would need to be controlled when towed, or after release, in cloud and/or at night, the instrumentation was fairly complete. That in earlier Horsas included an artificial horizon, a vertical speed indicator and a turn indicator, as well as an airspeed indicator, altimeter and compass, with appropriate panel lighting. Later Horsas, such as the one in which I flew in 1945, appear to have had a towing-cable angle indicator in the position previously occupied by the artificial horizon. This was probably just as useful; if a choice had to be made, the turn indicator would have provided the essential instrument-flying guidance. The split flaps, wheel brakes and undercarriage jettison jack were pneumatically operated from a pre-charged air-bottle, so the instruments included an air-pressure gauge; the airbrakes were mechanically operated.

The cantilever high wing of the Horsa was made up of three sections with split flaps between the ailerons and fuselage and with airbrakes, operated by cable, in the form of slotted grids which were normally flush with the wing under-surface. The fuselage was in three portions: a main cabin section as a plain semi-monocoque cylinder: an aft portion as a conical structure; and a nose section including the cockpit and, on the port side, the main loading door, which also formed a loading ramp. The bolts securing the joint between the main fuselage and the tail section were designed so that they could be released quickly, after controls and cables had been cut, or disconnected, for rapid unloading in action. There were hatches in the wing centre-section and below in the aft section of the fuselage, which could be used by a gunner. Just before the Horsa became operational test pilot Ron Clear found that in a very steep descent the tailplane twisted to make the pull-out most hazardous. Drastic action was taken to fit 'vee' struts to replace single struts on every tailplane.

The maximum troop-carrying capacity of the Horsa was 25, plus two pilots, with benches along each side of the fuselage accommodating up to 20 troops, three sets across the cabin aft, and two removable seats forward of the main door. There was a second door, to starboard.

The main gear of the tricycle undercarriage was jettisonable for landing on rough ground, when a central shock-absorbing skid and the nosewheel took over. This capability was not much used in practice; provided that the ground was reasonably open, the pilots preferred to have the better control which a braked undercarriage could provide.

Brig-Gen Chatterton OBE, DSO, who commanded the Glider Pilot Regiment, said that the Horsa gave great service to the Airborne Forces and its building was one of the supreme efforts of the Second World War.

Horsa I. Span 88 ft (26·8 m); length 67 ft (20·4 m); height 19 ft 6 in (5·9 m); wing area 1,104 sq ft (102·5 sq m). Empty weight 8,370 lb (3,800 kg); loaded weight 15,500 lb (7,030 kg); wing loading 14·1 lb/sq ft (68·6 kg/sq m). Normal gliding speed 100 mph (161 km/h); normal maximum towing speed 150 mph (241 km/h).

Horsa II. Dimensions, weights and performance as for Horsa I except: length 67 ft 11 in (20·7 m); height 20 ft 4 in (6·1 m); loaded weight 15,750 lb (7,144 kg).

The first prototype Ambassador, G-AGUA, flies past for the benefit of photographers on its initial flight at Christchurch, Hampshire.

AS.57 Ambassador

Some aircraft become legendary in their time—and the AS.57 was one of them—though not all the legends are capable of surviving an unexpurgated statement of the facts of their histories. A score of circumstances and events led to the near-canonization of the Ambassador in its heyday, but one fact has made at least a near-reality of the legend. Of the 23 which were built, including three prototypes, 18 were still flying more than 15 years after their entry into airline service and nearly 20 years after the initial flight of the first prototype. The Ambassador survived to honourable retirement after a longer-than-normal working life in spite of a succession of troubles and disasters which it suffered during development and the effects of an unnaturally truncated production programme. That is the real legend.

The AS.57 came into existence as a result of one of the five recommendations of the initial Brabazon Committee, set up in the mid-war years to consider future peacetime British transport aircraft requirements. Airspeed was asked to work on the design of a DC-3 replacement—Type 2 in the first recommendations. A small design team was set up in 1943 under A. E. Hagg at Fairmile Manor, Cobham, Surrey, to work on the project. Arthur Hagg, who had headed the design department at de Havilland, under Captain (later Sir Geoffrey) de Havilland and C. C. Walker, from 1920 to 1936, had been working (as aeronautical consultant to D. Napier & Son) with two members of the Airspeed design team, on the AS.56 fighter project to be powered by the Napier Sabre with a fan-cooled annular radiator. He joined Airspeed officially on 1 January, 1943, as technical and design director. By the end of that year the Brabazon project had been developed considerably from the original 32,000 lb Bristol Hercules engined proposal.

The situation, as it was early in 1944, can best be understood by quoting parts of a memorandum from the Director-General of Civil Aviation, W. P. (later Sir William) Hildred. This then-secret document, dated 3 January, 1944, was entitled 'Post-war British Civil Aircraft' and it said that the British Government had decided that 'work on the design of a limited number of aircraft for civil use should proceed in so far as this can be done without interfering with war production . . . [and] that

During the period on the ground after its initial flight, the Ambassador prototype, G-AGUA, was fitted with spinners and attractively styled. This is one of a series of magnificent air-to-air photographs taken on one of its early flights. Almost the only jarring pictorial feature was its jettisonable crew-escape door on the starboard side.

certain work should be done on the adaptation of existing types for use as transport aircraft during the interim period after the war before the new types are ready.' These decisions, the memorandum continued, were taken following the report of the committee under the chairmanship of Lord Brabazon. A second committee under Lord Brabazon had already looked more closely into the requirements, including those for powerplants.

For the record, the interim types, at the time when the memorandum was written, were: (1) A 70,000 lb pressurized transport based on the Lancaster IV for one-stop North Atlantic services; this was to be the Avro Lancastrian. (2) The Avro York, which was already in production, based on the Lancaster I. (3) A civil version of the Handley Page Halifax. (4) A civil version of the Short Shetland flying-boat, which was then about to make its first flight. (5) The Short Sunderland flying-boat, which, modified for passenger carrying, was already in service with BOAC.

Of the Type 2, the AS.57, which was to be developed as the Ambassador, Hildred's memorandum had this to say:

Another in a later air-to-air series of G-AGUA showing the characteristic Airspeed styling. G-AGUA is posed in this picture with the port propeller feathered. (*Charles E. Brown 6229-2.*)

'The type is intended for short/medium-stage operation. The manufacturers, Airspeed (1934) Ltd, supported by the de Havilland Aircraft Co, have submitted an outline design and the Brabazon Committee have prepared a list of requirements on which the detailed specification is being based. It is a twin-engined, all-metal aircraft of about 40,000 lb all-up weight, with a pressure cabin if desired, tricycle undercarriage, cruising speed of about 200 mph, good single-engine performance, and a payload over a still-air range of 1,000 miles of 7,000 lb, including about 30 passengers. Adequate heating and ventilation will be provided and the aircraft will be suitable for operation in cold or tropical climates. It should be in production in about four years' time.'

Although the AS.57 had already grown in size considerably beyond that of the DC-3 replacement visualized by the first Brabazon Committee, the thinking in 1944 was still tending towards a spaciousness for individual passengers—a spaciousness which was later to be seen to be economically unacceptable. Cabin plans produced by Airspeed in April of that year, for instance, included one for 24 passengers—presumably for operation over long hauls on the BOAC Empire routes. However, for shorter-haul work in Europe and elsewhere, layouts with seating arrangements for 40 passengers were then also being proposed.

Almost from the start of development of the AS.57, Hagg—supported on some, but not on all, sides—had insisted that the airlines were underestimating the traffic likely to be available in post-war years. For domestic services and even for continental operations the British railway companies (then planning for an air transport future) were thinking in terms of a fleet in which the biggest aircraft would accommodate no more than 25 passengers. The Civil Aviation Department of the Air Ministry and even BOAC (BEA did not then exist) considered that the proposed 40-seat AS.57 was too large for European services and that there just would not be the

The first two prototype Ambassadors, G-AGUA and G-AKRD, flying together near Christchurch, Hampshire.

traffic available to fill the aircraft at a reasonable operating frequency and consequent utilization. How wrong they were to turn out to be.

But not everyone was being so very much cleverer; Airspeed themselves were then working out operating costs on a basis of annual utilizations of 4,000 or even 5,000 hours—rates which had still not been reached, even on long-haul operations, 20 years later. However, the importance of high utilization was at least being accepted, and Airspeed were among the first manufacturers to make a strong and calculated case for the lower costs of big-capacity civil aircraft and for the superior economics offered by higher cruising speeds when these were obtained by reduced drag and greater overall efficiency. It is difficult to realize that, even in 1944, a high cruising speed was still looked upon in Britain as an expensive air transport commodity—as it had been for a decade or so since the then managing director of Imperial Airways, in a many-times-quoted lecture, had 'proved' this to be so.

The Airspeed design team was already installed at Christchurch in 1944, and by the end of that year, despite doubt and criticism, the AS.57 was already being planned as a high-level cruise (20,000 ft), 240 mph, 40-passenger transport with an overheads-inclusive seat-mile cost of 1·3d per passenger-mile for 1,000-mile sectors. Its projected existence had been announced at the year's end company general meeting, and outline operating-cost figures had been made available early in 1945. An initial mock-up had been built by November 1944 for checking the flight-deck layout and for obtaining the comments of prospective buyers. The name Ambassador, as a natural successor to the Courier and Envoy, had been chosen by the summer of 1945, and in October work at Christchurch was well under way on structural-test sections and prototype jigs, and the technical aviation journals were allowed to inspect the mock-up and to discuss plans with the designers.

All the essential features of the Ambassador had then been finalized—though its gross weight (then proposed at 45,000 lb), payload and seating capacity were to be greatly increased before the definitive version, following the building of a third prototype, went into service with British European Airways more than six years later. At that time, October 1945, the first prototype was planned as an unpressurized 36-seater with two Bristol Centaurus and development flying was in progress with these engines in a Vickers Warwick bomber. Proposals for the second of the two prototypes on order were still uncertain, but the intention was that this should have a fuselage structure designed for pressurization. At the annual general meeting at the end of the year, the chairman, then Alan S. Butler, said that it might be fitted with propeller-turbines, and the wing structure was, in fact, designed and initially built to take four Napier Naiad turboprops—the engines then being considered for the later development programme. Rolls-Royce Darts were planned for the Vickers VC2 Viceroy, later named Viscount, and Armstrong Siddeley Mambas for the Armstrong Whitworth Apollo—the two aircraft which were being developed to meet the 2B specification proposed by the second Brabazon Committee.

The first flight of the first prototype Ambassador, G-AGUA, was made on 10 July, 1947, from the grass field at Christchurch, by George Errington, Airspeed's chief test pilot, accompanied by J. Pears as flight observer and engineer. By normal standards of such always-tense events, this 45-minute

The flight deck of the prototype Ambassador was one of the first to be laid out as a result of airline pilot and other consultations during the mock-up stages. The pedal-type braking system was still unusual in British aircraft of that period.

flight was successful although not without incident. Immediately after take-off the Ambassador shed the spring tab on the centre rudder, and later, for a while, the electrical systems partially failed. For a month or so afterwards, G-AGUA remained in the Christchurch flight hangar undergoing resonance tests. Various modifications were also made, including the locking of the centre rudder and deletion of the spring tab; the fitting of geared tabs on the outer rudders; and the installation of the propeller-reversing system which had not been available for the first flight. The prototype was flying again in good time to be demonstrated at the Society of British Aircraft Constructors' show at Radlett in September, where, in the static exhibition, the actual cockpit structure and controls of the second prototype had been built-up for display on the company's stand.

The second prototype Ambassador, G-AKRD, fitted up for de-icing/ice-ingestion simulation trials when being used as a flying test-bed for the Bristol Proteus propeller-turbine.

An order was still being awaited for a production go-ahead when, on 22 November, after about 50 hours in the air, the Ambassador suffered its first test-flight setback. While cruising at high speed the bolts holding the port main undercarriage jack-supporting tripod failed. The leg dropped and locked down—luckily without pulling the wing off. The hydraulic lines were pulled away and all fluid lost, so that neither the starboard leg nor the flaps could be lowered and the Ambassador had to be landed on the irrevocably locked port leg. There was no wing or engine-nacelle damage. The inevitable fuselage-belly damage was repaired and the starboard propeller replaced within 18 days.

This demonstration of the still-doubtful crash-survival characteristics of the high-wing layout was unlikely to have influenced BEA's decision, early in December 1947, to order the Ambassador. Under pressure from the Ministry of Aircraft Production, the decision was made in understandable doubt about the economic viability of the propeller-turbine-powered

In the passenger cabin of the furnished second prototype Ambassador, G-AKRD, during a demonstration flight made in Ireland in January 1950, carrying representatives of Aer Lingus, one of whose stewardesses is the central figure.

alternatives. The order for a conventional, if advanced, piston-engined aircraft certainly caused convulsions within BEA and nearly resulted in Vickers stopping work on the turboprop Viscount. As it turned out, the decision left Airspeed with the uneconomic production of 20 aircraft while convincing BEA and Vickers of the need to go ahead with bigger-capacity versions of the Viscount 630—the 700/800 variants which later sold in hundreds rather than in tens. Had the Ambassador not been a year or more late in development and in entering service with BEA, the situation might still have been very different, with a Dart-powered variant to follow the initial Centaurus piston-engined version.

As existing in December 1947, the Ambassador was, after all, an advanced design, and the proposals for the production version took advantage of the higher powers promised for the Centaurus engine and of the structural changes stemming from design work on the proposed AS.60 Ayrshire military transport variant. The basic design in mid-1945 was for a clean aircraft with a high wing of high aspect ratio with near-laminar-flow characteristics, a tricycle undercarriage with steerable nosewheel, integral fuel tanks and a number of other original features. The developed production Ambassador was, in 1947, already being planned for gross weights of 47,000 lb, rising initially to 49,000 lb and later to 52,500 lb when using Centaurus 630/660 engines with a take-off power of 2,800 hp or more.

Early during its flight development, the Ambassador had been shown to possess rather remarkable asymmetric (engine-out) control properties down to very low speeds. Figures published after only 50 hours or so of test flying showed that the prototype was controllable, with the propeller of the critical engine feathered and using take-off power on the other, down to speeds as low as 110 kt. The chief test pilot, George Errington, had previously completed a very comprehensive series of engine-out controllability tests with the Vickers Warwick used for Centaurus engine development, and he and the chief aerodynamicist, J. F. Foss, were especially interested in the problems and requirements involved. At the SBAC exhibition and flying display at Farnborough in September 1948, Errington completed a demonstration flight with the second prototype on one engine throughout—a performance which had never been attempted before and never repeated since. The port propeller was feathered before the start of the take-off run, during which the Ambassador was kept straight with the steerable nosewheel, and remained so throughout the flight and until the completion of the landing run.

This second prototype, G-AKRD, was, in its way, the most remarkable of all the Ambassadors built. It flew for the first time on 26 August, 1948, and, unlike G-AGUA, was pressurized and in due course fully furnished for passenger demonstration flights. With the possible exception of the prototype turboprop Viscount 630, it provided the quietest and smoothest ride for passengers of any propeller aircraft. Within reason, weight and expense were not spared in the furnishing and soundproofing, and the Centaurus 630 powerplants were necessarily quieter and smoother than

The first Airspeed-designed powerplant built around the Bristol Centaurus 661 was flight-tested initially in the port nacelle of the original Ambassador prototype, G-AGUA, which was also fitted with the production-type undercarriage.

G-AKRD flying with Bristol Proteus propeller-turbines. Note how the original Ambassador styling scheme was continued, with a paint scheme to reduce the apparent bulk of the powerplants and retain the good lines of the aircraft. (*Flight 30709*[s].)

the fully developed and more powerful 660 engines of the production version. After completing its work with Airspeed, G-AKRD went to Bristol for Proteus turbine and DH propeller trials in 1953 and to Rolls-Royce in 1958 for Tyne turboprop development and remained with Rolls for tests with later Dart variants until after 1968, giving 20 years of service. Unmodified and with an under-strength wing, G-AKRD could never have been used for commercial operations and was flown throughout its long life with a special category certificate of airworthiness and with its maximum weight limited to 45,000 lb.

During 1948 the first prototype, G-AGUA, had continued to bear the brunt of development flying. Tests had shown it to be up on performance estimates both for climb and cruise, with very low minimum control speeds. The rate of climb with the starboard engine stopped and propeller feathered, for instance, was 260 ft/min at a height of 10,000 ft when using maximum cruise power on the 'good' engine. On 17 November it was flown for the first time at the maximum weight, 52,000 lb, then planned

Ambassador G-AKRD was also used from 1958 for Rolls-Royce Tyne propeller-turbine tests and is flying here with the Ministry of Aviation registration G-37-3. (*Flight 37580*[s].)

for the production aircraft. Although the second prototype was already flying, G-AGUA was used because it had the means of carrying and jettisoning water ballast not available on G-AKRD. The take-off (at a considerable overload weight for the first prototype) was made from RAF Beaulieu because Christchurch had a grass strip only 5,050 ft in length. A run of only 2,700 ft was, however, required at Beaulieu and the Ambassador was landed, after jettisoning some water ballast, at, again, a very high overload weight of 50,000 lb.

Meanwhile BEA had signed, on 23 September, 1948, an order for 20 of the developed version of the Ambassador and the plans involved service introduction in 1951—a date which Airspeed were not in fact able to meet. A number of difficulties, delays and minor disasters caused the introduction to be a year or so late. The first of the difficulties became apparent in 1949 with the successive failures of full-span wing specimens in the strength-test rig at the RAE Farnborough. The initial specimen had failed at a little less than 75 per cent of 'proof' load (the minimum permissible target, representing a 50 ft/sec up-gust on the fully loaded aircraft at maximum cruising speed) and detail modifications had not resulted in an improvement of this failure level in two other tests at Farnborough.

The structure of the high aspect ratio, semi-laminar-flow wing of the Ambassador differed considerably from then accepted design practice. The skin panels were thick and designed to take, with the span-wise stringers, more than 85 per cent of the load and the centre-section/outer-wing joint was made through this skin-stringer structure. Additional technical help was brought in by de Havilland and some fairly drastic measures taken to distribute the loads more evenly at the points of failure. A modified full-span wing finally passed its strength test on 6 December, 1949, with ultimate failure at a loading some 20 per cent in excess of proof. Earlier, the (water-dunked) fuselage pressure tests had been successful, with the main fuselage specimen reaching 9·8 lb/sq in (in Portsmouth docks) and the control cabin specimen (in a tank at Hatfield) reaching 9·9 lb/sq in before failure—both figures very well in excess of the pressure differential of 4·16 lb/sq in to be used in service.

Following a successful but unproductive demonstration with the second prototype in Ireland, in an effort to interest Aer Lingus, during January 1950, this aircraft was the victim of another minor but troublesome incident on 13 March. During a simulated take-off engine-failure demonstration at Hurn Airport, Bournemouth, G-AKRD sank back on a rising runway. Temporary repairs were made to the damaged fuselage and a new port propeller fitted for a ferry flight back to Christchurch, where it was grounded for several weeks while full repairs were completed.

Two more accidents in 1950 did nothing to help to win the race against

'Finished with engines' – G-ALFR at Christchurch on 13 November 1950. (*Airspeed*)

time. Early in July the production prototype, G-ALFR, later named *Golden Hind*, which had made its first flight in May that year, suffered a failure of the starboard undercarriage leg, with consequent damage to the underside of the fuselage, starboard engine nacelle and propeller. The same aircraft was later, on 13 November, involved in a very heavy landing at Christchurch during pre-certification trials. The causes of this were multiple. There were very gusty cross-wind conditions and the approach may have been a little on the slow side—but there were many other factors involved. At any rate, the descent could not be checked, the Ambassador hit the ground hard and both engines fell out following failure in tension of the upper longeron attachments. It was repaired and re-engined in very quick time and was flying again before the end of the year.

This extraordinary accident—which appeared disastrous when it happened, but which did practically no damage to G-ALFR apart from its powerplants and their ancillaries—was the indirect result of the pressure then being applied to the delayed test programme. BEA had earlier asked Airspeed to try to extend the centre-of-gravity limit further forward so that there would be less restriction on passenger seating. On the day in question the Air Registration Board's test pilot was due to assess the handling at forward C.G. limits, and the tests, which involved landings

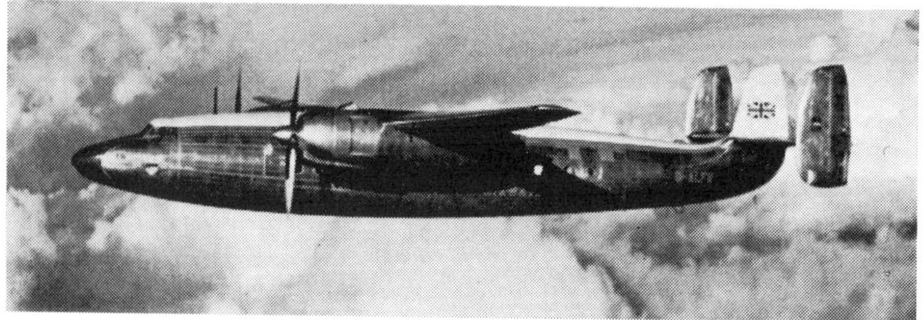

The definitive Ambassador G-ALFR, emphasizing the fact that the Ambassador was one of the most handsome civil airliners ever produced.

with full flap, power-off, had not yet been completed. According to R. E. Clear, the Airspeed test pilot who was given, at short notice, the work of completing the tests, the accident was the result of an error in the C.G. position and fading elevator control at large 'up' angles—compounded by the gusty, cross-wind conditions prevailing, and an over-reading air-speed indication because of static-system error. The C.G. had been moved forward in increments by shifting sandbag ballast between each test and for this landing too many bags had been moved forward, so that the C.G. was some 2½ per cent further forward than had been intended. Plenty of elevator movement remained—as confirmed by desynn readings during previous landings—and it was not realized that the final 4 degrees or so of up-elevator movement would have no appreciable effect in checking the descent and initiating the flare-out.

When Ron Clear realized that the elevator was not doing its work after starting to check at 50 ft, he opened the throttles from idle to the take-off power setting. There was the usual slight delay before the engines woke up and they were developing full power when the nosewheel hit the ground at a measured 14 g. The oleo was fully compressed and the power arrived just as the nose of the aircraft was being rotated upwards by the recoil of

One of BEA's Elizabethans on the apron at Frankfurt Rhein-Main Airport during a proving flight in 1952. (*BEA 4132.*)

the oleo. The result was that the engines 'just went straight ahead' and the Ambassador, now a glider, bounced over them and climbed to about 40 ft despite full down elevator—the C.G. now being well aft of the limit after shedding its two engines.

There was a lighthearted sequel to this when George Errington—always with a flair for doing the right thing—arranged for Ron Clear to be presented with a miniature ship's telegraph unit with its signal set at 'Finished with Engines'.

While the programme of tests with this production prototype had been proceeding, work was well under way on the production lines at Christchurch. Both G-AMAD *Sir Francis Drake*—made in advance of the remainder so that it could start proving trials—and the first in registration sequence, G-ALZN *Elizabethan*, BEA's flagship for the fleet, were well on the way towards completion. The first made its initial flight on 12 January, 1951, and *Elizabethan* on 10 April of that year. Contractually, the first production aircraft was scheduled for delivery to BEA on 15 January, 1951, and five by 15 March that year.

Between 10 May and 14 May inclusive, G-AMAD put in 52½ hr on proving work with a mixed Airspeed and BEA flight-deck team—an average of 10 hr per day—and 160 of the 250 hours required by the ARB had been completed by 20 May. Things were really beginning to move.

After the initial contractor's tests, G-ALZN was loaned to BEA on 22 August for training and taken over by Capt. C. E. F. Riley, then flight captain of the airline's No. 8 (Elizabethan) flight. At that time Airspeed (now the Airspeed Division of de Havilland) hoped to deliver five before the end of the year and the remainder during 1952. However, none were delivered officially before 1952, and the last three, including G-ALZN, did not reach BEA until the first quarter of 1953. Among problems still being met was overcooling and associated excessive drag of the powerplants, designed and built by Airspeed around the basic Centaurus 661 engine. The first of these powerplants, with practical and attractive 'four-petal' cowlings, had been flown in the port nacelle of the original workhorse prototype, G-AGUA, which had also been fitted with the production undercarriage and used for tests of the thermal de-icing system before being retired and dismantled in 1951.

The tropical trials with the production prototype G-ALFR at Wadi Seidna, Khartoum, in August and September 1951, demonstrated again the importance of moving only with small increments of change into unknown areas of the flight envelope—in this case tests in high ambient temperatures of the order of 35 °C (95 °F). These trials also showed how a determined crew can circumvent unexpected technical difficulties by the development of special handling techniques and how stringent new conditions can introduce mechanical troubles not previously experienced—in this case brake failures. In addition to normal take-off and landing measurements, the trials included, of course, those of engine-cut take-off, accelerate-stop and single-engine landing distances. The team consisted of four observers and a flight engineer, and was led by R. E. Clear, with B. A. Powell as extra test pilot.

During the engine-cut take-offs—of which thirty-eight were made, including eight which were camera-observed—it was found that the engine-cut speed was extremely critical in relation to its effect on the

The ingenious and practical petal cowling arrangement of the Bristol Centaurus 661 powerplant is seen in this picture taken while under maintenance at Wadi Seidna, Khartoum, during the tropical trials with G-ALFR in 1951.

distance to unstick—especially if the cooling gills were at anything but a minimum possible opening. In two of the measured runs at a weight of 49,000 lb there was a difference of 1,800 ft in distance from cut to unstick for one of only 2 kt in the calculated engine-cut speed. After a cut at 106 kt indicated, the distance to unstick was 2,880 ft, whereas with a cut delayed by 1½ seconds to 108 kt, indicated, the distance was only 1,044 ft. This unexpectedly poor acceleration from a cut at the pre-calculated speed for the weight and temperature led to one very 'hairy' incident. Ron Clear's test report tells the story:

'During one practice run at 49,000 lb in which the starboard engine was cut at 105 kt ASI, using 10 degrees gill, the unhappy situation developed in which the aircraft could not accelerate to normal unstick speed within the limits of the runway, while, by the time this was evident, insufficient room was available for stopping without retracting the undercarriage. The take-off was therefore continued and, as the last 100 yd of runway were being used, with the ASI at 106 kt, the undercarriage was retracted with the wheels still on the runway. Fortunately the aircraft did not sink sufficiently for the propellers to foul the ground while crossing the over-shoot area, during which time the aircraft was persuaded to accelerate (by holding down) to normal take-off safety speed and the climb-away started before reaching some low scrub bushes.'

The special and difficult handling techniques mentioned had to be developed to deal with inadequate oil cooling during the engine-cut tests, when the oil temperature of the live engine reached its permitted limit before sufficient height had been gained for the safe unfeathering of the critical (starboard) engine, which had been cut. The technique involved the minimum use of the port engine before and after the single-engine take-off and initial climb. The Ambassador was taxied out on the starboard engine, and the port engine was started only when lined-up and after take-off clearance had been obtained. As soon as the initial climb had been completed, and the starboard engine unfeathered, the port engine was throttled back as far as was practicable for a continued climb. Afterwards the aircraft was dived until the port oil temperature had dropped to a reasonable figure. The landing was then made as quickly as possible and the port engine switched off for the taxi-in.

The positioning flights to and from Khartoum, on 13–14 August and 19–20 September, 1951, respectively, were free from trouble and provided a good idea of the Ambassador's performance on long stages in varying conditions. On the three-stage outward journey, via Rome and El Adem, the average true airspeed was 219 kt, and the ground speeds varied between 218 and 224 kt.

The passenger-cabin layout of the BEA Elizabethan made practical use of the 'framed' centre-section area by using a Pullman-type table/seat layout. The seats forward of the Pullman group—behind the camera in this picture—were aft-facing. (*BEA 3699.*)

One of the last of the twenty production Elizabethans to be built and the last in service with BEA was G-AMAF, *Lord Howard of Effingham*, seen here with the port propeller feathered.

There are some differences in the various reports of the first series of genuine scheduled flights by BEA with the Elizabethan. But taking, as we must, the airline's own records, there was a short period of *ad hoc* service in September 1951—after which the aircraft, being used on loan, were returned to the makers to cure radio and other faults. The first scheduled London–Paris service was flown on 13 March, 1952. At the end of that month BEA had six Elizabethans, G-AMAD, G-ALZP, G-ALZR, G-ALZS, G-ALZT and G-ALZU, on loan for training and initial operations. In the first full three weeks of service they carried 3,430 passengers and clocked up about a million passenger-miles. With the Elizabethan the Silver Wing service to Paris—a luxury midday 'special' first provided by Imperial Airways 25 years before—was re-introduced on 16 June. It was an all-first-class flight, carrying a maximum of 40 (instead of the normal 47/49) passengers, who were provided with a hot luncheon and champagne 'on the house' during an intentionally slowed-down 90-minute schedule.

The Elizabethan, notwithstanding troubles, delays and modification costs, gave BEA a passenger-attraction edge on all competitors, but the airline kept it in service for only a little more than six years. The Viscount 700, introduced in 1953, had even greater passenger appeal, and Air France were also operating these turboprop transports. In 1957 BEA decided to withdraw the Elizabethans gradually and the last scheduled service was flown from Cologne to London on 30 July, 1958. Their safety and traffic record had been extremely good. By that date only two, G-AMAB and G-ALZU, had been written off—the first in a non-fatal incident on an attempted single-engine overshoot at Düsseldorf in 1955—in 90,000 flights during which about $2\frac{1}{2}$ million passengers had been flown over about 1,000 million passenger-miles at an average load factor of 67·5 per cent. The Düsseldorf accident was caused by one propeller going into reverse pitch, introducing so much drag that the Elizabethan could not maintain height. The technical reason for this pitch-reversal was never fully explained, and restrictions on the use of reverse pitch remained throughout the later use of the aircraft.

Like most other aircraft in airline service, the Elizabethans had their lucky escapes. On 11 August, 1954, G-ALZN, the flagship, in cloud at about 7,000 ft during let-down into Le Bourget, Paris, collided with the Air France DC-4 F-BBDP on an Orly–Düsseldorf service. *Elizabethan* lost a seven-inch strip from her wing tip, but was landed at Le Bourget without further incident. About two years later, on 27 March, 1956, an Elizabethan flying to London from Belfast was in near-collision with a de Havilland Vampire fighter over Daventry; one passenger was injured in the avoidance manoeuvre.

Although the AS.57 Ambassador/Elizabethan was to continue in service for more than ten years after the 1957 withdrawal decision, its future (or lack of it) had been decided seven years before that. In 1951 two overseas airlines had been near to signing orders—Australian National Airways (later Ansett-ANA) and Central African Airways of Rhodesia. In the circumstances, both airlines were probably well out of the deal. At that time there were many technical difficulties still to be resolved, and there was no certainty that a relatively small manufacturer, even with the backing of the parent de Havilland organization, could provide technical and spares support. Nevertheless, ANA was then a firm prospective buyer and the Airspeed director in charge of sales, P. E. Gordon-Marshall, was on the spot (in two senses) when a cable arrived for him in Australia to say that Ambassador production was to be discontinued after the 20 had been built for BEA.

There was a major, and not too successful, departure from the original styling when Butler Air Transport of Australia bought three Ambassadors in 1957. This one is VH-BUI (ex G-ALZK *Sir Philip Sidney*); the others were VH-BUJ and VH-BUK. This picture was taken in September 1958 after the BAT Ambassadors had been withdrawn from service and flown back to Britain.

In this formation of the three aircraft powered experimentally with Napier Eland propeller-turbines, Ambassador G-ALFR, originally the production prototype, is flanked by a Convair CV-340 and a Vickers Varsity.

Life for the AS.57 began again when various airline and other operators bought BEA's Elizabethans, which had plenty of time left in them structurally and whose Centaurus engines were already running to 1,700 hr between overhauls. By the end of BEA's 1958–59 financial year seven of the remaining 18 Elizabethans had been sold. Three went to BKS Air Transport, the British independent operator—one in July 1957 and two in May 1958; three to Butler Air Transport in Australia in June 1957 (at a reported price of £150,000 each), entering service on 5 August, and one to Rolls-Royce in that same month. The remaining Elizabethans were then in storage at Cambridge aerodrome. By mid-1960 two had been sold to Shell Aviation, one more to BKS, two to the Royal Jordanian Air Force and six were still awaiting disposal. All were sold before April 1961.

The BEA sales offer of Elizabethans in 1957 had included availability dates, with details of the working hours remaining and of the modification programme. A continuing operating life to 30,000 hr was expected, with modifications to the integral-tank bays, the lower wing-skin and centre-section structure. The ARB was prepared, after modifications, to clear the aircraft for another 12,000 hr. By February 1957, six aircraft had been modified for extended life at a cost of about £300,000 to BEA.

The production prototype, G-ALFR, had meanwhile been loaned in 1954 to the Napier engine company by the then Ministry of Supply for development flying with Eland turboprop engines, other examples of which

The first Ambassador to be bought by BKS Air Transport, G-AMAD, was based at Newcastle-upon-Tyne for the operation, from August 1957, of the service to Dublin which was previously flown with Douglas DC-3s.

were already flying in a Vickers Varsity and a Convair 340. This conversion was demonstrated at the 1955 SBAC Display at Farnborough. The 3,000 hp Elands were fitted as complete powerplants ahead of the existing fireproof bulkheads so that they could, if necessary, be removed complete and replaced by Centaurus engines at short notice if BEA (who had previously used G-ALFR for development and training flights) needed to supplement their fleet with this Ministry-owned '21st' Elizabethan which was not included in their original order. While the engine-change modifications were being completed, G-ALFR was also brought up to BEA fleet standards. The extra fuel needed for the turboprop development flying was provided by two removable tanks in the centre-section stub wings.

After completing its work with the Eland turboprops, G-ALFR was sold to Dan-Air Services in February 1961. Dan-Air converted it to airline

The BKS Air Transport Ambassador G-ALZW seen on the apron at Flesland Airport, Bergen, in June 1958 after the inaugural service from Newcastle.

standards on a long-term basis at their overhaul and maintenance base at RAF Lasham. It was ready for service in January 1964 and operated with the carrier for more than three years before being withdrawn in the autumn of 1967. The second (non-standard) prototype, G-AKRD, had previously, as already recorded, been modified for Bristol Proteus development tests and, later, for Rolls-Royce Tyne and Dart tests.

In 1960, Ambassador owners—the original name of the AS.57 can justifiably be used now that BEA were no longer operating them—were Dan-Air (3), Rolls-Royce (1), BKS (4), Overseas Aviation (4), Shell Aviation (2), and the Royal Jordanian Air Force (2). Butler of Australia had withdrawn their aircraft from service in August 1958 and four others

Dan-Air Services introduced the Ambassador into service in 1960 after the three Butler Air Transport aircraft had been bought in November 1959. The airline eventually had the biggest Ambassador fleet since the BEA era. Dan-Air's G-ALZX is seen here at Gatwick Airport, the airline's base. The last Ambassador, ex-Dan-Air, is at Duxford and in 1991 was being renovated by the Duxford Aviation Society.

were still awaiting sale at a reported price of £69,500 each. The Overseas aircraft were never in fact used by this operator, but were sold later to others, including Globe Air of Switzerland.

BKS put their first Ambassador, G-AMAD, into service on the Newcastle–Dublin run on 9 August, 1957, taking over from DC-3s. By June 1958, the airline had three in service, and a Newcastle (Woolsington)–Bergen (Flesland) operation had just been inaugurated. BKS's Ambassadors were laid out with 55 lightweight seats, pruning 800 lb or so from the previously equipped empty weight.

It was not until seven years later that the remaining Ambassadors were gradually being withdrawn from airline service—or relegated to all-cargo duties. Even at the end of 1966 there were still 18 on the ARB register of certificated civil aircraft, including the second prototype workhorse, G-AKRD. In addition to the two, G-ALZU and G-AMAB, which had been destroyed in accidents during BEA service, another, Dan-Air's G-ALZX, was damaged beyond economical repair in an overrun accident at Beauvais, France, on 14 April, 1966, and a fourth, G-AMAF, had been

Another British independent who made good use of the Ambassador was Autair International, one of whose aircraft, G-ALZS, is seen here on the apron at Glasgow Airport, Abbotsinch, during the inaugural service on the Luton–Blackpool–Glasgow route in May 1966. (*Flight*.)

grounded in 1962 and cannabalized for spares. One, G-ALZP, was in use by Decca for radio/radar demonstrations and executive flying under a private C of A, and another, Dan-Air's G-AMAA, was also being used only for executive and similar transport purposes. Still in airline service were Dan-Air's G-ALFR, G-ALZN, G-ALZO, G-ALZY, G-AMAE, G-AMAG and G-AMAH; Autair International's G-ALZS, G-ALZV and G-ALZZ; and BKS's G-ALZR, G-ALZT, G-ALZW, G-AMAC and G-AMAD. By the autumn of 1967, G-ALZW had been withdrawn from use and G-AMAD was being converted for all-cargo operations. Sadly enough, G-AMAD was to be written-off in an accident at London's Heathrow Airport on 3 July, 1968, when the attachment of the port flap actuating rod failed through fatigue when approaching Runway 28R. The consequent retraction of the port flap caused the Ambassador to roll uncontrollably to the left. The aircraft had only recently been converted at Southend for BKS Air Transport's bloodstock and cargo division and had made its first post-conversion flight on 10 June.

BEA's Elizabethan *Sir Thomas Gresham*, G-AMAG, was bought by Shell Aviation in 1959 and used by them as an executive transport until 1966 when it joined the fleet of Dan-Air Services. It is seen here at Woolsington Airport, Newcastle, in January 1968. (*R. M. Rayner*.)

One of the first Ambassadors to be put into service by BKS Air Transport was G-ALZW, BEA's *Sir Francis Walsingham*, in the livery used in September 1964 when this photograph was taken. (*R. M. Rayner.*)

BKS Air Transport's Ambassador G-ALZR, taken over in 1963, had earlier been used by Rolls-Royce for Tyne propeller-turbine tests, flying under the Ministry of Aviation registration G-37-4. Note the changed livery in this June 1968 photograph taken at Newcastle when it was operating with the airline's Cargo Division. (*R. M. Rayner.*)

This picture of Ambassador G-ALZR, taken in March 1969, shows it in the final styling used by BKS Air Transport. It was then operating in the airline's Bloodstock and Cargo Division. (*Air Portraits.*)

Early in 1969 there were nine Ambassadors on the ARB register. These were the second prototype workhorse, G-AKRD, still with Rolls-Royce; Decca's G-ALZP, restricted to aerial work; Autair's G-ALZZ; and Dan-Air's G-ALZN, G-ALZO, G-ALZR, G-ALZY, G-AMAE and G-AMAH.

There is little doubt that BEA, despite delivery delays and the cost in time and expense of later modifications, made money overall out of their fleet of 20 Ambassador/Elizabethans—and they certainly gained prestige and passenger approval to provide much later revenue. Most, if not all, of the airlines who later bought and operated the units of the disbanded fleet probably made a profit from the Ambassador as such—if not on their total business. The only positive losers were Airspeed and their parent company de Havilland.

It is difficult to believe, living in the present world of high-cost jet transports with big prospective earning powers, that the initial price of the Ambassador was £128,000 per unit—or, say, £300,000 at today's values. On the pre-production aircraft (bought at a higher price) and the first four production aircraft, Airspeed's estimated loss was about £250,000. Some of this loss may have been recovered on lower man-hour and other costs for the remaining 16 aircraft which were built. The losses on the three prototypes, the first two of which at least were paid for on a fixed-cost basis, may, too, have been recovered from income-tax repayments from war-time earnings. But, overall, Airspeed lost a lot of money on the total operation. Even if the Korean war had not, indirectly, led to the decision by the parent company that productive capacity at Christchurch and Portsmouth was needed for more important and profitable work, the failure, in real effect, of the Ambassador project would have killed Airspeed.

Many of the technical features of the AS.57 Ambassador have already been described or referred to when necessary to explain points in the narrative of the development and history of this outstanding transport aircraft. By way of conclusion, and before giving the outline data, it will be helpful to summarize these features, including those which have not found a natural place in the narrative.

For instance, the high aspect ratio wing was designed for laminar flow—though it is doubtful whether this was achieved to any really useful extent despite the use of an advanced method of construction, using heavy-gauge skin. The wing consisted of a centre-section, carrying the engine nacelles, which was attached to massive fuselage frames at the spar stations. The detachable extension wings were attached by span-wise bolts. The extension wings were of two-spar construction, with built-up ribs and closely spaced Z-section extruded-alloy span-wise stringers. The thickness of the skin and the pitching of the stringers were graded along the span so that the skin and stiffeners were designed to take some 90 per cent of the bending loads. The fuel was carried in integral tanks. Thermal de-icing, using combustion heaters, was used for the wings, tailplane and fins, with electric de-icing for the propellers.

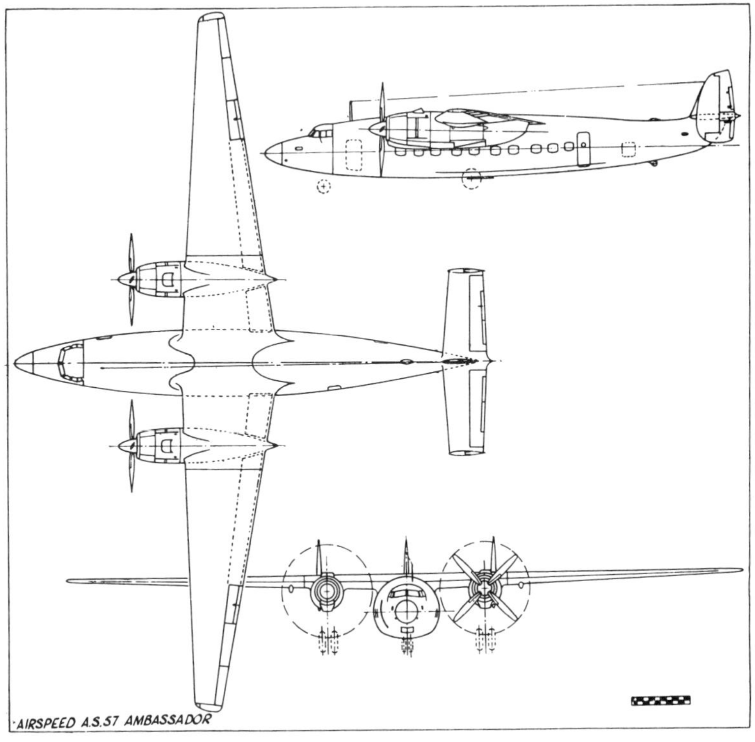

The fuselage cross-section was basically of two intersecting part-circles, with a 'flattened' base curvature, giving adequate width at the floor level and no depth of unusable volume below. The structure embodied vertical frames and bulkheads, longitudinal stringers of double-angle section, and a riveted skin. An Airspeed-Dowty undercarriage, with twin mainwheels, and twin steerable nosewheels, was hydraulically operated, with the flaps, brakes and nosewheel steering, by pressure from an electrically driven power-pack, with hydraulic accumulators, in the nose. Emergency lowering was by gravity and air drag. Two engine-driven blowers provided the pressurization, giving the cabin ground-level conditions up to 9,000 ft. and a pressure equivalent of 8,000 ft when cruising at 20,000 ft.

The Airspeed-designed and built powerplants were based on the 2,700 hp Bristol Centaurus 661 eighteen-cylinder, two-row sleeve-valve radials with two-speed blowers. The two integral tanks were of 500-gallon capacity and there was provision for two 300-gallon bag tanks in the centre-section. The figures which follow are those based on the measurements using the production prototype in 1951.

Span 115 ft (35·05 m); length 81 ft (24·69 m); overall height 18 ft 4 in (5·57 m); wheelbase 24 ft 5·6 in (7·4 m); track 27 ft 6 in (8·38 m); gross wing area 1,200 sq ft (111·48 sq m); mean chord 10 ft 5 in (3·18 m); aspect ratio 11. Basic operational weight 35,884 lb (16,277 kg); disposable load 16,116 lb (7,310 kg); loaded weight 52,000 lb (23,590 kg); maximum landing weight 50,000 lb (22,680 kg); power loading (at 52,000 lb) 10 lb/bhp (4·5 kg/bhp); wing loading (at 52,000 lb) 43·3 lb/sq ft (211·5 kg/sq m). Take-off distance to 50 ft (15·2 m) at maximum weight 3,270 ft (997 m); take-off to 50 ft at maximum weight, one engine inoperative, 4,590 ft (1,399 m); rate of climb after take-off, one engine inoperative, at maximum weight, 420 ft/min (2·13 m/sec); continuous climb at 5,000 ft (1,524 m) at maximum weight 1,520 ft/min (7·72 m/sec); continuous climb at 5,000 ft, one engine inoperative, at maximum weight, 360 ft/min (1·83 m/sec). Landing distance from 50 ft (15·2 m), at 50,000 lb (22,680 kg), 2,565 ft (782 m). Maximum weak-mixture cruising speed, at 20,000 ft (6,096 m) and weight of 50,000 lb (22,680 kg), 300 mph (483 km/h); at 60% METO power, 279 mph (450 km/h). Ultimate range, no allowances, with maximum payload of 11,650 lb (5,285 kg) cruising at 280 mph (450 km/h), 720 miles (1,159 km); as above, cruising at 220 mph (354 km/h), 900 miles (1,448 km); with full tanks and 7,900 lb (3,583 kg) payload at 280 mph (450 km/h), 1,560 miles (2,511 km); as above, with full tanks at 220 mph (354 km/h), 1,950 miles (3,138 km).

AS.65 Consul

The proposal which eventually led to the AS.65 Consul, a civil conversion of the AS.10 Oxford trainer, was first made in 1940 during an Airspeed board meeting at which post-war civil prospects were being discussed. At this meeting W. F. 'Bill' Shaylor, then commercial manager, said that the Oxford was an obvious candidate for conversion to civil use during the interim post-war period when circumstances would be difficult and suitable aircraft in very short supply—or words to that effect. Whether anyone in that boardroom realized that it would be more than five years before such a conversion would be possible is not recorded. When eventually the war was over, Airspeed were, however, quick enough off the mark with the business of buying back Oxfords from the Government, complete or in process of construction, and with making the necessary modifications to produce an aircraft designed to meet the pressing demand, correctly forecast, for a smallish low-priced general-purpose twin-engined airliner. The

The prototype AS.65 Consul in the 'lightning flash' styling which was to become very familiar. This first Consul was converted from Hatfield-built Oxford V3679 and did not have the longer, baggage-hold nose of later versions. It was used first by the Bata Shoe Co. (*Charles E. Brown 6104–11.*)

first, G-AGVY, ex-V3679, a de Havilland-built Oxford, was certificated in March 1946 and sold to the Bata Shoe Company for management commuting between their factories.

The interesting thing about the market-demand estimates for a civil Oxford conversion was the belief that it would be required not only for charter and feederline work, but also as a private executive transport. Although there were many owners of light aircraft in pre-war days in Britain and Europe, the numbers of owners of really practical, small multi-engined airliners, which would now be described as executive or corporate transports, could be counted on the fingers of one or, at the most, two hands. Airspeed saw this prospective market clearly. The original descriptive brochure, issued in February 1946, described the Consul as being of likely interest not only to charter and other operators, but also to private owners and 'business houses requiring aerial transport for their senior executives'. This was something which, for once, could reasonably be described as a breakthrough in aircraft sales thinking.

Because the modifications and alterations required for civil certification and use were of a relatively minor nature, and because the Oxfords and their engines were bought back from the Government for not so very much more than the proverbial song, the selling price could be extremely attractive even by immediately post-war standards. This practical five/six-passenger, fully-equipped twin was being offered for £5,500, excluding radio, but including essential loose equipment, such as covers and a dual-control set—and at a reasonably handsome profit for the makers.

The flight-deck of the first Consul with a single-pilot layout based on that of the Oxford and retaining the standard RAF instrument-flying panel. Radio equipment is below the right-hand panel which carried the engine instruments. (*Charles E. Brown 339–30.*)

The Consul's passenger cabin was separated from the crew compartment by a light partition with central double door. This is the interior of the ambulance version as laid out for 'sitting' cases with the folding seats in position.

Altogether, according to Airspeed records of 1951, 161 Consuls and variants, excluding 46 Oxford conversions for special purposes, were sold, 150 of them within about 18 months of the first appearance of the type. Most of them were civil-registered initially, or at some stage in their working lives. Fifteen years later, in 1960, there were at least nine Consuls still in service with British and foreign operators. With the known demand and at such a comparatively low first cost, they could be built 'for stock' and about 50 were produced at Portsmouth between May and December 1946.

This picture shows the upward-opening door of the ambulance version of the Consul. This particular Consul (Turkish Air Force No. 123) was originally intended for the Turkish Air Force but probably remained with Airspeed as G-AJWV.

The structural alterations made in the Oxford-to-Consul conversion included cut-outs for two additional passenger windows, one on each side of the fuselage forward of the rear spar station; a longer (duralumin) nose, with hinged cap for access to a forward luggage compartment (on all but the prototype); a partition between cabin and cockpit; and a re-setting of the tailplane to permit a centre of gravity limit more forward than that of the Oxford. This forward extension of the C.G. not only gave greater flexibility of loading, but also, and more important, increased the fore-and-aft stability, thus improving the instrument-flight handling characteristics, particularly during the climb.

For charter work the Consul could be laid out with five passenger seats —two on the front spar, one on the starboard side of the rear spar and two on a double, bench-type seat aft. A sixth seat could also be installed on the port side of the rear spar. Luggage was accommodated in the nose and between the rear seats and the aft bulkhead, with 10 cu ft available in each

One of the special Consuls produced in 1949 for the Burmese Air Force with two fixed forward-firing guns under the fuselage and provision for eight 25 lb rocket projectiles, which it is carrying in this picture.

area. The cockpit was normally laid out for one pilot, with the radio operator in the second pilot's (once the instructor's) seat on the right. The partition between the passenger compartment and the cockpit was windowed and had 19 in-wide central double doors. In the days when the Consul first appeared there was only a limited range of colours and quality of fabrics for furnishing, and all the earlier aircraft, at least, had an exterior finish of dark blue and gold or silver cellulose, with leather upholstery and trimmings, detachable carpets and headcloth to match.

Later variants of the AS.65 included an ambulance, with a large upward-opening door and accommodation for two stretcher cases and one or two sitting cases; a convertible version, which also had the large door and could be used for cargo-carrying or communications work; an executive aircraft, with four passenger seats, a lavatory and extra luggage space; and a military version which was, to some extent, a reversion to the Oxford.

The Alvis Leonides powered Consul which, flown by Airspeed test pilot R. E. M. B. Milne, averaged 188 mph in the *Daily Express* Hurn (Bournemouth) to Herne Bay, Kent, race in September 1950. It is seen here on the starting line with the Mamba-powered Miles Marathon beyond. Originally NJ318, this Consul was registered G-AKCW and re-numbered VX587 when acquired by the Ministry of Supply for Leonides development tests. (*Flight 24996s*.)

This last, as supplied to the Burmese Air Force, had two fixed forward-firing ·303 guns, provision for eight 25 lb rocket projectiles and a rear gun-turret; the armament was tested at the Aeroplane and Armament Experimental Establishment, RAF Boscombe Down, in the late autumn of 1949. Another Consul, originally NJ318 and civil-registered G-AKCW, was taken over by the Ministry of Supply as VX587 and fitted by Airspeed with Alvis Leonides engines, making its first flight on 9 November, 1948, It was later handed over to Alvis for continued work under its civil registration.

The extended nose with door for baggage stowage is shown in this picture of one of the seven Consuls used by Westminster Airways for charter and taxi work. It is seen being unloaded at Helsinki. (*Courtesy John Stroud.*)

On the whole, the safety record of the Consul was good—and certainly as good as could be expected in view of the wide variety of its duties, the unlikely places to which some of them went and the paucity of radio aids. This question of safety, or otherwise, is mentioned because the impression was gained in the late 1940s that there were too many accidents involving Consul operators. In fact, five of the first ten aircraft to be built were written-off in accidents—but during a wide spread of years (1946–52). Of the total of 20 or so accidents recorded (excluding those involving aircraft in dangerous areas such as Indo-China), 14 occurred during the period 1946–49 when up to 150 Consuls were in more or less continuous use in various parts of the world.

The Consul was Airspeed's only financially successful civil transport venture. This sad fact of history is an ironical one for a company which

Morton Air Services, the first new British independent operator to be formed after the war (on 1 January, 1946), eventually operated eight Consuls, including this one, which was the second to be bought by the carrier and is seen here at Croydon Airport, Morton's base. (*Richard Riding.*)

British Aviation Services of Blackbushe was another early Consul operator. Their first is seen here on the apron at Croydon Airport. (*Richard Riding.*)

Thomas Barclay, operating as International Airways from Croydon Airport, was also an early Consul operator. This Consul was named *Blanche Fury*. (*Richard Riding.*)

The first of seven Consuls, G-AIOL, operated by Steiner's Air Service of Speke Airport, Liverpool, was appropriately named *Liverpool Hawk*. (*Richard Riding*.)

Another of Morton Air Services' Consuls, G-AIOS, on the apron in front of the then-familiar control tower of Croydon Airport. (*Richard Riding*.)

Among the last Consuls to be bought were the five used by the Ministry of Civil Aviation's Flying Unit based first at Gatwick and later at Stansted Airport. They remained in service from 1947 to 1956. (*Richard Riding*.)

One of the first Consuls to be prepared for sale abroad was initially registered in 1946 for a now-forgotten buyer in Monte Carlo. The sale was not, however, completed and the registration MC-ABA was removed later in the year. (*Flight 19730s.*)

had always been civil-orientated. But it is symptomatic of the situation in the aircraft manufacturing industry. The backing of military contracts not only keeps the wheels of production turning, but provides the money for essential research and development.

It is sad, also, to look through the list of Consul operators and to realize that none of the companies in the embryonic British air-charter industry are still surviving. Of the dozen companies who bought Consuls in those early days only one was still operating under its original name in 1968,

At least four Consuls went to Spain. EC-ACZ, seen here at Gatwick, was acquired by Iberia early in 1948. (*John Stroud.*)

though three others existed, so to speak, in spirit as hidden parts of the organizations into which they were, long ago, absorbed. Altogether, these 12 companies bought and operated 69 Consuls—or between a third and a half of the total number sold. The biggest fleets were those of Air Enterprises of Croydon (7); Chartair of Thame and Croydon (9); the one named survivor (until its absorption into British United Island Airways in 1968), Morton Air Services of Croydon (8); and Westminster Airways of

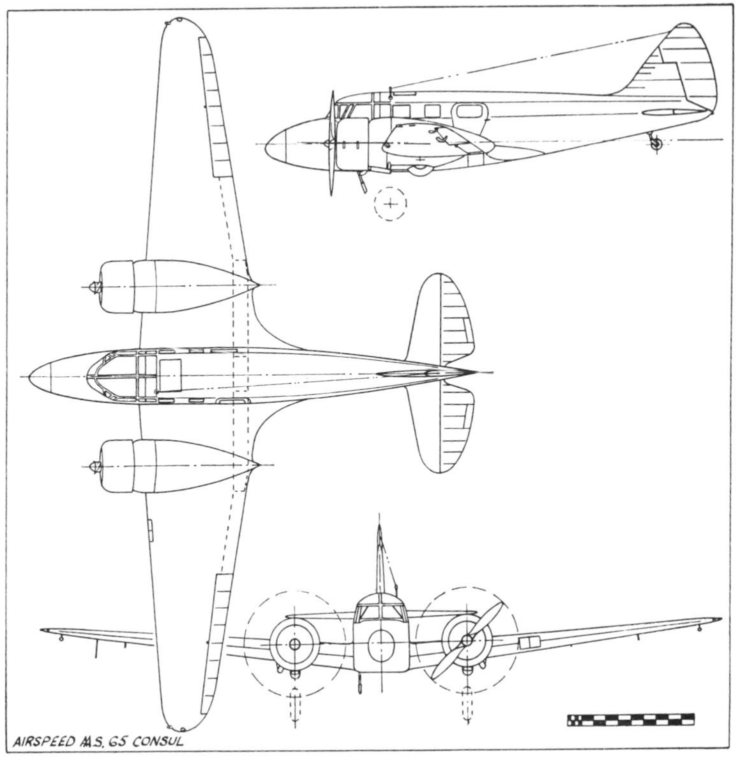
AIRSPEED A.S. 65 CONSUL

Blackbushe and Croydon (7). At that time only the State airline corporations were permitted to operate scheduled services within or from Britain, so the Consuls were used by their British operators almost exclusively for much-needed charter, executive transport and air-taxi services. However, Chartair, Bowmaker and British Aviation Services' Malta associate had Consuls based at one period at Luqa aerodrome, Malta, and operated semi-scheduled services for Air Malta to North Africa, Sicily, Italy and Greece.

Most of these British charter companies using Consuls in the 1946–49 period were formed in 1947, when plenty of these aircraft were becoming available, but Morton, which was formed as early as 1 January, 1946, had to wait six months for Consul deliveries. British Air Transport, of Redhill, with five Consuls in service, was the only one of them to have been in operation in pre-war days. The now-forgotten Westminster Airways was formed in 1946 by a group of British Members of Parliament, led by Air Cdre. A. (later Sir Arthur) V. Harvey, one-time manager of the Far East Aviation Co and adviser to the then Southern Chinese Air Forces. The others among the 12 were Atlas Air Services, Hornton Airways, International Airways, the Lancashire Aircraft Corporation, Steiners Air Service (Liverpool) and Transair, which was later to be taken over by what is now British United Airways. One still-surviving overseas operator of Consuls is Malayan Airways (now Malaysia-Singapore Airlines) who used two, VR-SCE and VR-SCF, for the initiation of their scheduled operations on 1 May, 1947.

Individual owners, however, provided many of the more vigorous Consul operations. One of these, O. H. Simpson, used G-AIKP (later ZS-BJX) for commuting between Britain and South Africa, putting in some 600 hr on this work, in which an average ground speed of 145 mph and a consumption of only 14·5 gallons per engine per hour were recorded.

Among Consuls used for training and similar purposes were the five, G-AJXE–G-AJXI, bought in 1947 towards the end of the production run, by the Ministry of Civil Aviation for use by the Civil Aviation Flying Unit in checking-out pilots for instrument ratings and calibrating ILS and other radio navigation aids. This fleet remained in service with the unit for nine years before being sold. Two were also bought second-hand by British South American Airways for instrument training; one of these, G-ALTZ, had previously been used, as EI-ADB, by Aer Lingus for training and charter work.

Two Consuls were used by Aer Lingus for training and charter. The other, EI-ADB, was later sold to British South American Airways, and used for training as *Star Monitor*. (*Courtesy John Stroud.*)

A version of the Consul was produced in mid-1947 with a large-aperture door for ambulance or cargo duties. This, the prototype ambulance version, was sold to a French operator for service in Indo-China.

A number of Consuls went, either new or second-hand, to French Indo-China, bought either by the Government or by Société Indochinoise de Transports Aériens (SITA), who bought at least seven, including the prototype ambulance version. Ten more were sold to Argentina.

Summarized historical details of most British and foreign civil-registered Consuls are in Appendix II (F).

AS.65 Consul (two Armstrong Siddeley Cheetah X moderately supercharged seven-cylinder air-cooled radials with Fairey Reed metal propellers; maximum rating, 395 bhp at 2,425 rpm and 2¼ lb/sq in boost at 4,300 ft (1,311 m)). Span 53 ft 4 in (16·3 m); length overall, tail down, 35 ft 6 in (10·8 m); height, tail down, 10 ft 1 in (3·05 m); wing area 348 sq ft (32·3 sq m); track 13 ft 5 in (4 m). Equipped empty weight 6,000 lb (2,720 kg); disposable load 2,250 lb (1,020 kg); loaded weight 8,250 lb (3,740 kg); wing loading 23·7 lb/sq ft (105·5 kg/sq m). Take-off distance to 66 ft (20 m), in 5 mph (8 km/h) wind, 1,725 ft (526 m); rate of climb, full throttle, sea-level, 1,230 ft/min (6·1 m/sec); climb at rated power, sea-level, 1,070 ft/min (5·5 m/sec), at 10,000 ft (3,048 m) 645 ft/min (3·3 m/sec); time to 10,000 ft (3,048 m) 10 min; landing run, zero wind, 825 ft (251 m); maximum speed at 4,800 ft (1,463 m) 190 mph (306 km/h); cruising speed, maximum weak mixture 2,100 rpm at 3,100 ft (945 m) 163 mph (261 km/h), at 10,000 ft (3,048 m) 155 mph (249 km/h), at 2,000 rpm and 10,000 ft (3,048 m) 145 mph (233 km/h); stalling speed, flaps down, 69 mph (111 km/h); range, no allowances, at 145 mph (233 km/h) and 10,000 ft (3,048 m), full tanks, 900 miles (1,448 km), range with 110 gal (500 litres) 635 miles (1,022 km).

Airspeed Projects

Of the 69 recorded Airspeed designations, excluding some 20 variants under these designations, only 17 were destined to be translated into hardware. But many of the projects were, in their several ways, as interesting as the aircraft which were actually constructed. All the usefully available information about them, culled from many sources, is included in the pages which follow. Existent general-arrangement drawings have been redrawn and reproduced where the importance or interest of the project seemed to merit such reproduction.

A few information gaps will be noticed in relation to the list of Airspeed type designations in Appendix I. Apart from two numbers which were not allocated—AS.13, for reasons, presumably, of traditional superstition, and AS.25, for other causes which have been lost in the mists of time—there were insufficient facts available about 11 others to justify individual entries in this section. Of these, the AS.3 is referred to anonymously in the company history and in the AS.1 and AS.4 narratives. This was the designation of the developed version of the two/three-seater high-wing cabin monoplane for the private owner on which Airspeed intended originally to base most of its initial efforts. The AS.7, of which there were two variants with different powerplants, was, as briefly mentioned in the AS.6 Envoy narrative, a projected military version of the Envoy.

The remaining nine projects which cannot be described in sufficient, if limited, detail to be dealt with individually include the AS.2, which was a glider or sailplane evidently intended to be a follow-up for the AS.1 Tern; the AS.11, which was to have been an all-metal version of the Courier aimed at the Canadian market; and the AS.12, which was a four-engined proposal about which no information has been discovered. The AS.26 was a projected vehicle-carrying biplane in which a wide fuselage was to have been of aerodynamic lift-generating section such as that of the Burnelli monoplane, which, of US origin, was later built in Britain as a one-off experiment by Cunliffe-Owen. Nothing can be discovered about the AS.28 other than the fact that it was a twin-engined transport project—possibly a development of the proposed AS.14. AS.61/62/63 were designations given respectively to conversions of the C-47 (DC-3) or RAF Dakota. After the decision had been made not to proceed with the AS.60

Ayrshire military freighter, the RAF had ideas for converting Dakotas for specialized military loads, and Airspeed was, presumably as some compensation for the loss of the AS.60 prospects, to have been given the design contract. Nothing appears to have come of the proposal. Finally, the designation AS.68 is believed to have been given to a version of the Ambassador with Bristol Proteus engines.

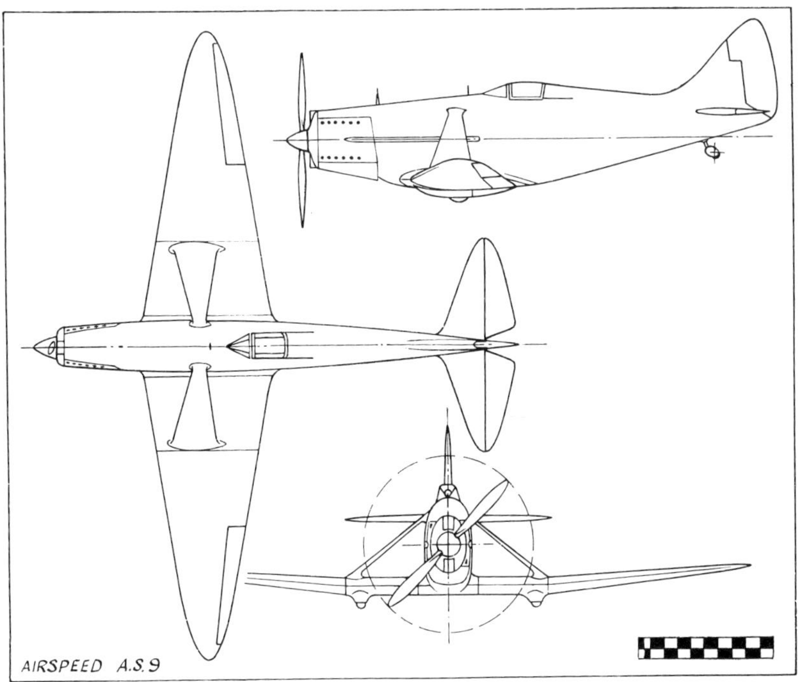

AS.9

Although the designation AS.7 had been given, as already recorded, to possible military variants of the AS.6 and work had been done, at five days' notice, to redesign the Envoy to meet an RAF Coastal Command specification, the AS.9 (*circa* 1935) represented the company's first *ab initio* military design. It was also the first of several attempts to enter the military, as opposed to the military trainer, market, which was, at least until the late 1930s, virtually closed to any but the old-established companies in the British aircraft industry.

The AS.9 was a strut-braced, low-wing interceptor fighter with (unusually for those days) a retractable undercarriage, flaps and controllable-pitch propeller. Powered either with a 650 hp Napier Dagger II twenty-four cylinder air-cooled H-type engine, as shown in the general-arrangement drawing, or a 700 hp Rolls-Royce Kestrel twelve-cylinder vee liquid-cooled engine, it was proposed as a relatively low-priced but advanced aircraft. The fuselage was to be of welded steel-tube construction with fabric covering and the wings of stressed-skin multi-cellular design in either wood or metal. It was laid out with two fixed guns, using interrupter gear for firing through the propeller, and the plans included the addition of up to six adjustable guns in the wings.

AS.9 (Napier Dagger). Span 43 ft (13·1 m); length 34 ft (10·4 m); wing area 245 sq ft (22·7 sq m). Empty weight 2,945 lb (1,336 kg); armament and equipment 975 lb (442 kg); pilot 180 lb (82 kg); fuel (100 gal, 454 litres) and oil 600 lb (272 kg); loaded weight 4,700 lb (2,132 kg); wing loading 19·2 lb/sq ft (93·7 kg/sq m); power loading 6·7 lb/hp (3 kg/hp). Maximum speed at rated altitude of 12,000 ft (3,658 m) 262 mph (421 km/h); cruising speed, at 75% power and rated altitude, 240 mph (386 km/h); landing speed, sea-level, flaps down, 58 mph (93 km/h); range, at 75% power and rated altitude with fuel as above, 485 miles (780 km); range with full tanks 610 miles (982 km); time to 10,000 ft (3,048 m) 6 min, to 20,000 ft (6,096 m) 12·6 min; service ceiling 27,500 ft (8,382 m).

AS.14 and AS.24

One of the most interesting and advanced of the Airspeed projects about which not much was heard, either at the time or later, was the AS.14—the originally named Ambassador of 1935. Information about it was given at the SBAC Display at Hatfield in 1936. This was, like its post-war namesake, a twin-engined high-wing cantilever monoplane, with retractable undercarriage and flaps, and with accommodation for 12–15 passengers and a two-pilot flight crew. At the time, no operator was sufficiently interested in the project, which got no further than the design and mock-up stage, and Airspeed was soon to be too heavily committed on military trainer development and production to be able to consider building a prototype, even if the money had been available.

Later references to the AS.14 described it as to be powered by two 930 hp Bristol Pegasus XC nine-cylinder radials, but the original outline specifications referred only to versions with two 550 hp Pratt & Whitney Wasp Junior nine-cylinder radials or two 620 hp Armstrong Siddeley Panther VI two-row fourteen-cylinder radials. The figures given in the data are for the version as projected with Wasp Juniors; the general-arrangement drawing, however, shows it with Pegasus engines. This version (drawing dated September 1936) had different dimensions. For the record these are also included in the data.

The AS.14 was to be of mixed construction, with the two-spar ply-covered wings of wood and the fuselage of welded steel tube in three sections. The split flaps and undercarriage were to be hydraulically operated. Trimming of rudder and elevator was by cockpit-adjustable tabs. In the 12-passenger version there was to be a compartment for light luggage and mail behind the flight deck and a buffet and lavatory at the rear of the passenger cabin. Aft of the cabin, accessible only from the outside, was a separate baggage compartment. Fuel capacity was for 300 gal (1,364 litres) in welded aluminium tanks between the wing spars.

A long-range mail-carrying version—the AS.24—was also proposed. This was to have been of similar construction, but with tankage for 670 gallons (3,046 litres) in the wings and the fuselage. In this it was proposed to have the flight deck differently arranged, with the first pilot's seat in the centre, the second pilot behind and slightly to the right and a navigator/radio operator behind and to the left of the second pilot.

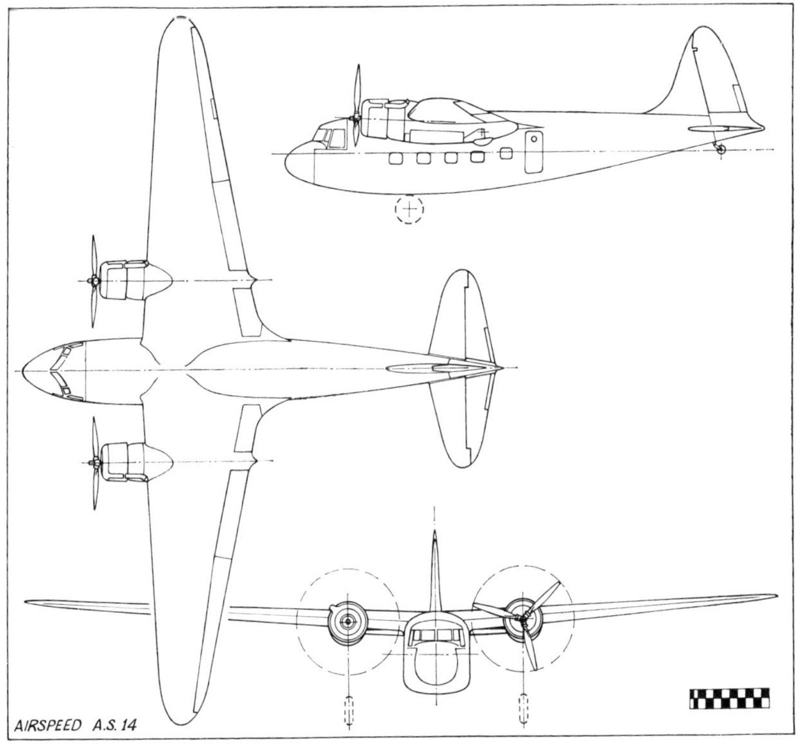

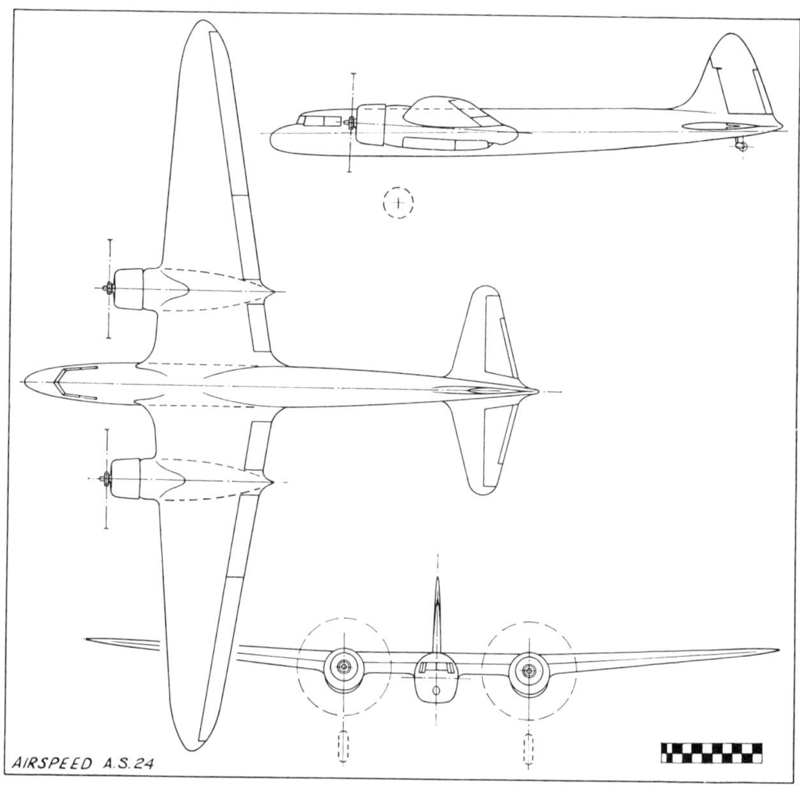

AS.14 (Pratt & Whitney Wasp Juniors). Span 73 ft 6 in (22·4 m); length 56 ft 3½ in (17·2 m); height 13 ft 2½ in (4 m); wing area 640 sq ft (59·5 sq m). Equipped empty weight 8,090 lb (3,670 kg); crew 330 lb (150 kg); fuel for 750 miles (1,207 km) 1,577 lb (715 kg); passengers (12) 1,980 lb (898 kg); baggage and cargo 553 lb (250 kg); loaded weight 12,530 lb (5,683 kg); wing loading 19·6 lb/sq ft (95·7 kg/sq m); power loading 11·4 lb/hp (5·2 kg/hp). Maximum speed at rated altitude of 5,000 ft (1,524 m) 206 mph (332 km/h); cruising speed at rated altitude and 62% power 177 mph (285 km/h); cruising speed at optimum altitude of 12,400 ft (3,780 m) and 62% power 184 mph (296 km/h); landing speed 59 mph (95 km/h); range with full tanks and 62% power, still air, 1,210 miles (1,947 km); single-engine ceiling 8,000 ft (2,438 m).

AS.14 (Bristol Pegasus XCs). Span 86 ft (26·2 m); length 60 ft 6 in (18·4 m); gross wing area 853 sq ft (79·25 sq m).

AS.24 (Pratt & Whitney Wasp Juniors). Dimensions as for Wasp Junior powered AS.14. Equipped empty weight 7,942 lb (3,602 kg); crew 510 lb (231 kg); fuel and oil 5,548 lb (2,517 kg); payload 1,000 lb (453 kg); loaded weight 15,000 lb (6,804 kg); wing loading 23·4 lb/sq ft (114 kg/sq m); power loading 13·6 lb/hp (6·2 kg/hp). Maximum speed at rated altitude of 5,000 ft (1,524 m) 200 mph (322 km/h); cruising speed at 62% power at rated altitude 171 mph (275 km/h); landing speed, sea-level, at 10,000 lb (4,536 kg), 58·5 mph (94 km/h); range at 62% power, rated altitude, full tanks, still air, 2,600 miles (4,184 km); range at optimum cruising speed at 15,000 ft (4,572 m) 3,000 miles (4,828 km); take-off run at maximum weight 1,290 ft (393 m).

AS.15

Early in 1935 Airspeed prepared designs for a high-performance general-purpose day/night bomber and troop carrier. This, designated the AS.15, was advanced for its day, with a retractable undercarriage and a thorough defensive armament system. It was to be powered by four radial engines of 1,300 hp each, of unidentified type. A civil airliner version, the AS.15A, was also projected. Figures are for the bomber as proposed in April 1935.

Span 166 ft (50·6 m); length 137 ft 6 in (41·9 m); height 25 ft (7·6 m); wing area 3,230 sq ft (300 sq m). Empty weight with fixed equipment 38,000 lb (17,237 kg); fuel and oil 10,890 lb (4,940 kg); crew 1,980 lb (898 kg); armament 7,130 lb (3,235 kg); loaded weight 58,000 lb (26,308 kg). Cruising speed at 75% power 195 mph (314 km/h); maximum speed at 5,000 ft (1,524 m) 215 mph (346 km/h); stalling speed 59 mph (95 km/h).

AS.16–23

The elements of the story of the abortive, January 1935, tie-up between Airspeed and Fokker of the Netherlands have already been given in the section covering the company's history. The various Airspeed type numbers allocated, from AS.16 to AS.23, are listed, with essential details, in Appendix I. They included the Douglas DC-2, the production version of the first aircraft which really brought air transport to life in the USA, for which Fokker held the manufacturing and sales rights in Europe. It was given the designation AS.23 by Airspeed, who had the right to manufacture and to sell it in the British Isles. The rights for the various Fokker-designed types also included sales within the British Empire. These seven types were the two four-engined high-wing transports, the Fokker F.XXII (Airspeed type AS.16) and F.XXXVI (AS.20); the D.XVII (AS.17), D.XIX (AS.19), D.XX (AS.21) Rolls-Royce Kestrel engined single-seat fighters; and the C.X (AS.22) two-seat Kestrel-engined fighter and its floatplane variant.

The nearest approaches to serious business under this arrangement were the prospects of making in the United Kingdom and selling D.XVII fighters to Greece, and of making DC-3s for a British airline. The deal with Greece fell by the wayside because of currency difficulties. The DC-3 prospect, involving the possible construction of 12 aircraft for British Continental Airways, had to be turned down because by then, in late 1936, Airspeed was very much too busy on other work—mainly that on the Oxford twin-engined trainer for which a big initial production order had been obtained.

AS.27

The designation AS.27 was orginally given to a project intended to meet a requirement for a slow-speed coastal patrol and general purpose aircraft. Designed in 1935, this was a highly unconventional single-engined biplane with its wing arrangement—following principles developed by H. B. Irving, the National Physical Laboratory aerodynamicist—intended to give the aircraft a wide speed range and good slow-speed stability. At about this time there was also a requirement for a 'special defence' aircraft which, flying in or above cloud, would trail a winched-out cable or cables, possibly carrying high explosive, to menace enemy bombers. The idea was that these aircraft would be flown by second-line pilots, although at that time no plans had been made to recruit and train such pilots. The largely abortive Civil Air Guard had yet to be formed, and the far from abortive Air Transport Auxiliary was not formed until war was imminent in 1939.

Another, very different, version of the AS.27 was therefore designed late in 1936. This, a characteristically handsome single-engined high-wing cabin monoplane, was considered likely to be more suited to the 'special defence' rôle, though design and development work on the Irving-wing biplane continued. Orders were placed by the Air Ministry for two prototypes of the AS.27, and RAF serial numbers K8846–8847 were allocated, but neither aircraft was built.

The Irving-wing AS.27, to be powered by a 225 hp Wolseley Aries, or 250 hp Wolseley Scorpio, both nine-cylinder radials, was a heavily staggered biplane, with the upper wing sharply tapered and with the lower wing, of more conventional planform, having a marked dihedral and forward sweep. A wide split-axle undercarriage with long-movement oleos was fitted. The cockpit was enclosed and the pilot would have had a good view forward and downward ahead of the lower wing. The estimated speed range of this version of the AS.27 was 43–121 mph.

The monoplane special defence project was to have been powered by a 350 hp Armstrong Siddeley Cheetah IX seven-cylinder radial, in a helmeted cowling. It was a clean high-wing cabin monoplane with single-strut bracing and cantilever undercarriage legs with internally sprung wheels. The engine was low-slung so that the single centrally-seated pilot would have had a good range of forward and downward view. The wing was tapered, with slots ahead of the ailerons and plain flaps inboard. The tailplane was a cantilever structure.

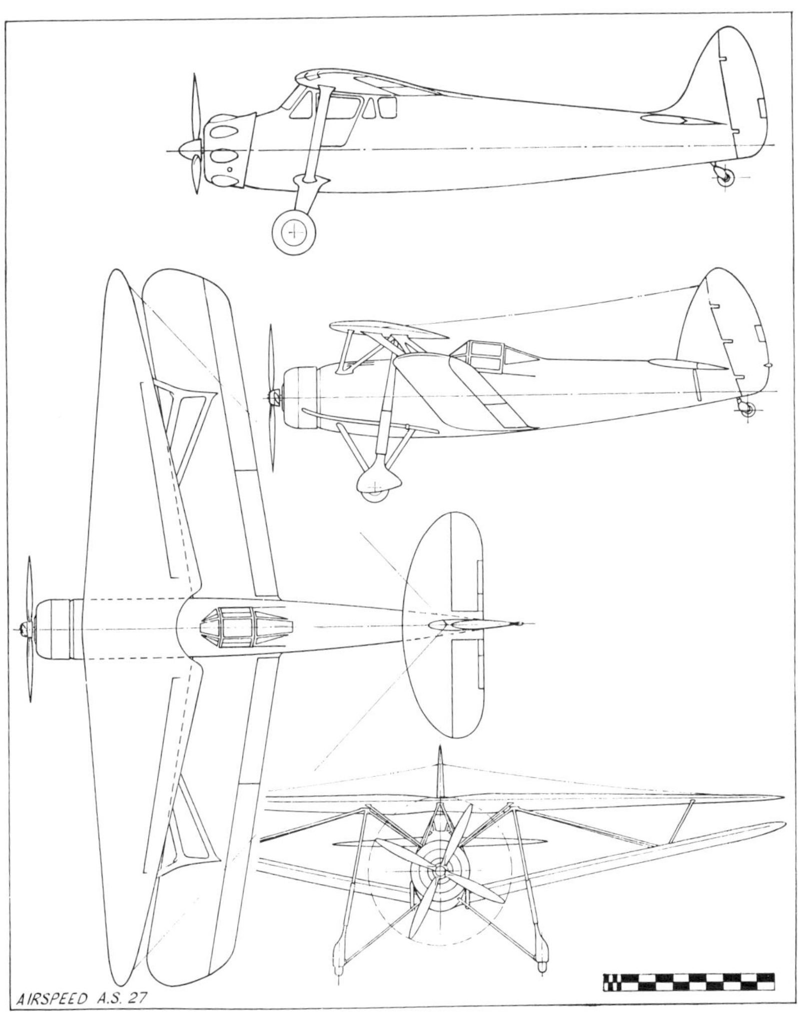

AS.27 Irving biplane (September 1935). Span 38 ft (11·6 m); length 29 ft 5 in (8·97 m); wing area 320 sq ft (29·7 sq m). Empty weight 1,691 lb (767 kg); pilot and parachute 200 lb (91 kg); fuel (42 gal, 190 litres) and oil (4 gal, 18 litres), 359 lb (163 kg); military load 300 lb (136 kg); loaded weight 2,550 lb (1,157 kg); wing loading 7·9 lb/sq ft (38·6 kg/sq m); power loading 11·3 lb/hp (5·1 kg/hp). Maximum speed 121 mph (194 km/h); stalling speed 43 mph (69 km/h); initial rate of climb 1,025 ft/min (5·2 m/sec).

AS.27 monoplane (January 1937). Span 50 ft (15·2 m); length 34 ft 6 in (10·5 m); total wing area 292 sq ft (27 sq m).

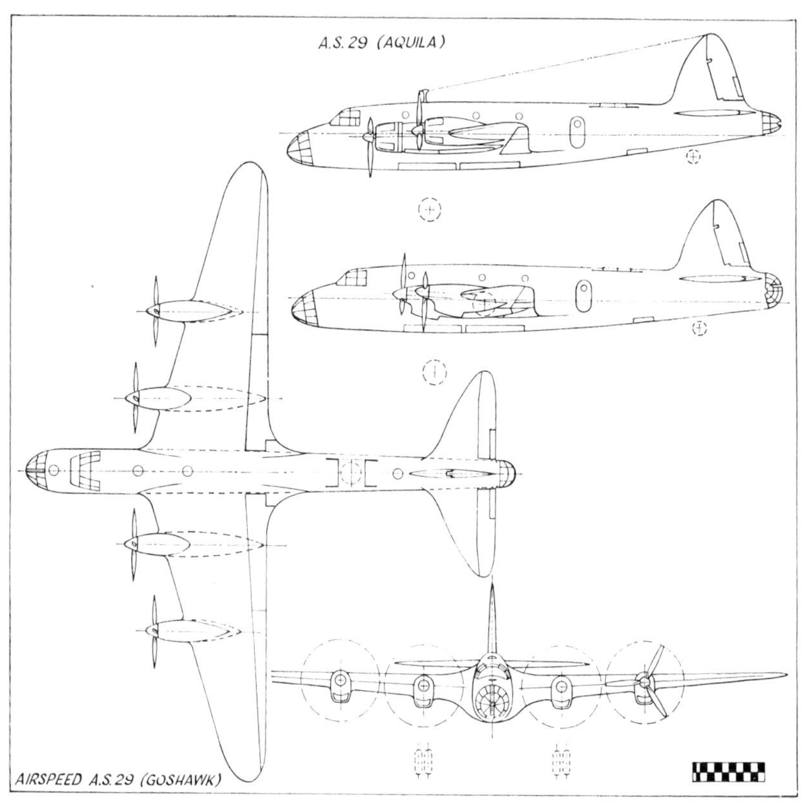

AS.29

Few people outside the company and the Air Ministry knew in 1935–36 that Airspeed's design staff were working on a very advanced high-speed four-engined bomber to meet specification B.1/35. As developed, it was an all-metal, cantilever mid-wing aircraft with slotted flaps and retractable tailwheel undercarriage. Great attention was paid to defensive armament and fields of fire from its retractable dorsal turret and nose and tail gun positions. The gross weight was to be 24,500 lb, including a military load of 3,600 lb, and its range estimated at 1,500 miles. The engines were to have been either 650 hp Bristol Aquila nine-cylinder sleeve-valve radials, or 850 hp Rolls-Royce Goshawk B twelve-cylinder vee liquid-cooled engines. The general-arrangement drawing shows the aircraft with Goshawks. A variety of bomb loads were proposed, and the main bays in at least one variant extended laterally up to the inner powerplants. A maximum of eight 500 lb bombs (with a normal load of four) or fourteen 250 lb bombs (normal, eight) could be carried in the main bays, with four 20 lb bombs in a subsidiary bay aft.

The stressed-skin extension planes were designed on a multi-spar principle while the centre-section had two main spars; the ailerons, Handley Page slotted flaps, and rudder were to be fabric covered. The fuselage was planned as a metal monocoque structure with the skin riveted to bulkhead rings and longitudinal stiffeners. The fin was designed as an integral part of the fuselage. The tailplane was of stressed-skin construction with fabric-covered elevators. The retractable twin-wheel undercarriage was to be electrically actuated. No order was placed.

Span 82 ft (25 m); chord 16 ft (4·9 m); overall length 66 ft 6 in (20·3 m); height 17 ft (5·2 m); overall wing area 875 sq ft (81·3 sq m). Military load 3,600 lb (1,633 kg); loaded weight 24,500 lb (11,113 kg); wing loading 28 lb/sq ft (137 kg/sq m); power loading 9·42 lb/hp (4·4 kg/hp). Maximum speed at 15,000 ft (4,570 m) 289 mph (465 km/h); cruising speed at 15,000 ft (4,570 m) 263 mph (423 km/h); stalling speed at sea-level 66 mph (106 km/h); service ceiling 32,600 ft (9,936 m); range 1,500 miles (2,414 km).

AS.31

Rarely has there been such a strange and ingeniously original aircraft project as the AS.31 fighter. This was a tractor monoplane, powered by an 880 hp Rolls-Royce Merlin E twelve-cylinder vee liquid-cooled engine, in which the tailplane, on twin tubular metal booms, carried the pilot in an egg-shaped streamlined nacelle. It was designed to meet Air Ministry specification F.35/35 and was the subject of Patent No. 470650 in the names of Airspeed and A. H. Tiltman. Among the advantages claimed for military purposes were a reduction in slipstream disturbance and drag in the area immediately behind the engine and propeller; a reduction in skin friction; and good fighting and flying view provided for the pilot, though this might in practice have been marginal in some circumstances.

Among the features of the AS.31 were a wide-track retractable main undercarriage (unusual still in 1936-era British military aircraft), a tail-wheel retracting into the rear part of the pilot's nacelle, and the burying of fuel, oil, armament, coolant-radiators and such items as oxygen bottles in the thick-section cantilever wing. Eight Browning guns were to be buried in the wings outboard of the booms. Split flaps were fitted across the trailing edge of the wing between the booms, with wide-span ailerons outboard.

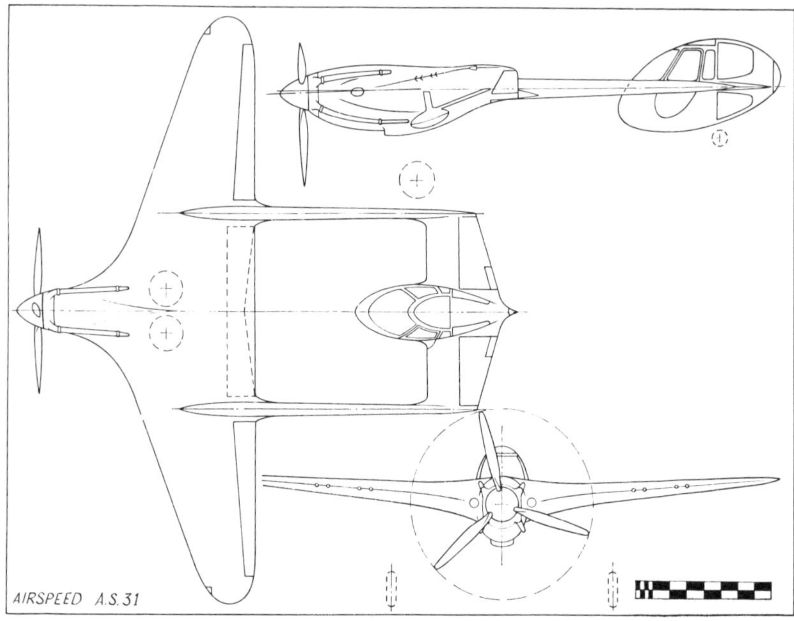

Curiously, no rudder or fin surface (apart from the nacelle itself) are indicated in the original prints from which the general arrangement, reproduced here, was developed. In level flight, the pilot's view, with his seat fully raised, was unrestricted above the wing and engine, and was restricted by little more than 9 degrees downwards on either side of the engine-nacelle cowling. With the seat in the lowest position the pilot's view under the wing and flap would probably have been adequate in the fully flared tail-down attitude but questionable during the final approach and hold-off.

Hessell Tiltman reported that the wind-tunnel model showed exceptional characteristics.

Span 33 ft (10·06 m); length 29 ft 6 in (8·99 m); wing area 195 sq ft (18·1 sq m).

AS.32–35

These type numbers were given to four projected civil transports of different layouts and capacities. The AS.32 and AS.33 were medium-sized, 24-seat, high-wing cantilever monoplanes to be powered by four 650 hp Bristol Aquila nine-cylinder sleeve-valve radials. The AS.34, 34A and 35 were each 12/15-seat airliners with four 350 hp Armstrong Siddeley Cheetah IX seven-cylinder radials, 305 hp Wolseley Scorpio II nine-cylinder radials and 205 hp de Havilland Gipsy Six II air-cooled inline engines respectively.

One surviving print, from a general-arrangement drawing of the AS.33 produced in October 1936, shows a clean, high-wing cantilever monoplane with twin fins and rudders, retractable tailwheel undercarriage and large-area plain flaps inboard of the ailerons. The design was described as that for an intermediate class airliner, and the proposed powerplants were Aquila AE-3Ms.

An interior layout drawing of similar date shows an arrangement for 21 passengers with the noisier centre-section and propeller-line areas used for two mail compartments, a galley, a lavatory and the entrance lobby. Forward of this 'working' area and aft of the two-crew control cabin were three rows of three-abreast (two and one) seats. Behind the area were three rows of four-abreast seats, including two rows in pairs on each side of the aisle and an aft continuous row of four against the bulkhead. Behind this passenger cabin was a luggage compartment reached through a separate external door.

AS.33 (October 1936). Span 109 ft (33·22 m); length 81 ft 6 in (24·85 m); height, tail down, 16 ft 6 in (5·03 m); tailplane span, between rudder centres, 32 ft 9 in (9·98 m); maximum width of fuselage 11 ft 6 in (3·5 m); wing area 1,560 sq ft (144·9 sq m).

AS.36

This project was designed to meet Air Ministry specification T.1/37 for an *ab initio* trainer similar to the Miles Magister which was designed to meet an earlier requirement (T.40/36). No prototype or other contract for the AS.36 was obtained by Airspeed, and basic training needs during the pre-war and war-time periods were met by the de Havilland Tiger Moth biplane and Magister low-wing cantilever monoplane. The AS.36 was to have been a rather more vigorous tandem-seat trainer powered by a 205 hp de Havilland Gipsy Six II air-cooled inline engine and was planned with flaps, twin fins and rudders, enclosed cockpits and advanced instrument-flying layout.

Construction was to be of wood, apart from the tubular-steel forward fuselage, with spruce structure, plywood-covered fuselage, wing leading edges and tailplane, and fabric-covered wings and rudder. The faired and spatted undercarriage was non-retractable, with single cantilever shock-absorber struts.

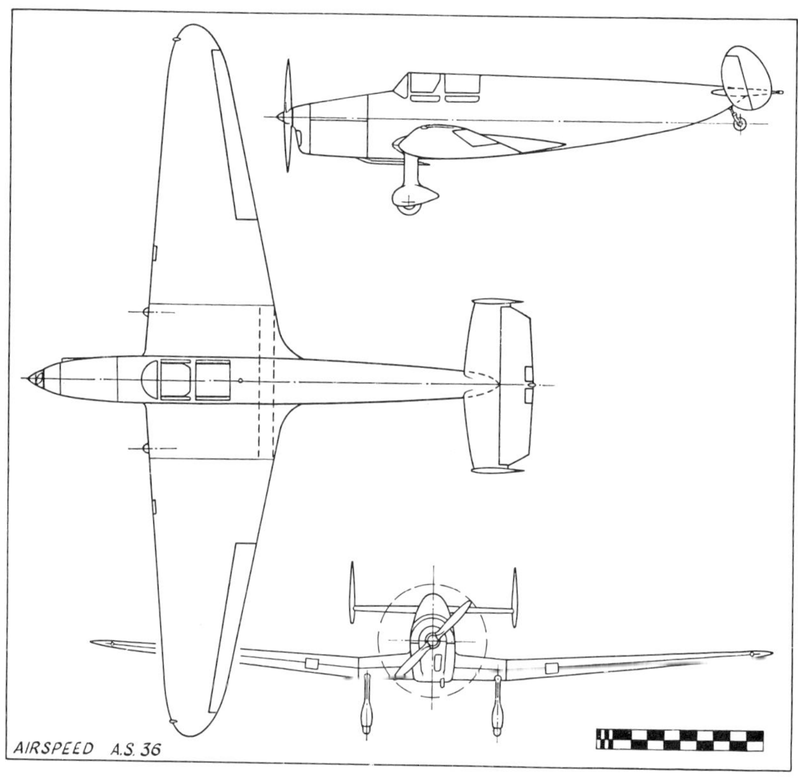

Span 42 ft (12·8 m); length 30 ft 9 in (9·37 m); wing chord 8 ft 7 in (2·6 m); wing area 250 sq ft (23·2 sq m). Loaded weight 3,060 lb (1,388 kg). Maximum speed, sea-level, 160 mph (258 km/h); cruising speed, sea-level, 140 mph (225 km/h); stalling speed, flaps down, 51 mph (82 km/h); landing run 600 ft (182 m); initial rate of climb 900 ft/min (4·5 m/sec); service ceiling 17,750 ft (5,410 m); endurance 4 hr, plus 15 min at full throttle.

AS.37

In August 1937 Airspeed completed preliminary designs for a radio-controlled flying-boat target aircraft to meet specification Q.8/37. This project, to be powered by a single 205 hp de Havilland Gipsy Six II engine, was reminiscent in layout of the 1927 Dornier Delphin III—though the AS.37 was smaller and, designed much more than a decade later, was more modern in overall concept. The engine, driving a tractor propeller, was in an over-wing nacelle within the mounting of which was the pilot's cabin. The aircraft had a cantilever wing, which merged into the clean hull and was designed to fold for shipboard stowage. Drawings show it with a tricycle undercarriage—presumably for initial land-based test-flying. In normal service the AS.37 would have been launched by catapult and, if not destroyed by practice gunfire, brought down on to the sea by radio control.

Span 28 ft (8·5 m); span folded 14 ft (4·3 m); length 25 ft 7 in (7·8 m); wing area including hull chines, 156 sq ft (14·5 sq m).

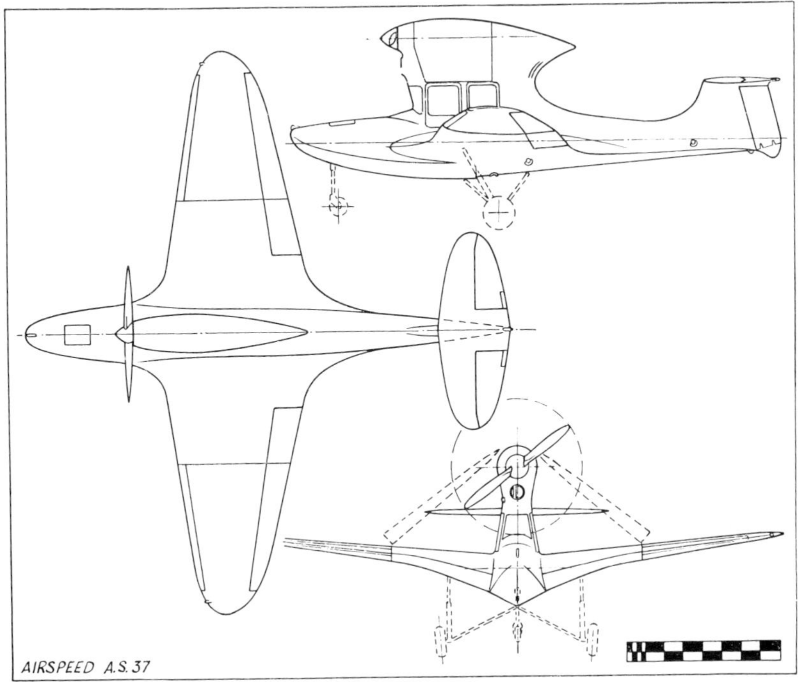
AIRSPEED A.S. 37

AS.44

By 1938 Airspeed was already considering the need for a successor for the Oxford, and, with customarily advanced thinking, it was to have had a retractable tricycle, or nosewheel, undercarriage. At least two designs were projected. One was a low-wing aircraft powered by two 500 hp Bristol Aquila nine-cylinder sleeve-valve radials. The other was a high-wing variant to be powered either by two 340 hp Armstrong Siddeley Cheetah IX seven-cylinder, or 440 hp Alvis Leonides nine-cylinder radials. Both were practical rather than handsome—with humped fuselages and 'inverted' twin fins and rudders to provide spin-recovery characteristics which had by then been found to be marginal in the Oxford.

AS.44 (low-wing version). Span 57 ft 6 in (17·5 m); length 41 ft 9 in (12·7 m); wing area 440 sq ft (40·88 sq m). Loaded weight 11,000 lb (4,990 kg); wing loading 25 lb/sq ft (122 kg/sq m). Maximum speed at 4,000 ft (1,219 m) 234 mph (377 km/h).

AS.47, AS.48 and AS.56

After the Airspeed design team had moved from Portsmouth to the de Havilland Technical School building at Hatfield in 1940, work began on projects powered by 2,200 hp Napier Sabre twenty-four cylinder H-type liquid-cooled engines. The first was an unusual and somewhat anachronistic high-speed twin-engined 'push-pull' bomber, the AS.47, and the others were single-engined fighters such as the AS.48. The work continued when the nucleus of what was later to be the Ambassador team joined A. E. Hagg, who was then a design consultant with Napiers, and the attractive-looking AS.56 fighter project resulted.

The AS.47 was a twin-boom, twin-fin device with a wide-track tricycle undercarriage, but otherwise somewhat reminiscent of the Fokker D.XXIII in that it had tractor and pusher engines with, between them, the crew of pilot and bomb-aimer/navigator. The pilot's cockpit, with its windscreen and canopy, was offset slightly to the port side of the nacelle,

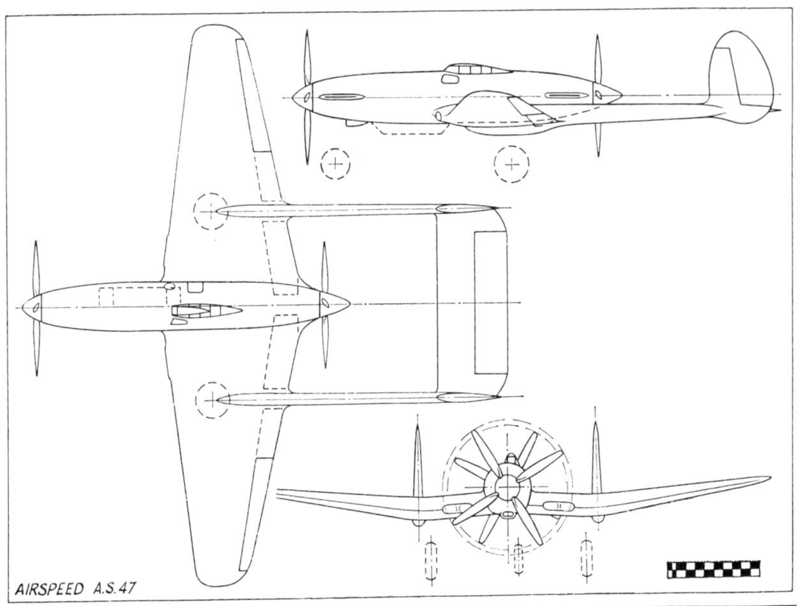

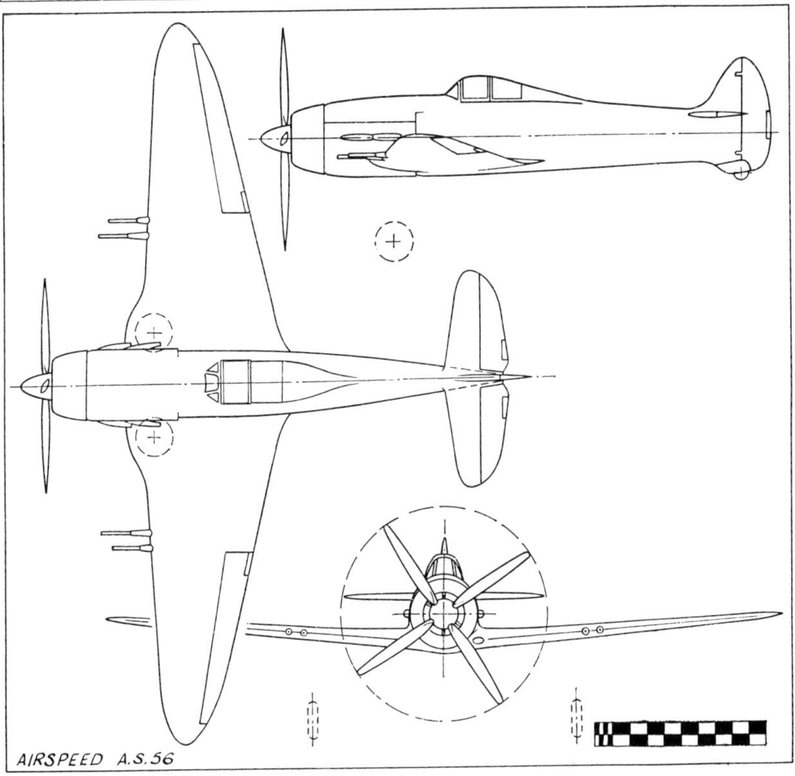

AIRSPEED A.S.56

and the bomb-aimer was accommodated to his right and below. No doubt means had been considered of abandoning the aircraft in emergency, but on the face of it the crew did not seem to have much chance unless the pusher propeller could somehow have been jettisoned by explosive means. The estimated performance was, however, attractive.

The AS.48, a single-seat night fighter, was more conventional and in appearance somewhat similar to the Hawker Typhoon. It was intended to be armed with six 20 mm cannon, but its drawing-board life ended with the realization that, to be successful, a night fighter had to carry a crew and radar equipment capable of hunting as well as of killing bombers. Had success attended the Turbinlite project, whereby single-seat fighters went into the kill after a radar-equipped aircraft had found and spotlighted the raider, there might still have been a place for the fast and heavily armed single-seater. But the weight and drag of the equipment prevented the Turbinlite aircraft from reaching the bombers, and the work was done more successfully by two-crew, radar-equipped Beaufighters and Mosquitos.

Other Sabre-engined fighter projects were also worked upon by the Airspeed team, including one with a well-faired fixed undercarriage and cranked wing. Both this and a retractable-undercarriage version had their radiators aft of the cockpit with cooling air ram-fed into an underside scoop and venting through slots in the tail. A verbal order was given officially at one stage to Airspeed for a day fighter which formed the basis for these undesignated projects, using wooden construction as a means of conserving strategic materials. The order was later revoked under pressure, it is believed, from another sector of the aircraft industry.

The day-fighting medium-altitude AS.56, worked upon later, was possibly more an exercise in design, making use of the new fan-cooled annular radiator for Napier Sabre IV engine developments, than a serious project study. Other features of the AS.56 included a wide-track undercarriage retracting inwards into the forward extending leading edge which can be seen in the general-arrangement drawing which is based on one completed in September 1942. Armament consisted of four 20 mm cannon. As an Airspeed design the fighter was dropped, but Napiers continued with the work on the cooling system.

AS.47. Span 58 ft (17·68 m); length 53 ft 9 in (16·38 m). Maximum speed at 18,500 ft (5,638 m) 470 mph (756 km/h). Range 1,000 miles (1,610 km) with 1,000 lb (454 kg) warload.

AS.48. Span 40 ft (12·2 m); length 40 ft (12·2 m).

AS.56. Span 40 ft (12·2 m); length 30 ft (9·1 m); wing area 237 sq ft (22·1 sq m). Maximum speed 492 mph (793 km/h) at 23,000 ft (7,010 m).

AS.49

Designed to meet Air Ministry specification T.24/40 for an intermediate single-seat fighter trainer, the AS.49 was a low-wing aircraft with fixed cantilever undercarriage and, in one form, a supercharged 295 hp de Havilland Gipsy Six IIIS (the RAF Gipsy Queen 51) with constant-speed propeller. Another version had a 250 hp Gipsy Six IV (the RAF Gipsy Queen 31). For simplicity, cheapness and the conservation of other materials, it was to be built largely of wood with a two-spar ply-covered wing in three sections and a ply-covered fuselage.

Progress on this design had gone quite a long way when, as recorded in the company history, bombs on Hatfield (where the Airspeed design team were then working) from a raiding Ju 88 destroyed the mock-up and caused a fire which burned the design calculations and drawings.

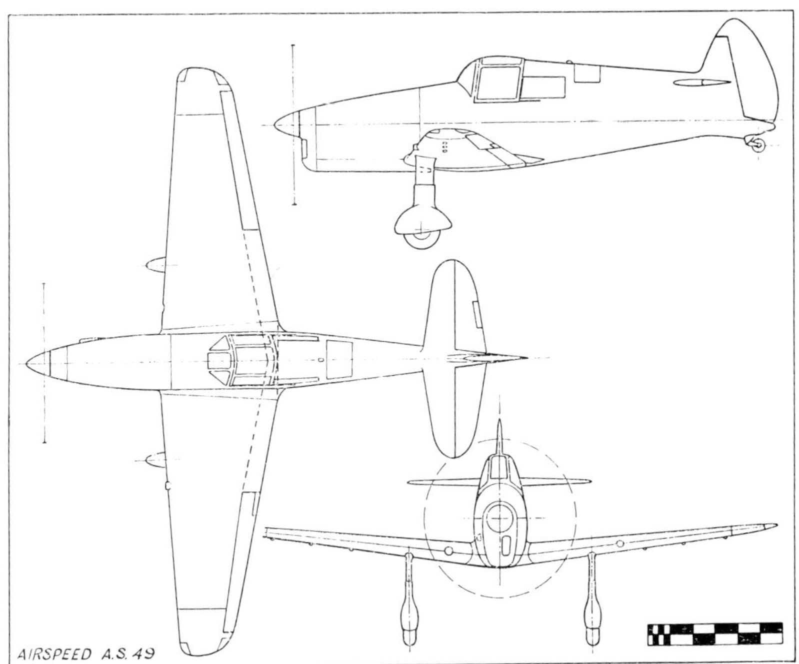

Span 25 ft (7·6 m); overall length 22 ft 7 in (6·87 m); wing area 98 sq ft (9·1 sq m). AS.49 (Gipsy Six IIIS). Loaded weight 2,540 lb (1,152 kg). Maximum speed at 8,000 ft (2,438 m) 228 mph (367 km/h); maximum economical cruising speed at 8,000 ft (2,438 m) 202 mph (325 km/h); rate of climb, sea-level, 1,940 ft/min (9·8 m/sec). Range at economical cruising speed at 8,000 ft (2,438 m) 390 miles (628 km) excluding 30 min climb.

AS.49 (Gipsy Six IV). Loaded weight 2,350 lb (1,066 kg). Maximum speed at sea-level 196 mph (315 km/h); maximum economical cruising speed at 6,000 ft (1,830 m) 177 mph (285 km/h); rate of climb at sea-level 1,250 ft/min (6·3 m/sec). Range at economical cruising speed at 6,000 ft (1,830 m) 360 miles (580 km) excluding 30 min climb.

AS.54

As a complementary aircraft to the Horsa troop-carrying glider, Airspeed also designed a two-seat training glider to specification TX.3/43. Its layout and planned handling features were intended not only for advanced training, but also to familiarize pilots in advance with the practical, but heavy and unsympathetic, control system of the Horsa and of other large transport gliders. Rare in a relatively small and clean glider, the layout involved, for this familiarization requirement, side-by-side seating for the instructor and pupil in an enclosed cabin ahead of the single-strut braced high wing. Provision was also made in the design for water-ballast loading. No order was received and no prototype was constructed.

The AS.54 was, like the Horsa, of wood and plywood construction more or less throughout, though a welded steel-tube fuselage was offered as an alternative. The wing was split spanwise into three sections, with the extension planes, outboard of the strut attachments, capable of being folded for stowage. Like the Horsa, it was to have had split trailing-edge flaps and dive-brakes. For take-off the undercarriage consisted of two self-jettisoning mainwheels, with a central skid and tail bumper for landing.

Span 36 ft (11 m); overall length 26 ft 10 in (8·16 m); height 10 ft 4 in (3·15 m); span, wings folded, 15 ft (4·57 m); maximum fuselage width 3 ft 9 in (1·14 m); wing area 157 sq ft (14·59 sq m). Loaded weight 1,880 lb (853 kg); wing loading 12 lb/sq ft (58·6 kg/sq m). Maximum permissible dive speed 200 mph (322 km/h); maximum permissible towing speed 150 mph (241 km/h); stalling speed 49 mph (79 km/h); steepest gliding angle 1:2.

AS.55

Prior to work on the AS.57 Ambassador, twin- and four-engined versions of a military transport project, the AS.55, were projected by Airspeed in the 1942–43 period. The twin-engined version was proposed with either 1,650 hp Bristol Hercules XIV fourteen-cylinder, or 2,000 hp Centaurus eighteen-cylinder sleeve-valve radials. The four-engined versions, of similar layout apart from a wider parallel-chord centre-section, were to be variously powered by 1,280 hp Rolls-Royce Merlin XX twelve-cylinder vee liquid-cooled engines; 1,085 hp Bristol Taurus XX fourteen-cylinder sleeve-valve radials; or 1,200 hp Pratt & Whitney R1830 Twin Wasp fourteen-cylinder radials. All were proposed with twin-wheel tricycle undercarriages.

Fading surviving prints of the AS.55 show the twin-engined Centaurus version as having a strong, though superficial, resemblance to the AS.57. It had a wide-span cantilever wing, tapered outside the centre-section, and twin fins and rudders. The fuselage, designed for cargo-carrying as well as passenger/trooping work, was of rounded square-section with large double-opening loading doors on the port side both forward and aft of the wing. In passenger-carrying or trooping forms all versions were shown with a seating capacity for 66 and a crew of three. The seats were in units of one, two, or three, arranged for three, four, or five passengers abreast according to their positions and the fuselage width.

During the middle war-years several undesignated transport projects were worked upon by Airspeed. There was, for instance, a twin-engined cargo transport with 1,560 hp Bristol Hercules XIs (drawing dated 23 June, 1942) with a high wing, a twin-boom tail and pod-type fuselage with hinged rear cone for direct loading. It was designed for a loaded weight of 44,000 lb and had a span of 112 ft.

Preliminary designs were also produced for a four-engined transport proposed by Sir Alan Cobham to meet the Brabazon Committee's recommendations (Types 3A/B) for Atlantic and Empire trunk route operations. It was laid out for the use of flight-refuelling techniques which were to be controlled by an operator in a compartment outside the pressurized area of the fuselage. With four Bristol Hercules engines it was to have had accommodation for 20 passengers in bunks for North Atlantic services, or for 40 sitting passengers on overland flights. The normal gross weight was to have been 63,060 lb, rising to 81,744 lb after air-refuelling. The span was 118 ft.

AS.55 (all four-engined versions). Span 138 ft (42 m); length 77 ft 9 in (23·7 m); wing area 1,710 sq ft (158·8 sq m).

AS.55 (four Merlins). Equipped weight, as freighter, 40,000 lb (18,145 kg); crew 800 lb (363 kg); fuel and oil for 1,500 mile (2,414 km) stage 11,200 lb (5,080 kg); payload 16,000 lb (7,257 kg); loaded weight 68,000 lb (30,844 kg).

AS.55 (two Centaurus). Span 134 ft (40·8 m); length 84 ft 6 in (25·8 m); wing area 1,500 sq ft (139 sq m). Equipped weight as freighter 36,030 lb (16,343 kg); crew 600 lb (272 kg); fuel and oil for 1,500 mile (2,414 km) stage 9,470 lb (4,295 kg); payload 19,900 lb (9,026 kg); loaded weight 66,000 lb (29,937 kg).

AS.59 Ambassador Mk II

As recorded in the section dealing with the AS.57 Ambassador, the possibility of fitting four propeller-turbines was considered early in the development life of the aircraft. Initial proposals, within the Government plan to have as many irons in the fire as was reasonably possible, involved the use of four Napier Naiads, thus giving this engine a possible civil future alongside the Rolls-Royce Darts to be fitted in the Vickers Viscount, and the Armstrong Siddeley Mambas in the Armstrong Whitworth Apollo, prototypes of which had also been ordered. The second prototype Ambassador did, in fact, have its outer wings designed and built initially with a structure capable of taking the mountings for two outboard Naiads.

The designation AS.59 was given to the projected propeller-turbine version, which might variously be powered by two Bristol Theseus, four Naiads, or four Darts. Only the Dart-engined variant, however, continued to be a live project as a possible successor to the piston-engined version and, known within the company as the Ambassador Mk II, remained so until the final decision was made in 1951 to discontinue production after the 20 aircraft for BEA had been completed.

Early in that year the proposal was to increase the maximum gross weight of the Dart-engined version to 54,500 lb—including the additional fuel (600 gallons) in centre-section bag tanks, for which provision had already been made—and to fit slotted flaps. With these and the additional available emergency power, it was estimated that, with four 1,400 hp Darts, the Mk II Ambassador would be able, at maximum weight, to clear a 50 ft screen in a distance of 3,000 ft in the engine failure case, or of about 3,300 ft in intercontinental temperature conditions. So as to take advantage of the higher payload potentialities and to balance the changed powerplant weight in relation to the piston-engined version, the fuselage would also have been lengthened, with additional sections fore and aft of the wing frames, to accommodate two extra seat rows (eight more passengers).

Because of the higher fuel consumption the performance gains were not, looked at in retrospect, necessarily worthwhile. The AS.59 would have had the advantages of a 15 kt higher maximum cruising speed (255 kt) and, no doubt, a smoother ride for the passengers, and would have carried a payload of 13,350 lb, but only over stage distances (with normal fuel allowances) up to about 350 naut miles. Beyond that range the payload would need to be reduced, and the Centaurus-powered Ambassador carried a higher payload on stages beyond 700 naut miles.

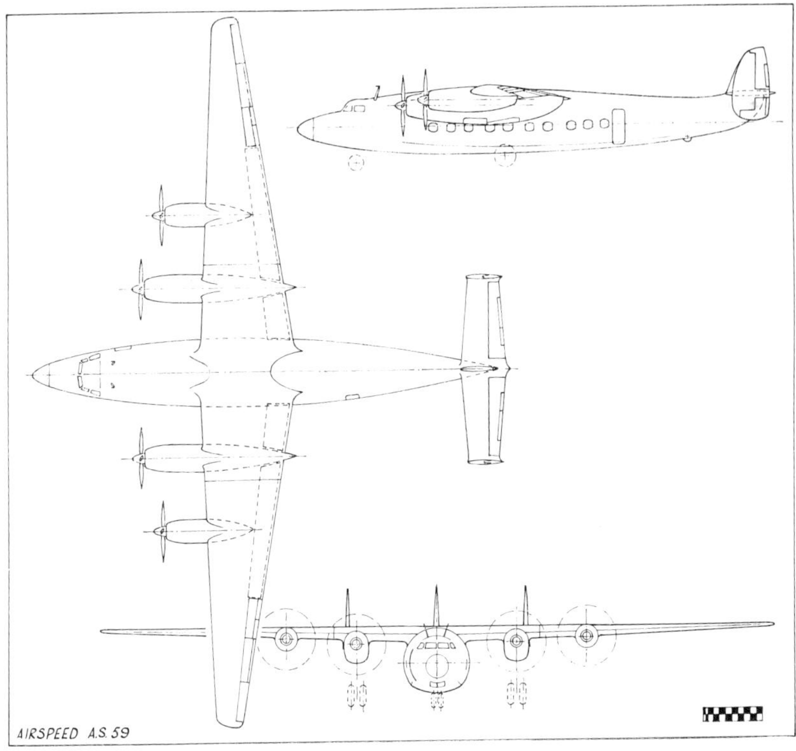

Length (approx) 87 ft (26·5 m); other dimensions as for AS.57. Equipped weight 33,125 lb (15,026 kg); disposable load 20,600 lb (9,344 kg); loaded weight 54,500 lb (24,721 kg); wing loading 45·5 lb/sq ft (222 kg/sq m). Cruising speed at 20,000 ft (6,096 m) 255 kt (473 km/h); take-off distance (ISA) 3,000 ft (914 m); climb to 25,000 ft (7,620 m) 27 min; landing distance from 50 ft (15·2 m) 2,400 ft (732 m); stage distance, SBAC fuel allowances and with maximum payload of 13,350 lb (6,056 kg), 350 naut miles (649 km), stage distance with full tanks and 7,600 lb (3,447 kg) payload, 1,060 naut miles (1,864 km).

AS.60 Ayrshire, AS.64, 66 and 67

Between 1945 and 1951 four numbered military transport or freighter variants of the Ambassador were designed in some detail, but were destined to come to nothing. Many hundreds of design and drawing office hours were spent on these projects and sales promotion efforts made in the hope of obtaining military and other orders in support of Ambassador production.

First and best known of these was the AS.60, named the Ayrshire, a military transport to specification C.13/45. Although not described fully by the technical press, it was the only one of the four projects about which some information was made publicly available. A model of the Ayrshire, as it was then conceived, was shown in 1946 both at the four-day exhibition at the RAE Farnborough and at the first post-war SBAC Display at Radlett.

As can be seen in the general-arrangement drawing, the Ayrshire had the Ambassador wings, powerplants (then 2,600 hp Bristol Centaurus 130s) and empennage, with a re-designed square-section fuselage. This had two

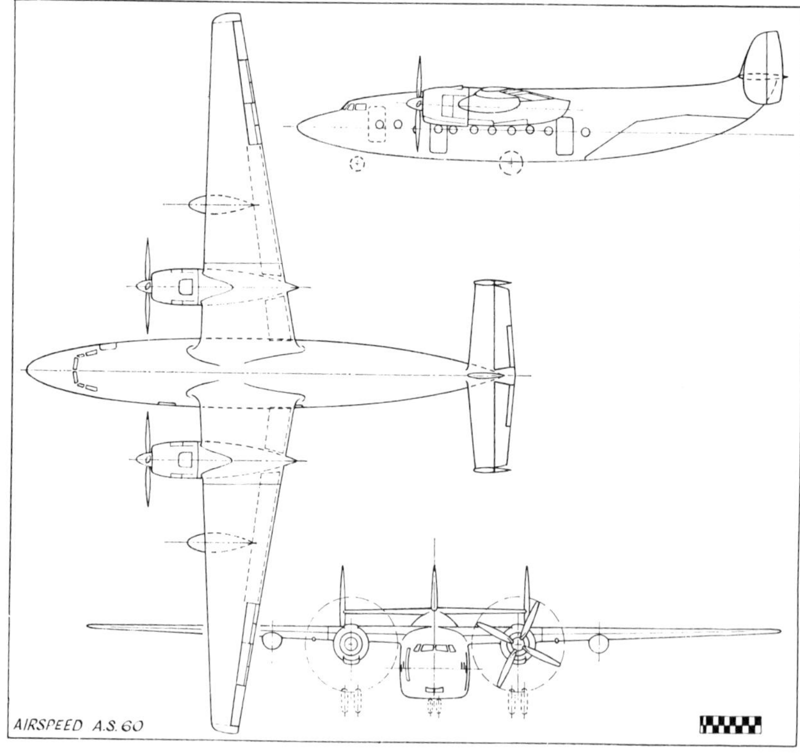

large outward-opening clam-shell doors beneath the deep-section rear fuselage which, when opened, provided direct, full-width entry into the fuselage for vehicles or other stores, and, when closed, formed an integral part of the fuselage structure. Work on this project—which was intended to have a maximum gross weight of 52,500 lb at a time when the Ambassador was planned for a maximum weight of 47,000 lb—led to some of the

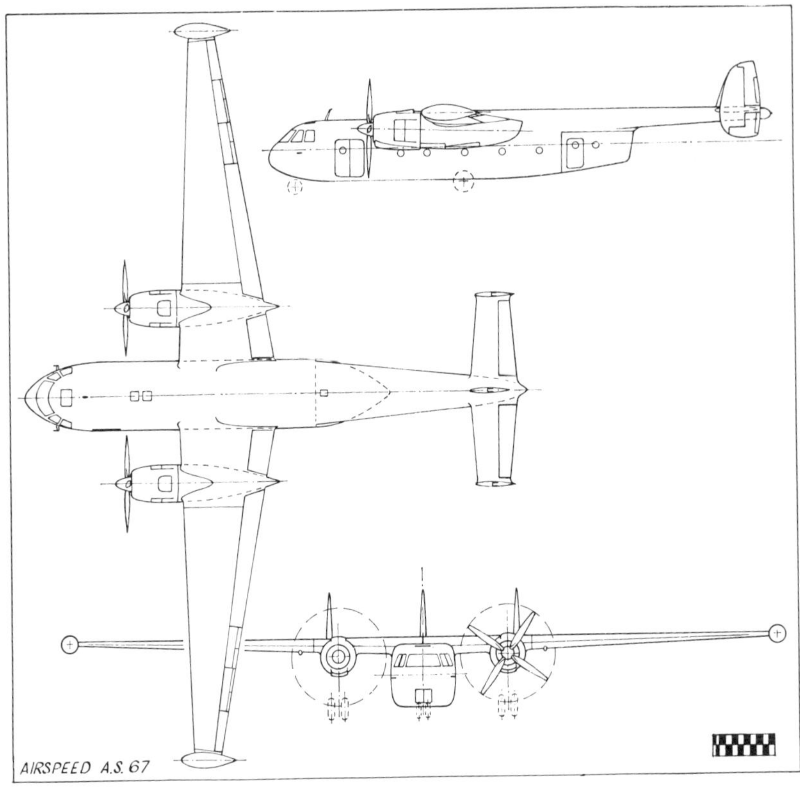

structural and other changes in the basic design of the AS.57 Ambassador which permitted the production version to be developed to take 52,000 lb and higher later loaded weights.

Other projects were the AS.64 for the RAF, to meet specification C.26/43; and the AS.66, a civil freighter with a fuselage shape and section similar to that of the Ayrshire, but without the special rear-loading doors; instead, side-loading was proposed with an 8 ft-wide double door on the port side. This version was planned early in 1947.

A much more ambitious project, stemming from the production Ambassador/Elizabethan, was the AS.67. In this, the wings, powerplants, empennage and systems of the developed AS.57 were retained, but the fuselage was completely redesigned on 'pod and boom' lines. With full-aperture rear loading under the boom tail, the AS.67 was intended either as a civil freighter or as a military transport adaptable for large-scale paratroop and (with the rear door removed) air-launching operations, and for glider-towing. A brochure describing the definitive version was issued on a confidential basis in April 1950.

This brochure explained that, with its high-wing layout and low floor level, the Ambassador's basic configuration was admirably adapted for freighter work, and the new fuselage made the most of these advantages. 'Not only is this fuselage of constant section throughout', the description ran, 'but there is a full-width, direct-loading door, and the floor height is less than three feet from ground level—so that it is practicable to use short, lightweight loading ramps which can be carried in the aircraft with a minimum loss of space and payload'. The fuselage was planned for a passenger-cargo rôle with quick convertibility. The fuel capacity included the normal integral tanks (1,000 gallons total), two 300-gallon bag tanks (already provided for) in the centre-section and, for overload long-range military work, two wing-tip tanks of 200 gallons each.

AS.67. Length 83 ft 4 in (25·4 m); height 20 ft 3 in (6·17 m); other overall dimensions and areas as for AS.57 Ambassador. Cabin length 37 ft 9 in (11·51 m); width 9 ft 6 in (2·9 m) throughout; floor width 8 ft 6 in (2·6 m) throughout; height 7 ft 8 in (2·33 m) throughout; volume 2,500 cu ft (73·05 cu m); main door size 7 ft 8 in by 9 ft 6 in (2·33 m by 2·9 m); floor height from ground level 2 ft 8 in (0·81 m). Operationally equipped weight, including 600 lb (272 kg) crew, 35,600 lb (16,148 kg); maximum landing weight 52,500 lb (23,814 kg); maximum payload 16,000 lb (7,257 kg); loaded weight, normal, 54,000 lb (24,494 kg); overload weight 60,000 lb (27,216 kg); wing loading, normal, 45 lb/sq ft (220 kg/sq m). Take-off distance to 50 ft (15·2 m), ISA, one engine out, 4,710 ft (1,436 m); landing distance from 50 ft (15·2 m) at maximum landing weight on dry concrete, brakes only, 3,195 ft (975 m). Still air range (AP970 definitions), with maximum payload of 16,000 lb (7,257 kg), 480 miles (770 km); payload with full normal tanks, for range of 2,660 miles (4,280 km), 6,650 lb (3,020 kg); range with wing-tip tanks and payload of 3,630 lb (1,650 kg) 3,410 miles (5,490 km). (Take-off and pay-load/range figures are for the normal maximum loaded weight.)

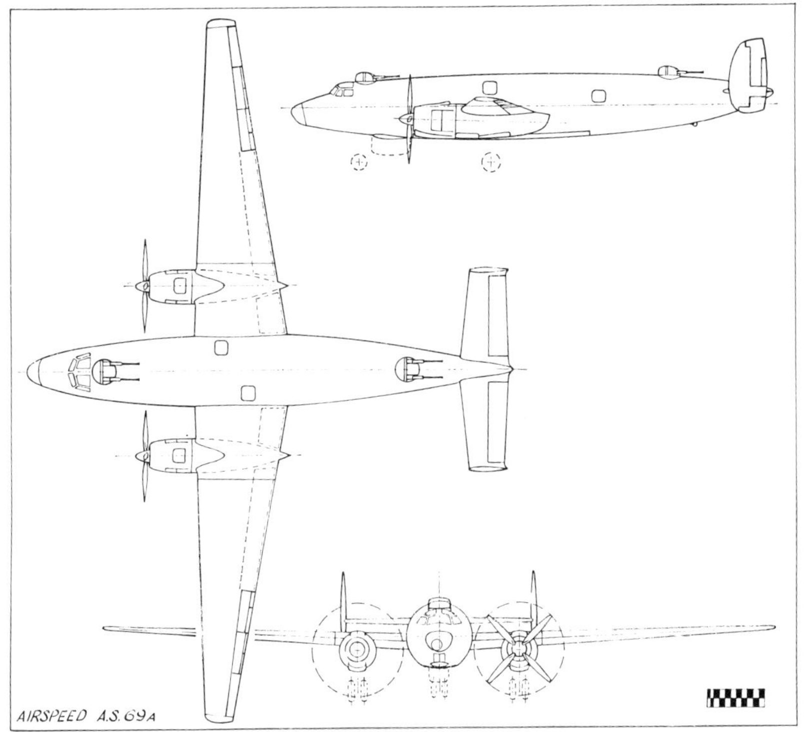

AS.69

A few months before the decision was made to abandon further development of the Ambassador, and any production beyond the 20 for BEA, the Airspeed design team had been working on a version, the AS.69, to meet Air Staff requirements for a marine reconnaissance aircraft. A secret preliminary brochure describing the proposals was issued in February 1951. So far as the records can tell us, this was the last projected variant of the Ambassador and the last Airspeed design apart from the very considerable amount of redesign work on basic de Havilland aircraft such as that leading to the Sea Vixen.

Two variants of the AS.69 were proposed. One retained the normal high-wing arrangement and was similar in general layout to the Ambassador. The other, the AS.69A, had the centre-section lowered to a mid-wing position, thus raising the fuselage. This made the bomb-bay more accessible for loading and provided a better field of fire from the two standard B-17-type twin 20 mm gun turrets, one forward of the tailplane and one immediately aft of the control cabin. The raised fuselage also permitted the aircraft to be loaded with the retractable air-to-surface-vessel (ASV) scanner, below and aft of the control cabin, in the extended position. This scanner was designed to be jettisonable so as to provide a forward parachute exit in addition to that in the floor at the rear of the aircraft.

Both variants used the Ambassador's centre-section, Bristol Centaurus 661 powerplants (with water injection) and extension wings, but the rear fuselage was modified and the increased-area tailplane lowered to provide a full field of fire from the dorsal turret. In the AS.69A the revised fuselage position would, however, have required a redesigned nosegear. The fuselage had a raised floor to accommodate the 30 ft by 8 ft bomb-bay (accommodating a maximum of 16 directional Sonobuoys and various combinations of anti-submarine weapons) and to allow the crew's quarters to be at the same level throughout the aircraft. Armament, in addition to the two gun turrets, could consist of eight 60 lb, 3-in rockets on either side of the forward fuselage. There were thirteen crew positions, and the layout was planned for a total crew of seven—pilot, Sonobuoy operator, aircraft navigator, tactical navigator, plotter (who would be captain of the aircraft), communications radio operator and gunner. The necessary range was provided by two additional 300-gallon bag tanks in the centre-section, for which provision had already been made, giving a total tankage of 1,600 gallons and an operational radius of 600 naut miles plus 2 hours' patrol, with a war load of 6,500 lb. The planned normal maximum take-off weight was 60,000 lb.

AS.69. Span 115 ft (35 m); length 82 ft 6 in (25·2 m); height (AS.69A) 22 ft (6·7 m); other overall dimensions and areas as for AS.57. Operationally equipped weight 41,463 lb (18,807 kg); bombs, fuel, oil, etc, 18,537 lb (8,408 kg); loaded weight 60,000 lb (27,216 kg). Take-off distance, both engines operating, ISA, sea-level, 5 kt wind, at 60,000 lb (27,216 kg), 3,900 ft (1,189 m); take-off distance, one engine inoperative 4 sec before unstick, ISA, sea-level, 5 kt wind, at 60,000 lb, 5,925 ft (1,806 m); landing distance from 50 ft (15·2 m), dry concrete, 2,610 ft (795 m). Operational radius at maximum weight 600 naut miles (1,112 km), plus 2 hr patrol at 160 kt (297 km/h).

APPENDIX I

Airspeed Type Summary

Type number	Type	Powerplants	First flight
AS.1	Tern. High-performance sailplane	—	1931
AS.2	Glider project	—	—
AS.3	Private-owner project	—	—
AS.4	Ferry. Three-engined short-stage ten-seat biplane	One de Havilland (DH) Gipsy III, two Gipsy II	1932
AS.5	Courier. Five/six-seat single-engined low-wing monoplane	Armstrong Siddeley (A.S.) Lynx IVC	1933
AS.5A	Courier	A.S. Lynx IVC	1933
AS.5B	Courier	A.S. Cheetah V	1933
AS.5C	Experimental and demonstration model	Napier Rapier IV	1934
AS.5J	Courier	A.S. Cheetah IX	1934
AS.6	Envoy. Twin-engined six/eight-seat low-wing monoplane	Wolseley A.R.9 Mk II	1934
AS.6A	Envoy	A.S. Lynx IVC	1934
AS.6B/C	Envoy seaplane projects	—	—
AS.6D	Envoy	Wright Whirlwind	1944
AS.6E	Envoy	Walter Castor II	1935
AS.6F	Envoy photographic survey project	—	—
AS.6G	Envoy	Wolseley Scorpio I	1936
AS.6H	Envoy	Wolseley Aries III	1934
AS.6J	Envoy	A.S. Cheetah IX	1934
AS.6JM/C	Envoy military/civil convertible	A.S. Cheetah IX	1936
AS.6K	Envoy	Wolseley Scorpio II	—
AS.7J	Military Envoy project	A.S. Cheetah VI	—
AS.7K	Military Envoy project	Wolseley Scorpio II	—
AS.8	Viceroy. Special Envoy for England–Australia race	A.S. Cheetah VI	1934
AS.9	Interceptor fighter project	Napier Dagger or Rolls-Royce (R-R) Kestrel	—
AS.10	Oxford I. Advanced twin-engined general-purpose trainer	A.S. Cheetah X	1937
	Oxford II. Pilot, navigation and radio trainer	A.S. Cheetah X	1938
	Oxford III. (Prototype only, P1864) Rotol constant-speed propellers and other changes	A.S. Cheetah XV	1940
	Oxford IV. Projected pilot-training version of Oxford III	—	—
	Oxford V. Version for overseas training schools (see also AS.46)	Pratt & Whitney (P & W) Wasp Junior	1942

Type number	*Type*	*Powerplants*	*First flight*
AS.11	All-metal Courier project for Canadian market	—	—
AS.12	Four-engined project	—	—
AS.13	Number not allocated	—	—
AS.14	Twin-engined 16-passenger high-wing transport project named Ambassador	P & W Wasp Junior, A.S. Panther VI or Bristol Pegasus XC	—
AS.15	Day/night bomber and troop-carrying project	—	—
AS.15A	Civil AS.15 project	—	—
AS.16	Fokker F.XXII 22-seat four-engined transport	P & W Wasp	—
AS.17	Fokker D.XVII single-seat fighter	R-R Kestrel IV	—
AS.18	Variant of AS.17	—	—
AS.19	Fokker D.XIX single-seat fighter	R-R Kestrel IV	—
AS.20	Fokker F.XXXVI 32-seat four-engined transport	Wright Cyclone	—
AS.21	Fokker D.XX single-seat fighter	R-R Kestrel IV	—
AS.22	Fokker C.X two-seat fighter	R-R Kestrel V	—
AS.22A	Fokker C.X floatplane version	R-R Kestrel V	—
AS.23	Douglas DC-2 to be built under licence	—	—
AS.24	Long-range mail-carrying version of AS.14	P & W Wasp Junior	—
AS.25	Number not allocated	—	—
AS.26	Vehicle-carrying project similar to Burnelli	—	—
AS.27	Special defence aircraft. Monoplane version	A.S. Cheetah IX	—
	Irving biplane version	Wolseley Aries or Scorpio II	—
AS.28	Twin-engined transport project	—	—
AS.29	Four-engined bomber to specification B.1/35	Bristol Aquila	—
AS.30	Queen Wasp. Radio-controlled target biplane to specification Q.32/35	A.S. Cheetah IX	1937
AS.31	Fighter project with twin booms and cockpit in tailplane	R-R Merlin E	—
AS.32	Projected 24-seat four-engined transport	Bristol Aquila	—
AS.33	Projected 24-seat four-engined transport	Bristol Aquila	—
AS.34	Projected 12/15-seat four-engined transport	A.S. Cheetah IX	—
AS.34A	Projected 12/15-seat four-engined transport	Wolseley Scorpio II	—

Type number	Type	Powerplants	First flight
AS.35	Projected 12/15-seat four-engined transport	DH Gipsy Six II	—
AS.36	Two-seat *ab initio* trainer project	DH Gipsy Six II	—
AS.37	Radio-controlled flying-boat target project	DH Gipsy Six II	—
AS.38	Projected communications version of AS.30 Queen Wasp	A.S. Cheetah X	—
AS.39	Fleet Shadower. Four-engined carrier-borne observation aircraft to specification S.23/37	Pobjoy Niagara V	1940
AS.40	Oxford civil conversion for radio research	A.S. Cheetah X	1938
AS.41	Oxford for engine test work (Miles Aircraft conversion)	Alvis Leonides	1947
AS.42	Oxford I to specification T.39/37 for New Zealand	A.S. Cheetah X	1938
AS.43	Survey version of AS.42	A.S. Cheetah X	—
AS.44	Projected Oxford replacements	—	—
	Low-wing version	Bristol Aquila	—
	High (shoulder)-wing version	A.S. Cheetah IX or Alvis Leonides	—
AS.45	Cambridge. Single-engined advanced trainer to specification T.4/39	Bristol Mercury VIII	1941
AS.46	Oxford V. Series I, Canadian version; Series II, non-winterized version	P & W Wasp Junior	1942
AS.47	Twin-engined (tractor and pusher) twin-boom bomber project	Napier Sabre	—
AS.48	Projected single-seat night fighter	Napier Sabre	—
AS.49	Projected single-seat fighter trainer to specification T.24/40	DH Gipsy Six IIIS, or Gipsy Six IV	—
AS.50	Production Queen Wasp trainer to specification T.24/40	A.S. Cheetah IX	—
AS.51	Horsa I troop-carrying glider to specification X.26/40	—	1941
AS.52	Horsa I bomb-carrying project to specification X.3/41	—	—
AS.53	Horsa I project for vehicle transport	—	—
AS.54	Projected two-seat training glider	—	—
AS.55	High-wing transport/freighter project in three versions	Four R-R Merlin XX, Bristol Taurus or P & W Twin Wasp. Two Bristol Hercules XIV or two Bristol Centaurus	—
AS.56	Projected single-seat fighter with annular radiator	Napier Sabre VI	—

Type number	*Type*	*Powerplants*	*First flight*
AS.57	Ambassador. Twin-engined 40/50-seat transport to specification C.25/43. Prototype	Bristol Centaurus 130	1947
	Production prototype and production series	Bristol Centaurus 661	1950
AS.58	Horsa II vehicle-carrying glider with hinged nose and twin nosewheels	—	1943
AS.59	Ambassador Mk II propeller-turbine project	Four R-R Darts	—
AS.60	Ayrshire. Projected military freighter version of Ambassador	Bristol Centaurus 130	—
AS.61	Dakota I (DC-3) conversion	—	—
AS.62	Dakota II (DC-3) conversion	—	—
AS.63	Dakota III (DC-3) conversion	—	—
AS.64	Ambassador project for RAF	—	—
AS.65	Consul. Civil conversion of Oxford	A.S. Cheetah X	1946
AS.66	Projected civil freighter version of Ambassador	Bristol Centaurus 130	—
AS.67	Projected civil freighter version of Ambassador with 'pod and boom' layout	Bristol Centaurus 661	—
AS.68	Projected propeller-turbine version of Ambassador	Bristol Proteus	—
AS.69	Projected marine reconnaissance version of Ambassador	Bristol Centaurus 661	—

APPENDIX II

Individual Aircraft Histories

II (A)

AS.4 Ferry

C/n	*Registration (Date of C of A)*	
4	G-ABSI (Apr 1932)	Prototype. Flew 5 April, 1932. Sir Alan Cobham's National Aviation Day and National Aviation Displays as *Youth of Britain II*; C. W. A. Scott Air Displays, Mar 1936; Air Publicity, Nov 1936; Portsmouth Southsea and Isle of Wight Aviation, 1939; impressed as AV968, 8 Nov, 1940; No. 474 ATC Sqn, Long Eaton, as 2758M, ground instruction airframe; struck off charge, 11 June, 1945.
5	G-ABSJ (June 1932)	National Aviation Day and National Aviation Displays as *Youth of Britain III* (later *Youth of Africa*); to Himalaya Air Transport and Survey Co as VT-AFO *Dragoman*, 1934.
6	G-ACBT (Feb 1933)	Midland and Scottish Air Ferries; remained at Renfrew, Glasgow, from end of 1934 until dismantled in 1940.
9*	G-ACFB (June 1933)	Midland and Scottish Air Ferries; C. W. A. Scott Air Displays, Apr 1936; Air Publicity, Nov 1936; C of A expired, Nov 1938; remained at Heston until impressed as DJ715, 18 Feb, 1941; dismantled and taken to No. 1037 ATC Sqn, Meir, Stoke-on-Trent.

* *C/n 7 was the first AS.5 Courier; C/n 8 was the Shackleton-Murray SM.1 built by Airspeed.*

II (B)

AS.5 Courier

C/n	*Registration (Date of C of A)*	*Variant*	
7	G-ABXN (Aug 1933)	AS.5	Prototype. First flight, 11 Apr, 1933; Sir Alan Cobham for flight-refuelling development trials, Jan 1934; force-landed Malta on flight to India, 24 Sept, 1934; repaired; North Eastern Airways, Mar 1937; Miss J. M. Parsons, Hanworth; impressed as X9427, 12 June, 1940, for Air Transport Auxiliary (ATA), at No. 3 (later No. 1) Ferry Pilots' Pool, White Waltham; withdrawn, Sept 1940.
10	G-ACJL (Aug 1933)	AS.5A	Aircraft Exchange and Mart, Sept 4, 1933; Mac.Robertson Trophy race to Australia, Oct 1934; re-registered VH-UUF, Nov 1934.

11	G-ACLR (Nov 1933)	AS.5A	Airspeed; Portsmouth Southsea and Isle of Wight Aviation (PSIOWA), Aug 1936; impressed as X9344, 18 Mar, 1940; ATA, White Waltham; Stn Flt, Exeter, 1942; crashed on take-off at Bolt Head, 1 Aug, 1942.
12	G-ACLF (Dec 1933)	AS.5B/A	R. K. Dundas for demonstrations in India; North Eastern Airways, Feb 1937; PSIOWA (re-engined with Lynx IVC); impressed as X9342, 18 Mar, 1940, for ATA, White Waltham; No. 25 OTU, 27 July, 1942; No. 5 MU, Kemble, 28 Nov, 1942; struck off charge, 12 Apr, 1944.
13	G-ACLS (Dec 1933)	AS.5A	Airspeed; Air Taxis, Oct 1934; crashed Grenoble, 17 Oct, 1934.
14	G-ACLT (Mar 1934)	AS.5A	PSIOWA (leased); North Eastern Airways, Feb 1937; PSIOWA; Air Taxis; impressed as X9394, 29 Mar, 1940, for ATA, White Waltham; written off in air raid, Apr 1942.
15	K4047	AS.5A	Air Ministry, Feb 1934; Airspeed for flap/slot modifications, 1935; RAE Farnborough for tests (Nov 1935–Oct 1936); RAF for communications.
16	G-ACSY (June 1934)	AS.5A	London, Scottish & Provincial Airways; crashed nr. Sevenoaks, Kent, 29 Sept, 1934.
19	G-ACSZ (June 1934)	AS.5A	London, Scottish & Provincial Airways; North Eastern Airways, Feb 1937; crashed nr. Doncaster, 29 May, 1937.
20	G-ACNZ (June 1934)	AS.5C/A	D. Napier & Son for Rapier IV engine tests and demonstrations; PSIOWA (re-engined with Lynx IVC); impressed as X9346, 18 Mar, 1940, for ATA, White Waltham (and ATA, Hawarden, June 1940); Airspeed for communications, 13 Mar, 1941; No. 5 MU, 18 Jan, 1944; struck off charge, 12 Apr, 1944.
22	G-ACVE (Aug 1936)	AS.5A	Airspeed; crashed at Portsmouth during take-off on unauthorized attempted flight to Spain, 20 Aug, 1936.
23	G-ACVF (Aug 1936)	AS.5B/A	Airspeed; North Eastern Airways, Feb 1937; PSIOWA (re-engined with Lynx IVC); impressed as X9437*, 14 Apr, 1940, for ATA, White Waltham (and ATA, Hawarden, June 1940); Boulton Paul, 28 Feb, 1942; No. 51 MU, Lichfield, 30 Sept, 1943; No. 5 MU, 5 Oct, 1943; sold to Sqn. Ldr. R. J. Jones, East Anglian Flying Services, 18 Jan, 1946 (only post-war Courier survivor); scrapped, 1949.
24	G-ACVG (Jan 1935)	AS.5J	R. K. Dundas; Maharajah of Jaipur as VT-AFY.
25	G-ACZL (Mar 1935)	AS.5A	PSIOWA, Apr 1935; impressed as X9345, 18 Mar, 1940, for ATA, White Waltham; written-off 15 Oct, 1940, while taking off after forced landing on flight to RAF Stradishall.
26	G-ADAX (Apr 1935)	AS.5A	PSIOWA, Apr 1935; impressed as X9347*, 18 Mar, 1940, for ATA, White Waltham; Airspeed for overhaul 17 Mar, 1941; struck off charge, 13 May, 1941.

27	G-ADAY (May 1935)	AS.5A	PSIOWA, Apr 1935; impressed as X9343, 18 Mar, 1940; ATA, White Waltham; No. 22 MU, Silloth, 12 Oct, 1940; No. 48 MU, Hawarden, 15 Oct, 1940; Airspeed for overhaul, 12 Mar, 1941; struck off charge, 13 May, 1941.

Variants: AS.5, Armstrong Siddeley Lynx IVC; AS.5A, Lynx IVC, 'English' model; AS.5B, Armstrong Siddeley Cheetah V, 'Colonial' model; AS.5C, Napier Rapier IV; AS.5J, Cheetah IX.

Many Couriers were registered first with Airspeed, but this is noted only when a reasonably long period was involved.

* *These serial numbers were transposed accidentally: G-ACVF should have been X9347 and G-ADAX, X9437; hence the post-war emergence of G-ACVF as G-ADAX until the error was rectified at C of A renewal, 19 Dec, 1946.*

II (C)

AS.6 Envoy and AS.8 Viceroy

C/n	*Registration (C of A)*	*Variant (Mark)*	
17	G-ACMT (9 Oct, 1934)	AS.6(I/II)	Prototype. Flew 26 June, 1934; modified to Series II (AS.6G) standard, 1936; Spain to civil war, Dec 1936; hit high ground and destroyed.
18	G-ACMU (Sept 1934)	AS.8	Viceroy. Flew Aug 1934; England–Australia Race, Oct 1934, withdrew at Athens; Spain, July 1936.
28	G-ACVH (6 Oct, 1934)	AS.6(I)	Wolseley Motors, Oct 1934; Airspeed, Mar 1936; force-landed Langstone Harbour, May 1936.
29	G-ACVI (6 Oct, 1934)	AS.6H/D(I)	Lord Nuffield, Oct 1934, as *Miss Wolseley*; tests included flight to Cape Town and return; Ansett Airways, Australia, as VH-UXM, Aug 1936; re-engined 1944 with Wright Whirlwinds (as only AS.6D).
30	G-ACVJ (29 Dec, 1934)	AS.6A(I)	R. K. Dundas, Jan 1935, for demonstrations in India; Commercial Air Hire, July 1936; Spain, Aug 1936.
31	G-ACYJ (9 Nov, 1934)	AS.6J(I)	C. T. P. Ulm as VH-UXY; lost on flight from Oakland, Cal, to Honolulu, Dec 1934.
32	G-ADAZ (28 Mar, 1935)	AS.6J(I)	North Eastern Airways, Apr 1935, as *Tynedale*; Air Service Training, Hamble, Nov 1938; impressed as DG663, 14 Feb, 1941; Air Transport Auxiliary, Hamble; No. 5 MU, Kemble, 6 May, 1941; Stn Flt, Northolt, 24 Jan, 1942; No. 5 MU, 19 Mar, 1942; No. 52 MU, 12 July, 1942; TFU, Defford; struck off charge, 14 June, 1943.

Variants: AS.6, Wolseley AR.9 Mk II; AS.6A, Armstrong Siddeley Lynx IVC; AS.6D, Wright Whirlwind; AS.6E, Walter Castor II; AS.6G, Wolseley Scorpio I; AS.6H, Wolseley Aries III; AS.6J, Cheetah IX; AS.6K, Wolseley Scorpio II; AS.8, Cheetah VI.

33	G-ADBA (18 Apr, 1935)	AS.6J(I)	Cobham Air Routes, leased Olley Air Service, May 1935; North Eastern Airways, Feb 1937; Air Commerce, Dec 1938; RAF as P5778, 14 Feb, 1939; No. 1 Electrical and Wireless School (EWS); No. 2 EWS; No. 9 FTS, 5 Dec, 1939; No. 2 EWS, 11 Dec, 1939; No. 8 MU, 14 Nov, 1940; No. 781 Sqn ATC, 21 Mar, 1941.
34	G-ADBB (6 Apr, 1935)	AS.6J(I)	North Eastern Airways, Apr 1935, as *Wharfedale*; Spain, Sept 1936.
35	G-ADBZ (13 Apr, 1935)	AS.6J(I)	North Eastern Airways, Apr 1935, as *Swaledale*; Air Dispatch on lease; crashed near Oxted, Surrey, 22 Jan, 1937.
36	G-ADCA (2 May, 1935)	AS.6A(I)	Portsmouth Southsea and Isle of Wight Aviation (PSIOWA), May 1935; Spain, Aug 1936; shot down.
37	G-ADCB (17 May, 1935)	AS.6(I)	Japan Air Transport as J-BDDO, Aug 1935.
38	G-ADCC (17 May, 1935)	AS.6(I)	Japan Air Transport posssibly as J-BDBO, 1935.
39	G-ADCD (31 July, 1936)	AS.6JC(II)	South African Airways, registered as ZS-AGA, 23 July, 1936; taken over by South African Air Force (SAAF) as 254, 10 May, 1938.
40	G-ADCE (17 May, 1935)	AS.6A(I)	Japan Air Transport, as J-BDEO, July 1935; known to have had Lynx IVC engines in service; probably re-engined in Japan.
41	— (15 June, 1935)	AS.6A(I)	Mitsubishi as J-BAOH and then Japan Air Transport.
42	— (18 July, 1935)	AS.6A(I)	Mitsubishi (possibly as J-BAOI) and then Japan Air Transport.
43	— (27 July, 1935)	AS.6(I)	Japan Air Transport as J-BDCO, June 1935.
44	ZS-ALD (19 July, 1936)	AS.6JM(II)	South African Air Force, probably as 251, July 1936; Air Survey Flight, Zwartkop, Pretoria; temporarily registered ZS-ALD.
45	ZS-AGD (15 Oct, 1936)	AS.6JC(II)	South African Airways, *Alex Biggar*, Oct 1936, registered 1 July, 1936; SAAF as 257, 4 May, 1938.
46	ZS-AGC (12 Oct, 1936)	AS.6JC(II)	South African Airways, Oct 1936, registered 1 Dec, 1936; SAAF as 256, 10 May, 1938.
47	OK-BAL (30 July, 1935)	AS.6E(I)	Československé Státní Aerolinie (ČSA), 6 Aug, 1935.
48	OK-BAM (30 Aug, 1935)	AS.6E(I)	ČSA, 9 Sept, 1935.
49	ZS-ALE (1 July, 1936)	AS.6JM(II)	SAAF, July 1936, probably as 252; Air Survey Flight; temporarily registered ZS-ALE.
50	ZS-ALF (26 June, 1936)	AS.6JM(II)	SAAF, June 1936, probably as 253; Air Survey Flight; temporarily registered ZS-ALF.

51	ZS-AGB (19 July, 1936)	AS.6JC(II)	South African Airways, *Sir Hercules Robinson*, July 1936, registered, 3 Nov, 1936; SAAF, as 255, 4 May, 1938.
52	G-AEBV (20 Apr, 1936)	AS.6J(II)	Brian Allen Aviation, May 1936; Spain, Aug 1936.
53	OK-BAN (17 Aug, 1936)	AS.6E(II)	ČSA, Aug 1936.
54	OK-BAO (3 Sept, 1936)	AS.6E(II)	ČSA, Sept 1936.
55	G-AEGF (29 Dec, 1936)	AS.6J(II/III)	British Scandinavian Airways (BSA), order cancelled. Probably one of two (with c/n 56 below) sold to E. Hoffman, Vienna, but impounded at Rotterdam (see Envoy narrative). Possibly one of two, PH-ARK and PH-ARL, registered unofficially in name of D. H. Reinders, The Hague, and based at Ypenburg aerodrome in 1937.
56	G-AEGG (30 Dec, 1936)	AS.6J(II/III)	BSA, order cancelled. Probably one of two sold to E. Hoffman. Possibly PH-ARK or -ARL (see entry above).
57	VT-AHR (27 Oct, 1936)	AS.6J(II)	Maharajah of Jaipur, Oct 1936; Indian National Airways; crashed 22 Mar, 1942.
58	OK-VIT (3 Dec, 1936)	AS.6E(III)	Steel and Iron Corp, Czechoslovakia, Dec 1936.
59	G-AFWZ (May 1937)	AS.6J(III)	Maharajah of Indore as VT-AIC; R. K. Dundas as G-AFWZ; impressed RAF, 21 Mar, 1940, as X9370; No. 24 Sqn, Hendon, 27 Mar, 1940; destroyed in air raid, Hendon, 7-8 Oct, 1940.
60	G-AENA (17 Sept, 1936)	AS.6J(III)	Portsmouth–Johannesburg race as *Gabrielle*; crashed Abercorn, Rhodesia, 1 Oct, 1936.
61	—	AS.6J(III)	Registered (with c/n 62) in name of E. Hoffman, but probably replaced by cancelled BSA aircraft (see c/ns 55 and 56 above). C/n given to first prototype Ambassador, G-AGUA.
62	—	AS.6J(III)	Registered in name of E. Hoffman (see c/n 61 above). C/n given to second prototype Ambassador, G-AKRD.
66	G-AEXX (7 May, 1937)	AS.6J(III)	First flight, 25 Mar, 1937; RAF Martlesham, 25 Apr, 1937; King's Flight, June 1937; No. 24 Sqn RAF, as L7270, 1939; re-registered G-AEXX post-war; G. F. W. Farquharson, 11 Feb, 1946; Sweden as SE-ASN, 19 June, 1946.
67	G-AEXE (13 May, 1937)	AS.6J(III)	Second of two Envoys bought by Military Governor of Kwangsi Province, China; left Portsmouth 15 June, 1937; believed crashed in 1938.
68	G-AERT (22 Jan, 1937)	AS.6J(III)	First of two Envoys flown out to Kwangsi Province, China; left Portsmouth 27 Jan, 1937.

No.	Registration	Type	Remarks
69	F-APPQ (5 Feb, 1937)	AS.6J(III)	Registered in name of E. Hoffman, but not delivered. Probably F-APPQ to Air Pyrénées, 20 Mar, 1937; French C of A tests Villacoublay, 21–26 Mar; Toulouse, 27 Mar, for Toulouse–Biarritz service; damaged in forced landing after attack by Spanish fighters, but no casualties.
70	F-AQAA	AS.6J(III)	Bought by Auguste Amestoy, of Bayonne. (70–74)
71	F-AQAB	AS.6J(III)	
72	F-AQCR	AS.6J(III)	
73	F-AQCS	AS.6J(III)	
74	F-AQCT	AS.6J(III)	
76	G-AFJD (Aug 1938)	AS.6J(III)	Taken on charge 28 Aug, 1938. Operated by RAF Communications Flight, New Delhi, serial N9107; struck off charge, 11 June, 1942.
77	G-AFJE (Aug 1938)	AS.6J(III)	As above, serial N9108; crashed Mingaladon, Rangoon, 24 Apr, 1942.
78‡	P5625 (8 Mar, 1939†)	AS.6J(III)	No. 3 FTS; Stn Flt, Northolt; Stn Flt, Plymouth, 6 July, 1939; No. 15 Gp Comm Flt, 1 Mar, 1940; No. 14 Gp Comm Flt, 18 June, 1940; Stn Flt, Gosport, 28 June, 1940; struck off charge, 8 Apr, 1943.
79‡	P5626 (8 Mar, 1939†)	AS.6J(III)	No. 1 Electrical and Wireless School; No. 10 FTS, 2 June, 1940; RAF Cranwell, 11 June, 1940; No. 45 MU, 21 July, 1940; registered post-war as G-AHAC, 1946; Brevet Flying Club, 24 Jan, 1946; Flight Plan, 22 July, 1946; N. C. Alderson, 19 Sept, 1946; Private Charter, 25 Mar, 1948; dismantled Tollerton, May 1950.
80‡	P5627 (8 Mar, 1939†)	AS.6J(III)	Stn Flt, Chatham; No. 16 Gp Comm Flt, Rochester, 5 Dec, 1939; No. 39 MU, 19 Nov, 1940; Stn Flt A, Gosport, 10 Apr, 1941; struck off charge, 4 July, 1942.
81‡	P5628 (8 Mar, 1939†)	AS.6J(III)	Stn Flt, Grantham; School of Technical Training.
82‡	P5629 (8 Mar, 1939†)	AS.6J(III)	Stn Flt, Turnhouse, 6 July, 1939; Stn Flt, Leuchars; No. 4 MU, 14 Sept, 1940; Fleet Air Arm (comm), 30 May, 1941.

† *Date when taken on charge by RAF.* ‡ *Unconfirmed.*

Mitsubishi-built Envoys (type-named Hina-Zuru, or Young Crane): J-BAOD, J-BAOF, J-BAOK, J-BAOL, J-BAOP, J-BAOQ, J-BAOR, J-BAOS, J-BAOV, J-BAOW (three sold to Japan Air Transport; four others operated by Manchurian Air Transport; others possibly to Japanese Navy).

II (D)

British Civil-registered Oxfords

Registration (Serial)	C of A Date (c/n)	
G-AFFM (L4538)	31 Aug, 1938 (75)	Airspeed; Secretary of State for Air (Dept of Civil Aviation) and British Airways; hit balloon barrage, 20 Nov, 1939.
G-AFVS (—)	30 June, 1939 (83)	Airspeed; intended for Canada for winterization trials, Aug 1939, but no evidence of its arrival.
G-AHDZ (ED190)	28 Mar, 1946	Scottish Aviation, Feb 1946; Union Aéromaritime de Transport (UAT) as F-BBIU, July 1954.
G-AHGU (V3815)	9 May, 1946 (3277)	Bristol Aeroplane Co; Air Couriers; Film Aviation Services, Gatwick.
G-AHTW (V3388)	19 June, 1946 (3083)	Boulton Paul Aircraft.
G-AHXA (V3870)	23 Dec, 1946	Brevet Flying Club, July 1946; Payloads (Charter), Dec 1946; Egypt as SU-AER, Aug 1947.
G-AIAT (NM387)	10 May, 1948	BOAC Initial Training Flight, Hurn, Aug 1946; Air Service Training (AST), Apr 1951.
G-AIAU (NM457)	24 Apr, 1948	BOAC, Aug 1946; Cyprus Airways, Feb 1953.
G-AIAV (NM536)	9 Mar, 1948	BOAC, Aug 1946; Hong Kong as VR-HFC, Sept 1951.
G-AIAW (NM649)	15 June, 1948	BOAC, Aug 1946; Short Bros; Sweden as SE-CAM, Nov 1954; Spain, Sept 1956.
G-AIAX (DF356)	29 July, 1949	BOAC, Aug 1946; AST, Apr 1951.
G-AIAY (DF521)	—	BOAC, Aug 1946; broken up, 1947.
G-AIRZ (HN610)	22 Feb, 1947 (2816)	BOAC, Aug 1946; Hunting Aero Surveys, Mar 1951; crashed Luxembourg, July 1952.
G-AITB (MP345)	29 May, 1947	AST, Nov 1946.
G-AITF (ED290)	27 Mar, 1947	AST, Nov 1946.
G-AIUH (NM277)	6 Jan, 1949	Reid and Sigrist, Oct 1947; Hunting Aero Surveys.
G-AIVY (—)	8 Mar, 1948 (828)	British South American Airways (BSAA) as *Star Mentor*, Nov 1946; BOAC; Cyprus Airways, Oct 1953.
G-AJGR (LX533)	4 July, 1947	Hunting Aero Surveys, Feb 1947; withdrawn, Feb 1952.
G-AJNC (ED251)	26 June, 1947 (5137)	Fairey Aviation Co, May 1947; Air Survey Co, S. Rhodesia, VP-YIY, Nov 1951.
G-AJWJ (LX119)	—	Miles Aircraft, June 1947, for Alvis Leonides test-bed conversion (U-7).
G-ALTB (PH321)	26 Jan, 1950	AST.

British Civil-registered Oxfords contd.

G-ALTR (PH368)	9 Jan, 1950	AST.
G-ALXV (X6811)	Jan 1950	Lancashire Aircraft Corp (LAC), Jan 1950.
G-ALXW (NJ352)	—	LAC; not converted for civil use.
G-ALXX (EB759)	—	LAC; not converted for civil use.
G-ALXY (AT660)	— (3830)	LAC; not converted for civil use.
G-AMCU	—	Airspeed; de Havilland Aircraft.
G-AMCV	—	Airspeed; de Havilland Aircraft.
G-AMCW	—	Airspeed; de Havilland Aircraft.
G-AMCX	—	Airspeed; Spain as EC-WGE.
G-AMCY	—	Airspeed; de Havilland Aircraft.
G-AMCZ	—	Airspeed; de Havilland Aircraft.
G-AMFJ	1951	Aerocontacts; Britavia; Israel Air Force, 15 Dec, 1951.
G-AMFK	—	Aerocontacts; Britavia; Israel Air Force, Dec 1951.
G-AMFL	1951	Aerocontacts; Britavia; Israel Air Force, 2 Mar, 1952.
G-AMFM	—	Aerocontacts.
G-AMHE	—	Aerocontacts.
G-AOUT	—	Eagle Aviation.

Non-British Civil-registered AS.10 Oxfords*

Serial (c/n)	*Registration (C of A issued)*	
V3325 (2960)	SE-BTP	Sweden; Finland as OH-VLT
BP857/ NZ1336	ZK-APX (22 Oct, 1947)	G. M. Gould, Wellington, N.Z., for light cargo operations; C of A cancelled 21 Oct, 1948; returned to RNZAF.
—	XA-FAO— XA-FAT	Mexico 1945, ex-Canada. Possibly Airspeed-built Mk V airframes in serials EB424-677.
HN368/ NZ1337	ZK-APY (2 Feb, 1948)	G. M. Gould, as above; C of A cancelled, 1 Feb, 1949; returned to RNZAF.
PK262	LN-LAD	Norwegian Air Lines (DNL); sold to Royal Norwegian Air Force (RNAF).
PK285	LN-LAE	DNL; sold to RNAF.

* *Excluding aircraft initially registered and operated in Britain.*

II (E)

AS.57 Ambassador/Elizabethan

C/n	*Registration (C of A date)*	
61	G-AGUA (RT665) (5 May, 1949)	First prototype. Flew, 10 July, 1947; dismantled, 1951.
62	G-AKRD (RT668) (4 Aug, 1949)	*Golden Lion*. Second prototype. Flew 26 Aug, 1948; special category C of A, 45,000 lb; de Havilland propeller tests, 1951; Bristol Proteus 705 development tests, 1953; Rolls-Royce Tyne development tests, Mar 1958 (MoA G-37-3); Rolls-Royce Dart development tests; still airworthy, 1969.
5210	G-ALFR (25 May, 1951)	*Golden Hind*. Production prototype. Flew May 1950; Napiers for Eland tests, 1955; Dan-Air, Mar 1961; conversion to airline standards completed, Jan 1964; withdrawn from use, Nov 1967.
5211	G-AMAD (19 Mar, 1952)	*Sir Francis Drake*. First production aircraft. Flew 12 Jan, 1951; route proving; BEA, 20 Mar, 1952; BKS, 23 July, 1957; withdrawn from passenger service, Oct 1967; converted to freighter; crashed Heathrow Airport, London, 3 July, 1968.
5212	G-ALZN (20 Aug, 1951)	*Elizabethan*. Flew 10 Apr, 1951; BEA on loan, 22 Aug, 1951; delivered, 31 Jan, 1953; Overseas Aviation, 10 Mar, 1961; Dan-Air, Apr 1962.
5213	G-ALZP (19 Dec, 1951)	*Sir Richard Grenville*. BEA, 28 Feb, 1952; Royal Jordanian Air Force (as 109) 13 Sept, 1960; King of Morocco (as CN-MAK); Decca Navigator, 1963; C of A restricted to aerial work only, 1968.
5214	G-ALZR (12 Feb, 1952)	*Sir Walter Raleigh*. BEA, 13 Feb, 1952; Rolls-Royce Tyne tests (MoA G-37-4), 30 Aug, 1957; BKS, May 1963; converted to freighter, Nov 1964.
5215	G-ALZS (24 Jan, 1952)	*William Shakespeare*. BEA, 25 Jan, 1952; Globe Air (HB-IEK), June 1960; Autair, 1963; damaged in accident at Luton, 14 Sept, 1967.
5216	G-ALZT (26 Jan, 1952)	*Sir John Hawkins*. BEA, 27 Jan, 1952; BKS, 5 May, 1958; withdrawn, Oct 1968.
5217	G-ALZU (5 Mar, 1952)	*Lord Burghley*. BEA, 5 Mar, 1952; crashed on take-off, Munich, 6 Feb, 1958.
5218	G-ALZV (5 Apr, 1952)	*Earl of Leicester*. BEA, 12 Apr, 1952; Overseas Aviation, 10 Mar, 1961; Globe Air (HB-IEM), 1961; Autair, 1963; withdrawn, June 1968.
5219	G-ALZW (28 Apr, 1952)	*Sir Francis Walsingham*. BEA, 28 Apr, 1952; BKS, 15 May, 1958; withdrawn, Oct 1967.
5220	G-ALZX (29 May, 1952)	*Sir John Norris*. BEA, 29 May, 1952; Butler Air Transport, Australia (VH-BUI), 6 June, 1957; Dan-Air, Nov 1959; damaged beyond repair in overrun accident at Beauvais, 14 Apr, 1966.

5221	G-ALZY (10 July, 1952)	*Sir Philip Sidney*. BEA, 10 July, 1952; Royal Jordanian Air Force (as 107), 26 Dec, 1959; Handley Page; Dan-Air, Feb 1963.
5222	G-ALZZ (6 Aug, 1952)	*Edmund Spenser*. BEA, 9 Aug, 1952; Overseas Aviation, 8 Nov, 1960; Globe Air (HB-IEL), 1961; Autair, 1963; on lease Skyways Coach Air for summer 1968; withdrawn at end of season.
5223	G-AMAA (2 Sept, 1952)	*Sir Francis Knollys*. BEA, 5 Sept, 1952; Shell Aviation 28 Jan, 1960; Dan-Air, 6 Oct, 1966; withdrawn, Nov 1967.
5224	G-AMAB (3 Oct, 1952)	*Sir Francis Bacon*. BEA, 4 Oct, 1952; forced landing near Düsseldorf, 8 Apr, 1955; written off.
5225	G-AMAC (1 Nov, 1952)	*Sir Robert Cecil*. BEA, 1 Nov, 1952; BKS, 21 June, 1960; withdrawn, 31 Oct, 1967.
5226	G-ALZO (25 Nov, 1952)	*Christopher Marlowe*. BEA, 25 Nov, 1952; Royal Jordanian Air Force (as 108), 5 May, 1960; Handley Page; Dan-Air, Feb 1963.
5227	G-AMAE (10 Dec, 1952)	*Earl of Essex*. BEA, 18 Dec, 1952; Butler Air Transport (VH-BUK) 6 June, 1957; Dan-Air, Nov 1959.
5228	G-AMAF (16 Jan, 1953)	*Lord Howard of Effingham*. BEA, 17 Jan, 1953, to 30 July, 1958 (last BEA Elizabethan in service); Overseas Aviation, 10 Mar, 1961; Globe Air (HB-IEI), but not delivered; BKS, for spares, 1962.
5229	G-AMAG (4 Feb, 1953)	*Sir Thomas Gresham*. BEA, 4 Feb, 1953; Shell Aviation, 8 Feb, 1959; Dan-Air, 3 June, 1966; belly-landed Manston, 30 Sept, 1968.
5230	G-AMAH (5 Feb, 1953)	*Sir Christopher Hatton*. BEA, 6 Mar, 1953; Butler Air Transport (VH-BUJ), 6 June, 1957; Dan-Air, Nov 1959.

II (F)

British-registered AS.65 Consuls

Many Consuls were initially registered in the name of Airspeed, but are not so noted unless kept for more than a short period.

Registration (Serial)	*C of A date (c/n)*	
G-AGVY (V3679)	15 Mar, 1946 (3204)	Prototype conversion of Hatfield-built Oxford without longer (baggage) nose of later versions. Bata Shoe Co, Mar 1946; Air Links, May 1947; Air Enterprises, Dec 1948; crashed in Lebanon, 11 Feb, 1949, on United Nations work.
G-AHEF (—)	16 May, 1946 (4044)	Airspeed for communications; de Havilland, Aug 1951.
G-AHEG (T1206)	26 Apr, 1946 (1052)	Airspeed; Airwork as demonstrator; Metal Containers, Apr 1948; Colley, June 1951; Swain Holdings, 1956.

G-AHEH (LX641)	22 May, 1946 (3362)	British Air Transport, Redhill; G. C. S. Pearson, Nov 1948; Rollason; Aerocontacts, Aug 1953.
G-AHFS (HN769)	15 June, 1946 (2942)	British Air Transport; Sweden as SE-BTU, Aug 1951.
G-AHFT (HN423)	24 May, 1946 (2593)	Morton Air Services, Croydon; crashed in English Channel, 14 June, 1952.
G-AHJX (LB529)	13 July, 1946 (541)	Morton Air Services, Croydon; crashed Guernsey, 12 May, 1950.
G-AHJY (HN471)	21 June, 1946 (2647)	Airspeed; Atlas Aviation, Elstree, Feb 1947; four other owners before going to Iceland as TF-RPM, Jan 1951; crashed, 12 Apr, 1951.
G-AHJZ (HN494)	26 June, 1946 (2686)	de Havilland; Groupe d'Études et des Consultations Aéronautiques, Toussus, as F-BFAT, Apr 1957.
G-AHMA (LX732)	29 July, 1946 (3428)	Airwork; G. J. Dawson (Atlas), Gatwick, July 1946; crashed Isère, France, 23 Dec, 1946.
G-AHMB (LX281)	29 July, 1946 (3112)	Airwork; to South Africa as *Southernaire*; Dennis Aviation, Croydon; Israel, Aug 1949.
G-AHMC (HN583)	4 July, 1946 (2778)	Airwork; Westminster Airways, Blackbushe, June 1946; H. White, Croydon, Dec 1947; Israel, June 1949.
G-AHMD (NM329)	2 Aug, 1946 (3545)	Airwork; Lancashire Aircraft Corporation; broken up Blackpool, 20 Apr, 1956.
G-AHRK (LX265)	18 July, 1946 (3096)	British Aviation Services, Blackbushe; Rhodesia as VP-RBM, Feb 1949; Silver City Airways as G-AHRK, Sept 1949; sold abroad, May 1952.
G-AHXP (HN840)	21 Aug, 1946 (2996)	Thomas Barclay (International Airways), Croydon, as *Blanche Fury*; sold abroad, May 1952.
G-AHYW (PG936)	3 Sept, 1946 (3923)	Portsmouth Aviation; force-landed 55 miles N.E. of Salisbury, Rhodesia, 16 Oct, 1946.
G-AHZV (RR356)	19 Sept, 1946 (4397)	Lancashire Aircraft Corporation; broken up, Mar 1946.
G-AHZW (LX260)	13 Sept, 1946 (3091)	Lancashire Aircraft Corporation; Skyways.
G-AIAH (PK252)	27 Sept, 1946 (4316)	Channel Islands Iron & Steel; Morton Air Services, Croydon, Sept 1946; training use only, 1958; broken up, 1959.
G-AIBC (RR358)	24 Sept, 1946 (4399)	Westminster Airways; three other owners before Aviation Traders, Southend; broken up, June 1952.
G-AIBF (LX726)	17 Aug, 1946 (3422)	British Aviation Services; Silver City Airways (Malta Airways); broken up, Apr 1954.
G-AICZ (PK253)	9 Sept, 1946 (4317)	Westminster Airways; SBAC Show, Radlett, Sept 1946; H. White; Israel, June 1949.
G-AIDW (HN783)	22 Aug, 1946 (2956)	G. J. Dawson; Dexford Motors, Southend; broken up, 1951.
G-AIDX (PK254)	7 Nov, 1946 (4318)	Intava; Anglo-American Oil; Esso; Switzerland as HB-LAT, Oct 1956.
G-AIDY (LX263)	3 Oct, 1946 (3094)	British Air Transport; crashed Berck, 14 June, 1948.
G-AIDZ (RR363)	8 Oct, 1946 (4404)	British Air Transport; Escadrille Mercure, Le Bourget, as F-BFVS, July 1951.

G-AIEA (PK256)	3 Oct, 1946 (4320)	British Air Transport; French West Africa as F-OAHJ with Oxford nose for photographic work, Oct 1950.
G-AIHC (PK248)	Oct 1946 (4312)	Belgium as OO-GVP; crashed Tumbur, Sudan, 6 Jan, 1947
G-AIIM (PK290)	Sept 1946 (4342)	Turkish Air Force.
G-AIIN (PK292)	28 Oct, 1946 (4344)	Westminster Airways; Airwork; Colman Myers, Bulawayo, as VP-YIC, Nov 1949; reg. South Africa as ZS-DDM. 5 Dec, 1949; returned as VP-YIC; to Israel.
G-AIIO (PK297)	Oct 1946 (4349)	Extractors (Hull); crashed, 17 July, 1948.
G-AIIS (RR357)	8 Oct, 1946 (4398)	Thomas Barclay, Croydon; broken up, Feb 1951.
G-AIKO (PK287)	5 Dec, 1946 (4339)	Chartair, Croydon/Thame; Air Jordan as TJ-ABE, Dec 1950; Aerocontacts as G-AIKO, Aug 1953; Aero-technico, Spain, as EC-AJV, May 1954.
G-AIKP (PK259)	Dec 1946 (4323)	O. H. Simpson, Gatwick, as *The Silver Lady*; South Africa as ZS-BJX, 1947 (reg. 5 Oct, 1946); used by Airspeed as G-AIKP in 1948; returned to South Africa; broken up, 1950.
G-AIKR (PK286)	5 Dec, 1946 (4338)	Chartair; Airwork, Jan 1947.
G-AIKS (PK288)	22 Nov, 1946 (4340)	Skytravel; Bowmaker, Blackpool, Mar 1951; Air Malta; broken up, 20 Apr, 1950.
G-AIKT (PK304)	27 Nov, 1946 (4356)	Ulster Aviation, Londonderry; Wirral Airways; Air Enterprises, Croydon, June 1951; Louis Newmark, Croydon.
G-AIKU (PK296)	5 Nov, 1946 (4348)	Butlins, Luton; S. E. Norman; Air Jordan as TJ-AAX, May 1951.
G-AIKX (PK302)	16 Dec, 1946 (4354)	Chartair; S. Hodge & Sons; H. A. J. Silley, Feb 1952; broken up, Aug 1956.
G-AIKY (PK260)	5 Dec, 1946 (4324)	British Aviation Services; Malayan Airways VR-SCD; W. S. Shackleton, Aug 1952; Aeroservices, May 1953; Israel, July 1953.
G-AIKZ (PK261)	5 Dec, 1946 (4325)	Skytravel; Bowmaker, Blackpool, June 1951; Air Malta; Italy as I-VALH.
G-AILA (PK258)	Sept 1946 (4322)	Sold abroad, probably Turkish Air Force.
G-AIOL (PK257)	5 Dec, 1946 (4321)	D. L. Steiner (Steiner's Air Service), Speke, as *Liverpool Hawk*; Thomas Barclay; sold abroad, Nov 1948.
G-AIOM (PK295)	5 Dec, 1946 (4347)	Chartair; crashed near Lyons, France, 24 Jan, 1948.
G-AION (PK300)	Oct 1946 (4352)	Aigle Azur, Indo-China, as F-BCJD, Dec 1946.
G-AIOO (PK305)	19 Dec, 1946 (4357)	Payloads (Charter); reg. South Africa as ZS-BNT (not used), 14 Feb, 1947; crashed Perpignan, 27 Nov, 1947.
G-AIOP (HN642)	19 Feb, 1947 (671)	Registered OO-MAB (not used); Hornton Airways, Gatwick; Transair Sweden, as SE-BTB, Nov 1951; broken up, Sept 1955.

G-AIOR (PK289)	23 Dec, 1946 (4341)	Dennis Aviation; sold abroad, Sept 1949.
G-AIOS (PK265)	20 Dec, 1946 (4329)	Morton Air Services; training use only, 1958; broken up, 1969.
G-AIOT (PK266)	2 Jan, 1947 (4330)	Patrick Duval, *City of Warwick*; Air Enterprises, Oct 1953; Central Aero Bureau, May 1956.
G-AIOU (PK303)	10 Jan, 1947 (4335)	Morton Air Services; crashed near Cairo, 24 May, 1948.
G-AIOV (PK309)	3 Feb, 1947 (4361)	Patrick Duval, *City of Worcester*; Air Enterprises, Oct 1953; to Italy as I-VALZ.
G-AIOW (PK301)	17 Jan, 1947 (4353)	Morton Air Services; broken up, June 1954.
G-AIOX (EB748)	19 Feb, 1947 (2188)	Transcontinental Air Services; Airspan Travel; Fly-, away, as *Gorgeous Gussie*; Air Jordan as TJ-ABD, Dec 1950.
G-AIOY (PK282)	10 Jan, 1947 (4334)	S. Yager, White Waltham, as *Carlos Amigos*; Solar Air Services, Sweden, as SE-BTD, Sept 1950; crashed near Gävle, Sweden, 14 July, 1951.
G-AIOZ (PK283)	23 Jan, 1947 (4335)	Grayson Air Services; I. R. K. McLaren, Croydon; crashed 29 Apr, 1947, on Botley Hill, Limpsfield.
G-AIRP (RR359)	2 Nov, 1946 (4400)	Payloads (Charter); Brevet Flying Club; broken up Southend, May 1951.
G-AIUR (HN174)	4 Feb, 1947 (967)	Chartair; withdrawn, 1950.
G-AIUS (HM757)	14 Feb, 1947 (750)	Air Kruise; Stewart Smith & Co; Silver City Airways, Mar 1954.
G-AIUT (LX666)	10 Feb, 1947 (3375)	Congo Charter Air Services; C. Myers, Rhodesia, as VP-YID, Nov 1949; Commercial Air Services, Johannesburg, 5 Dec, 1949, as ZS-DDN; crashed Bulawayo, 20 June, 1950.
G-AIUU (W6562)	11 Apr, 1947 (5104)	Thomas Barclay, Croydon.
G-AIUV (HN191)	11 Apr, 1947 (5098)	Hornton Airways; sold abroad, Apr 1950.
G-AIUW (PH503)	11 Apr, 1947 (5100)	Hornton Airways; Transair; sold abroad, May 1950.
G-AIUX (LB527)	15 Apr, 1947 (5106)	Chartair; British South American Airways as *Star Master*; BOAC (training flight); East African Airways as VP-KMI, May 1954.
G-AIUY (HN323)	17 Apr, 1947 (5116)	Olley Air Service, Croydon; Cambrian Airways, Feb 1953; Morton Air Services, Oct 1953; broken up, 1956.
G-AIUZ (V4125)	11 Apr, 1947 (5105)	Transair, Croydon; crashed Berne, Switzerland, 5 Nov, 1948.
G-AIVA (BG152)	5 May, 1947 (5102)	Transair; S. J. Cooke, Dec 1951; sold to Spain, Feb 1953.
G-AJAX (LX599)	15 Oct, 1946 (3331)	Originally registered as MC-ABA (then Monte Carlo), but purchase not taken up; Airwork; Atlas Aviation; three other owners; sold abroad, Apr 1949.
G-AJFZ (T1013)	20 Feb, 1947 (5097)	P. H. Meadway, Portsmouth, as *Monica*; broken up. July 1949.

G-AJGA (X6740)	8 May, 1947 (5117)	Northern Air Charter; Astral Aviation; Lancashire Aircraft Corp; broken up, Mar 1956.
G-AJGB (LX156)	30 May, 1947 (5110)	D. L. Steiner, Speke, Liverpool; Thos. Barclay; withdrawn, 1950.
G-AJGC (LW833)	22 Apr, 1947 (5119)	D. L. Steiner; crashed La Rochelle, 13 Nov, 1947.
G-AJGD (HN633)	16 May, 1947 (5120)	D. L. Steiner; Olley Air Service; crashed Chiswick, London, 15 July, 1949.
G-AJGE (R5973)	30 May, 1947 (5121)	Pullman Airways; lost in Mediterranean, Benina–Castel Benito, 27 Feb, 1948.
G-AJGF (HN199)	22 May, 1947 (5122)	Patrick-Laing Air Services; leased to Transair, 1949; sold abroad, Aug 1949.
G-AJGG (HN733)	10 June, 1947 (5123)	Chartair; Air Jordan as TJ-ABG, Dec 1950; Adie Aviation as G-AJGG, Sept 1952; Rombaldi, Toussus, Paris, as F-BGOP, Mar 1953.
G-AJGH (AT676)	22 May, 1947 (5124)	British Aviation Services; sold abroad, Sept 1947; Air Charter as G-AJGH, Apr 1948; sold abroad, June 1950.
G-AJGI (LW832)	9 May, 1947 (5125)	D. L. Steiner; Mrs E. Wheeler; B. R. W. Betts; crashed France, 14 Nov, 1947.
G-AJLH (NJ376)	17 June, 1947 (5126)	Northern Air Charter; Astral Aviation; Lancashire Aircraft Corporation; dismantled for spares, May 1951.
G-AJLI (LX760)	4 June, 1947 (5127)	Westminster Airways; Fairflight; S. J. Cooke, Sept 1951; to Spain, 16 Feb, 1952.
G-AJLJ (HM627)	22 May, 1947 (5128)	Air Enterprises; dismantled, 1950.
G-AJLK (HN780)	10 June, 1947 (5129)	Westminster Airways; two other owners, then Air Jordan as TJ-ABF and, later, as TJ-AAY.
G-AJLL (HN479)	6 June, 1947 (5130)	Chartair; Aigle Azur, Indo-China, as F-BCJE, Jan 1949.
G-AJLM (LW899)	17 June, 1947 (5131)	Portsmouth Aviation; J. T. Donaldson as *Eagleways*; Turkey as TC-GOK, Aug 1952.
G-AJLN (V4159)	10 July, 1947 (5132)	Transair; Airspeed; English Electric, Preston; Aerocontacts, Apr 1953; Israel, May 1953.
G-AJLO (X6859)	May 1947 (5133)	Airspeed; Belgian Air Force, Congo, as C-34, Leopoldville, 1948; South Africa, 13 Aug, 1955; Natal Airlines, Durban, as ZS-DNL; broken up, Aug 1958.
G-AJLP (DF402)	22 May, 1947 (5135)	Prince Aly Khan; B. R. W. Betts; Flyaway; Air Jordan as TJ-ABC, Sept 1950; South Africa, 13 Aug, 1955, Natal Airlines, as ZS-DNM; broken up, Aug 1958.
G-AJLR (R6079)	10 June, 1947 (5136)	Olley Air Service; Cambrian Airways, Feb 1953; Morton Air Services, Oct 1953; All Power Transformers, Sept 1956.
G-AJND (EB718)	May 1947 (5138)	D. L. Steiner; sold abroad, probably to Burma Corporation, as XY-ABJ, Nov 1947.
G-AJNE (LW900)	25 June, 1947 (5139)	D. L. Steiner; Air Enterprises, June 1953; Crewdson, June 1955; Airwork, Nov 1956.
G-AJNF (HN847)	23 June, 1947 (5145)	Milburnair; R. K. Dundas; Maharajah of Bikaner as VT-CRG, Jan 1948.

G-AJNG (DF522)	27 June, 1947 (5146)	Chartair; Westminster Airways; British Aviation Services; Airtech; Chartair; Sweden as SE-BUP, Mar 1952; broken up, Apr 1955.
G-AJNH (HN915)	June 1947 (5150)	Soc Indochinoise de Transports Aériens (SITA) as F-BDPY, July 1947; damaged Tongking, Annam, 18 May, 1949.
G-AJNI (DF515)	June 1947 (5157)	SITA as F-BDPV, July 1947; damaged Gia Lam, Haiphong, Annam, 28 June, 1949.
G-AJNJ (EB908)	June 1947 (5158)	Airspeed; sold abroad, Nov 1947.
G-AJNK (MP347)	13 Jan, 1948 (5159)	R. K. Dundas; Maharajah of Bundi as VT-CZQ.
G-AJNL (HN831)	June 1947 (5160)	Airspeed; sold abroad, probably to Burma Corporation, as XY-ABK.
G-AJWP (NM642)	June 1947 (5161)	SITA as F-BDPX, July 1947; damaged Namdinh, Annam, 16 Mar, 1949.
G-AJWR (HN829)	July 1947 (5162)	Airspeed ambulance prototype; SITA as F-BEDP, Oct 1947; damaged by fire, Tan-Son-Nhut, Saigon, 26 Oct, 1950.
G-AJWS (HN756)	14 Nov, 1947 (5170)	E. A. R. van den Bergh; Robert Bouchier as F-OAGD; de Havilland as G-AJWS, Oct 1953.
G-AJWT (HN713)	4 Sept, 1947 (5169)	Airspeed; United Air Services, Tanganyika, as VR-TAR; damaged Mombasa, 4 Mar, 1948.
G-AJWU (HN917)	Aug 1947 (5180)	Sold abroad, probably to Burma Corporation, as XY-ABI.
G-AJWV (HM636)	Aug 1947 (5172)	Airspeed; sale abroad not taken up; dismantled Portsmouth, July 1949.
G-AJWW (HN717)	Oct 1947 (5173)	To France as F-BEDT.
G-AJWX (NJ302)	Nov 1947 (5174)	United Air Services, Tanganyika, as VR-TAS.
G-AJWY (EB974)	Mar 1948 (5175)	United Air Services, Tanganyika, as VR-TAU; Air Jordan as TJ-ABA, Sept 1950; crashed Jerusalem, 31 Oct, 1950.
G-AJWZ (AT657)	Apr 1948 (5176)	Govt of French Indo-China as F-OABU, Apr 1948; crashed Mar 1952.
G-AJXE (HN734)	23 Sept, 1947 (5164)	Ministry of Civil Aviation (MCA), Civil Aviation Flying Unit (CAFU), Gatwick/Stansted; T. D. Keegan, 1956.
G-AJXF (NM314)	9 Oct, 1947 (5165)	MCA, CAFU; Skyways, 1956.
G-AJXG (NM334)	6 Nov, 1947 (5166)	MCA, CAFU; BKS Air Transport, 1956.
G-AJXH (HN719)	4 Nov, 1947 (5167)	MCA, CAFU; Eagle Aviation, Mar 1956.
G-AJXI (V4283)	6 Nov, 1947 (5168)	MCA, CAFU; W. S. Shackleton, Sept 1956; for survey, French West Africa, with Oxford nose as F-BHVY, Feb 1957.
G-AKCK (HN827)	Apr 1948 (5177)	Govt of French Indo-China as F-OABT, 28 Apr, 1948.

G-AKCV (NM593)	Oct 1948 (5178)	Airspeed; Belgian Air Force, Leopoldville, probably as C-32.
G-AKCW (NJ318)	Dec 1948 (5179)	Airspeed; Ministry of Supply as VX587 for Alvis Leonides engine testing; Alvis as G-AKCW, May 1953.
G-AKSA (—)	May 1943 (5188)	Airspeed; Burma, 11 Aug, 1949.
G-ALTZ (HN844)	30 June, 1947 (5134)	Aer Lingus as EI-ADB; BSAA as G-ALTZ *Star Monitor*, 1949; BOAC; L. Berner & Co, June 1956.
G-AMBT (—)	1950 (5202)	Airspeed; Indo-China as F-OAHG.
G-AMBU (—)	1950 (5243)	Airspeed; Indo-China as F-OAHH.
G-AMID (—)	16 May, 1951 (5250)	Airspeed; de Havilland, Sept 1951; to France as F-BGPF, Mar 1952.

Principal Consul operators (numbers in parentheses) were:

Air Enterprises (7)*; Atlas Air Services* (4)*; British Air Services* (4)*; British Air Transport* (5)*; Chartair* (9)*; Hornton Airways* (3)*; International Airways (Barclay)* (5)*; Lancashire Aircraft Corporation* (6)*; Morton Air Services* (8)*; Steiner's Air Service* (7)*; Transair* (5)*; Westminster Airways* (7).

Non-British Civil-registered AS.65 Consuls*

Serial (c/n)	*Registration*	
AT657† (5176)	F-OABU	Govt of French Indo-China; crashed Mar 1952.
DF515† (5157)	F-BDPV	Soc Indochinoise de Transports Aériens (SITA), Saigon, Indo-China.
EB732 (5171)	F-BDPU	SITA, Indo-China.
EB974† (5175)	VR-TAU	United Air Services (UAS), Tanganyika.
HM629	XY-ABC	Burma Corporation
HM848	F-BECD	—
HN530	F-BDPS	SITA, Indo-China.
HN717† (5173)	F-BEDT	—
HN827† (5177)	F-OABT	Govt of Indo-China.
HN831† (5160)	XY-ABK	Burma Corporation.
HN844† (5134)	EI-ADB	Aer Lingus, Dublin; later G-ALTZ.
HN915† (5150)	F-BDPY	SITA, Indo-China.
HN917† (5180)	XY-ABI	Burma Corporation.

HN980 (5153)	EI-ADC	Aer Lingus, Dublin.
LX729	F-BCJL	SITA, Indo-China.
LX735 (5108)	VT-CJB	Airways (India).
MP302 (5096)	VR-SCF	Malayan Airways.
NJ302† (5174)	VR-TAS	UAS, Tanganyika.
NJ309 (5181)	EC-ACZ	Iberia, Spain.
NM523	VT-CJA	Airways (India).
NM642† (5161)	F-BDPX	SITA, Indo-China.
PH178 (4031)	VR-SCE	Malayan Airways.
PK248† (4322)	OO-GVP	To Belgium; crashed in the Sudan, 6 Jan, 1947.
PK300† (4352)	F-BCJD	Aigle Azur, Indo-China.
— (5189)	ZS-DNK	Belgian Air Force C-33; reg. South Africa, 13 Aug, 1955, with Natal Airlines, Durban; scrapped, Aug 1958.
— (5190)	ZS-DNJ	Belgian Air Force C-31; reg. South Africa, 13 Aug, 1955, with Natal Airlines; crashed Matatule, 8 May, 1956.
— (5202)†	F-OAHG	Govt of Indo-China, 1950.
— (5243)	F-OAHH	Govt of Indo-China, 1950.

* *Excluding aircraft which were initially operated or demonstrated under British registrations. For these, see the full listing under alphabetical registration sequence. All Consuls appear to have been registered first in Britain except when orders were received in advance of such registration. Ten Consuls (c/n 5140–44 and 5152–56), were, for instance bought by the Argentine Aeronautical Purchasing Commission in 1947; C of As were issued between 27 June and 8 Dec, 1947, but they were not registered in Britain.*

† *Entries so marked can also be found in the full listing. Although initially British-registered, their first operational use was under the non-British registrations.*

APPENDIX III

AS.10 Oxford I and II; AS.46 Oxford V: RAF Serials by Manufacturers and Marks

Airspeed

Oxford I

Quantity	*Serials*
136	L4534 (prototype) –L4669. (L4538 used as civil transport, G-AFFM; L4539 used for McLaren undercarriage experiments; L4556–4557, L4592–4593 not delivered to RAF).
50	L9635–9650, L9692–9703 (intermediate trainers), L9651–9660, L9680–9691 (advanced trainers).
5	N1190–1194 (advanced trainers).
71	N6250–6270 (less turrets), N6271–6299, 6320–6340 (N6327 had experimental twin fins and rudders).
130	P1865–1899 (P1865–1866 converted to Mk V; P1894 to Royal Netherlands Air Force, 1946, as Mk V). P1920–1969, P1980–2009, P2030–2044 (P1984, 1993 and 2002 transferred to Iranian Air Force as 801–803. P1945, 1953, 1963, 1983, 1989–1992, 1996–1999, 2004–2009, 2030–2044 transferred to Royal New Zealand Air Force (RNZAF) as NZ255–258, NZ261–268, NZ271–291 respectively).
80	P8822–8830, P8855–8868, P8891–8916, P8995–8998, P9020–9046 (50 to RNZAF).
6	R4062–4065 (to RNZAF), R4066–4067 (to Rhodesia).
200	R5938–5979, 5991–6038, 6050–6059, 6070–6114, 6129–6163, 6177–6196 (R5938–5941 to Rhodesia).
145	R9974–9988; T1001–1028, 1041–1047, 1112–1141, 1167–1180, 1264–1288, 1308–1332 (T1265, 1269, 1270, 1272 to RNZAF).
3	X1038–1040 (replacements for P1984, 1993, 2002 to Rhodesia).
250	X6520–6564, 6589–6623, 6643–6692, 6726–6750, 6764–6813, 6835–6879 (X6765 to Royal Netherlands Air Force, 1946).
4	AP654–657 (to blind-approach training flights).
175	AS474–523 (AS504 fitted with Gipsy Queen engines), 537–571, 591–640, 665 704 (AS592 was prototype Mk V).
400	BF782–831, 845–889, 904–953, 967–999; BG100–101, 113–132, 149–183, 196–245, 260–274, 546–575, 588–637, 649–668 (BF807, 825, 858–859, 861, 867; BG100, 115, 118, 171, 213, 263, 610 converted to Mk V).
230	EB414–423 (to South Africa), EB689–703, 717–761, 777–826, 838–870, 884–930, 946–975 (EB849, 884, 888, 894, 915, 924, 953, 962–966, 968 converted to Mk V).
450	HN217–239, 254–284, 298–346, 363–386, 405–441, 467–495, 513–554, 576–614, 631–671, 689–738, 754–790, 808–855 (HN217, 235–237, 280, 306, 340–341, 343, 346, 367, 533, 542, 549, 551, 602, 605, 790 converted to Mk V; HN691, 771, 826 to Royal Netherlands Air Force, 1946).
50	LB469–492, 513–538.

450	LX156–199, 213–245, 258–289, 301–333, 347–369, 382–401, 415–448, 462–489, 502–541, 555–582, 595–617, 629–648, 661–699, 714–746, 759–777 (LX366–369, 382–401, 415–416, 467–470, 510–512, 561–565 to Turkish Air Force; LX417–422 to Portuguese Air Force; LX423–426 to Free French Air Force in Africa).
450	NM217–254, 270–314, 329–370, 385–429, 444–488, 509–550, 571–615, 629–676, 681–720, 736–760, 776–810 (NM532–533 destroyed by fire before delivery; NM520 to Royal Netherlands Air Force, 1946).
400	PG925–956, 968–999; PH112–157, 169–215, 227–268, 281–327, 339–379, 391–425, 447–489, 502–535 (PH528–535 converted to T. II and renumbered VB861–868 in 1945).
50	PK248–269, 282–309 (many converted post-war to AS.65 Consul).
50	RR321–367, 380–382 (remainder of order for 450, in serials RR383–906, cancelled; RR347–348 to Royal Netherlands Air Force, 1946).
3,785	

Airspeed **Oxford II**

Quantity	*Serials*
69	N6341–6349, 6365–6384, 6400–6439.
70	P1800–1849, 1860–1864 (P1864 was Mk III prototype, converted, with P1865–1866, to Mk V), P2045–2059 (transferred to RNZAF as NZ1201–1215).
70	P8831–8854 (P8832–8833 fitted out as ambulances), 8917–8931, 8964–8994.
155	T1048–1082, 1097–1111, 1181–1215, 1243–1263, 1333–1348, 1371–1404 (T1373 converted to Mk V).
250	X6880–6884, 6932–6981, 7031–7075, 7107–7156, 7176–7200, 7231–7265, 7278–7317.
175	AS705–709, 726–745, 764–813, 828–877, 893–942 (AS732 transferred to USAAF).
200	BG275–304, 318–337, 349–398, 415–459, 473–522, 541–545 (BG301, 423, 444, 445, 509, 521 converted to Mk V).
989	

Airspeed **Oxford T. II**

Quantity	*Serials*
9*	VB861–868 (ex-PH528–535), 869 (VB862–869 sold back to Airspeed for AS.65 Consul conversion).

* *One only, VB869, built as T. II from scratch; remainder converted (see Oxford I serials).*

Airspeed **Oxford V (excluding conversions)**

Quantity	*Serials*
190	EB424–461, 483–518, 535–584, 599–640, 654–677 (all but two to Canada as airframes).

de Havilland Aircraft **Oxford I and II**

Quantity	Serials (c/ns in parentheses)
200	N4560–4609 (2400–2449), 4630–4659 (2575–2604), 4681–4700 (2605–2624), Mk I; N4720–4729 (2450–2459), 4730–4739 (2460–2469), 4754–4803 (2470–2519), 4824–4853 (2520–2549), Mk II. N4655 converted to Mk V.
75	P6795–6819 (2550–2574), 6831–6880 (2625–2674), intermediate Mk I/II version.
150	R6211–6235 (2675–2699) Mk II; R6236–6248 (2700–2712), Mk I; R6263–6299 (2713–2749), 6317–6341 (2750–2774), Mk I; R6342–6358 (2775–2791), Mk II; R6371–6403 (2792–2824), Mk II. R6211–6226 to RNZAF; R6269 to Royal Netherlands Air Force in 1946.
500	V3145–3194 (2825–2874), 3208–3247 (2875–2914), 3267–3296 (2915–2944), 3310–3328 (2945–2963), 3329–3230 (2964–2965), 3331–3332 (2966–2967), 3333 (2968), 3334–3353 (2969–2988), Mk I; V3502–3540 (2989–3028), 3555–3589 (3029–3063), Mk II; V3354–3359 (3064–3069), 3375–3404 (3070–3099), 3418–3442 (3100–3124), 3456–3480 (3125–3149) Mk I; V3590–3604 (3150–3164), 3623–3647 (3165–3189), 3665–3694 (3190–3219), 3719–3748 (3220–3249), 3768–3792 (3250–3274), 3813–3862 (3275–3324), Mk II.
350	AR756–790 (3325–3359), 804–853 (3360–3409), 870–889 (3410–3429), 909–953 (3430–3474) 968–982 (3475–3489), Mk I. AS144–150 (3490–3496), 151–153 (3514–3516), Mk I; AS154–167 (3500–3513), 168–170 (3497–3499), 170–188 (3517–3534), 201–230 (3535–3564), 254–278 (3565–3589), 297–331 (3590–3624), 347–396 (3625–3674), Mk II. AS376 was completed as a Mk V.
240	AT439–488 (3675–3724), 502–536 (3725–3759), 576–625 (3760–3809), 641–685 (3810–3854), 723–742 (3855–3874), 760–799 (3875–3914), Mk I (the original order was for 475 Mk I and 475 Mk II in serials between AT439 and AV502, but remaining 235 Mk I and all Mk II were cancelled).
1,515	

Standard Motors **Oxford I**

Quantity	Serials
300	V3865–3914, 3933–3957, 3972–3996, 4016–4065, 4079–4103, 4124–4173, 4192–4241, 4259–4283.
250	DF220–264, 276–314, 327–367, 390–433, 445–489, 501–536 (DF257, 410, 479 to Royal Netherlands Air Force in 1946).
50	LB401–429, 442–462.
150	MP275–314, 338–376, 391–430, 444–474 (MP428, 461 to Royal Netherlands Air Force in 1946).
750	

Percival Aircraft **Oxford I**

Quantity	*Serials*
80	ED197–204, 215–236, 251–300.
375	HM603–650, 666–700, 721–767, 783–813, 827–875, 889–918, 945–990 (HM610, 725 to Royal Netherlands Air Force in 1946); HN111–149, 163–212 (HN131, 172, 182 to Royal Netherlands Air Force in 1946).
235	LW727–759, 772–799, 813–835, 848–879, 891–927, 948–973, 985–999 (LW819, 864 to Royal Netherlands Air Force in 1946); LX113–152.
85	NJ280–322, 345–382, 397–400 (NJ318 re-numbered VX587; remainder of order for 250, serials within NJ401–607, cancelled).
775	

Percival Aircraft **Oxford II**

Quantity	*Serials*
25	P1070–1094.
100	W6546–6595, 6608–6657.
100	AB639–668, 685–729, 749–773 (AB650 to USAAF).
100	AP387–436, 451–500 (AP474 used by BOAC for crew training).
150	BM671–720, 737–785, 801–844, 871–877 (BM825 to Fleet Air Arm; BM713 and 830 converted to Mk V).
100	EB978–999. ED108–157, 169–196.
575	

Percival Aircraft **Oxford V (excluding conversions)**

Quantity	*Serials*
6	LW928–930, 945–947.

APPENDIX IV

AS.51 Horsa I and AS.58 Horsa II: Manufacturers and RAF Serials

Horsa I

Prototypes (Airspeed assembled)

Quantity	*Serials*
3	DG597, 603, 609 (prototypes to specification X.26/40; first flight, 12 Sept, 1941).
4	DK346, 349, 353, 358.
—	
7	

Harris Lebus and others

Quantity	*Serials*
300	DP279–294*, 303–315, 329–353, 368–399, 412–440, 484–506, 513–562, 567–575, 592–631, 644–681, 689–713 (DP593–598, 614, 617, 701 transferred to USAAF).
636	LG550, 662–699, 713–749, 761–798, 814–856, 868–896, 911–952, 966–999; LH113–154, 167–189, 202–249, 263–301, 316–359, 373–415, 429–476, 490–536, 549–583, 597–601 (LG511–534, 547–549, 551, 593, 616–658 cancelled out of original order for 750).
100	RJ245–287, 290–316, 330–359.
325	RN523–568, 583–625, 638–679, 693–738, 752–795, 809–850, 865–902, 918–941.
100	RX595–634, 647–688, 700–717.
——	
1,461	

* *A few of the early production Horsas were assembled by Airspeed at Portsmouth; all others were assembled by RAF maintenance units—initially Nos 15 and 27—until production was under way at the Airspeed shadow factory at Christchurch.*

Made and Assembled by Airspeed at Christchurch

Quantity	*Serials*
50	HS101–150 (HS110, 119, 138, 139, 147 shipped to USA in 1943).
220	LH942–976; LJ101–144, 157–193, 206–241, 256–291, 303–334 (LJ271 converted to Mk II).
100	PF690–725, 739–770, 786–817.
100	RJ111–143, 150–196, 212–231.
—–	
470	

Austin Motor Company

Quantity	*Serials*
100	DP714–726, 739–777, 794–841 (DP725 to USAAF).
200	HG736–770, 784–819, 831–880, 897–944, 959–989.
300	

Horsa II

Harris Lebus and others

Quantity	*Serials*
206	PW637–678, 693–735, 742–790, 812–847, 862–897.
450	RX718–735, 749–779, 792–835, 848–889, 902–937, 949–998.
	RZ112–156, 170–203, 215–259, 280–325, 338–380, 393–408.
600	TK828–869, 882–913, 927–963, 978–999.
	TL114–157, 173–215, 229–261, 274–312, 328–369, 384–427, 440–481, 495–536, 549–587, 602–643, 659–691, 712–735.
15	TT353–367 (remainder of order for 400, in serials TT368–974, cancelled).
1,271	

Austin Motor Company

Quantity	*Serials*
65	LF886–923, 937–963 (20 to USAAF).

Airspeed at Christchurch

Quantity	*Serials*
175	RN309–349, 362–405, 418–459, 473–520.
50	RX534–583.
225	

Aircraft resulting from Recommendations of Second Brabazon Committee (1943)

Type No.	*Initial Proposals (Jan 1944)*	*Developments and Offshoots*	
1	Non-stop North Atlantic project. Bristol Aeroplane Co submitted design for 240,000 lb aircraft powered by eight Bristol Centaurus engines coupled in pairs and carrying 50 passengers in bunks. Two prototypes ordered later	First prototype Bristol 167 Brabazon with Centaurus engines completed and flown. Second prototype with eight coupled Proteus propeller-turbines not completed	
		Ministry of Aircraft Production specification for multi-engined long-range flying-boat	Saunders-Roe SR.45 Princess prototype with ten Proteus propeller-turbines, eight coupled in pairs. One of three completed and flown
2	Short/medium-haul 'DC-3 replacement'. Airspeed selected as manufacturer. 40,000 lb Hercules-powered twin proposed with payload of 7,000 lb and accommodation for about 30 passengers. Two prototypes ordered later	*Type 2A* Airspeed AS.57 Ambassador with two Centaurus engines. 45,000 lb gross with 8,000 lb payload (40 passengers)	Production Ambassador/Elizabethan; 52,000 lb gross; 11,650 lb payload, including 47 passengers
		Type 2B Vickers Viscount 630 prototype; four Dart propeller-turbines	Production Viscount 700 and 800
		Armstrong Whitworth Apollo prototype; four Armstrong Siddeley Mamba propeller-turbines	

3A	Four-engined 100,000 lb aircraft for one-stop Atlantic and long-haul Empire services. A. V. Roe selected as designers	3A and 3B proposals cancelled BOAC medium-range Empire specification	Bristol 175 Britannia; four Bristol Proteus propeller-turbines
3B	Four-engined 70,000 lb aircraft for medium-haul Empire services with 40-60 passengers. No designer selected		
4	Experimental transport with 'new methods of propulsion'. No designer selected. Range and speed prospects being studied	Turbojet passenger airliner by de Havilland Aircraft	DH Comet 1 with four DH Ghost turbojets
5A	Twin- or four-engined, 15,000 lb, 14-passenger feederliner. No designer selected	Marathon by Miles Aircraft and Handley Page (Reading); four DH Gipsy Queen piston engines. Prototype also with two Armstrong Siddeley Mamba propeller-turbines	
5B	Twin-engined all-metal feeder, charter and taxi aircraft with 8,000 lb gross and carrying 8 passengers over ranges up to 300 miles. De Havilland selected as designers	DH Dove; two Gipsy Queen piston engines	

Bibliography

A Time to Fly, Sir Alan Cobham; Shepheard-Walwyn, 1978
Airspeed, the Company and its Aeroplanes, D. H. Middleton; Terence Dalton Ltd, 1982.
Slide Rule, Nevil Shute (Norway); William Heinemann Ltd, 1964.

Index